Life's a Pitch

'A marvellous book about selling, and life, and who
we are and how we tick . . . dazzling' Tom Peters,
author of *In Search of Excellence*

'You can never look upon a sale in quite the same way
again. Buy *Life's a Pitch* and be enlightened'
Adrian Wooldridge, *Economist*

'Entertaining, balanced and provocative' *Kirkus Reviews*

'Like Malcolm Gladwell, Philip Delves Broughton is
drawn to success stories where natural talent takes
second place to hard work. His enthusiasm and
admiration are contagious' *Publishers Weekly*

Philip Delves Broughton is the author of the international bestseller *What They Teach You at Harvard Business School*, named Business Book of the Year by the *Financial Times* and *USA Today*. He was born in Bangladesh and grew up in England. He served as the New York and Paris bureau chief for the *Daily Telegraph*, and now writes for publications including the *Financial Times*, the *Evening Standard* and the *Wall Street Journal*. In 2006 he received an MBA from Harvard Business School. He is married with two sons.

Life's a Pitch

WHAT THE WORLD'S BEST SALES PEOPLE

CAN TEACH US ALL

PHILIP DELVES BROUGHTON

PORTFOLIO
PENGUIN

PORTFOLIO PENGUIN

Published by the Penguin Group
Penguin Books Ltd, 80 Strand, London WC2R 0RL, England
Penguin Group (USA) Inc., 375 Hudson Street, New York, New York 10014, USA
Penguin Group (Canada), 90 Eglinton Avenue East, Suite 700, Toronto, Ontario, Canada M4P 2Y3
(a division of Pearson Penguin Canada Inc.)
Penguin Ireland, 25 St Stephen's Green, Dublin 2, Ireland (a division of Penguin Books Ltd)
Penguin Group (Australia), 250 Camberwell Road, Camberwell, Victoria 3124, Australia
(a division of Pearson Australia Group Pty Ltd)
Penguin Books India Pvt Ltd, 11 Community Centre, Panchsheel Park, New Delhi – 110 017, India
Penguin Group (NZ), 67 Apollo Drive, Rosedale, Auckland 0632, New Zealand
(a division of Pearson New Zealand Ltd)
Penguin Books (South Africa) (Pty) Ltd, Block D, Rosebank Office Park,
181 Jan Smuts Avenue, Parktown North, Gauteng 2193, South Africa

Penguin Books Ltd, Registered Offices: 80 Strand, London WC2R 0RL, England

www.penguin.com

First published as *The Art of the Sale* in the United States of America by The Penguin Press,
a member of Penguin Group (USA) Inc. 2012
First published as *Life's a Pitch* in Great Britain by Portfolio Penguin 2012
002

Printed in Great Britain by Clays Ltd, St Ives plc

A CIP catalogue record for this book is available from the British Library

ISBN: 978–0–670–92151–5

www.greenpenguin.co.uk

MIX
Paper from
responsible sources
FSC
www.fsc.org   FSC™ C018179

Penguin Books is committed to a sustainable
future for our business, our readers and our planet.
This book is made from Forest Stewardship
Council™ certified paper.

ALWAYS LEARNING   **PEARSON**

For Margret, Augie, and Hugo

You can get all A's and still flunk life.

WALKER PERCY

You call yourself a salesman, you sonofabitch?

DAVID MAMET, *GLENGARRY GLEN ROSS*

CONTENTS

LIFE ON STEROIDS

Life's a pitch—and then you buy.

BILLY MAYS, THE INFOMERCIAL KING

I imagined when I went to Harvard Business School to study for my MBA that sales would be part of the curriculum. But it wasn't. In fact, the subject is absent from most MBA programs. If you accept the idea that business is about selling things and making things, and that everything else is secondary, then this absence makes no sense. When I asked one of my Harvard professors to explain it, he told me that if I really wanted to study sales, I could pay for a two-week evening course somewhere. You could say the same thing about a lot of what the school taught, but no one was suggesting we go and learn strategy at night school.

In his book *Birth of a Salesman*, the Harvard Business School professor Walter Friedman observed that "while business schools have continued to offer some type of sales management instruction—usually within a larger marketing course—they do not offer courses in salesmanship skills. The topic remains, just as it was in the 1910s, more suitable for popular how-to books and memoirs of successful salespeople than for academic classes. Economists, for their part, still tend to ignore the role of salesmanship in the economy." Part of the problem is institutional. In order to get tenure at a business school, you need to be published in a handful of journals, which focus on finance, marketing, strategy, and operations, leaving little room or serious consideration for articles on selling. So for reasons that have nothing to do with the relevance of selling in business, selling is an orphan in business academe.

The effects of this omission are grave. Many supposedly well-educated people in the business world are clueless about one of its most vital functions, the means by which you actually generate revenue. The absence of knowledge about sales has opened a class division between salespeople and the rest of business. Salespeople are often seen as operating by different rules and needing different motivators from other employees. They need conventions in Las Vegas and complex commission structures. They need to be goaded to perform and reined in when they sell too hard. They are patronized as "feet on the street" by those who prefer to imagine that business can be conducted by consultants with dueling PowerPoint presentations. Salesmen themselves use terms that diminish the complexity of what they do. IBM salespeople used to talk of "pushing metal" (mainframe computers), and Xerox salespeople of "slamming boxes" (photocopiers).

When Bank of America rescued Merrill Lynch from imminent bankruptcy at the depth of the financial crisis in late 2008, Merrill Lynch's brokers derided Bank of America's retail bankers as "toaster salesmen." Bank of America's chief executive, Kenneth Lewis, was similarly described as a "former shoe salesman," in contrast to Merrill Lynch's Harvard- and Goldman Sachs–trained boss, John Thain.

Lewis had indeed sold shoes while he was in high school; he had been paid a commission of 36 cents per pair. He'd also sold Christmas cards door-to-door and while in college worked at a municipal bond firm and as a reservations agent for United Airlines. Good for Lewis, one might think, to have risen up the hard way. So why reduce him to a "former shoe salesman"? Anyone who has actually started, bought, or run a business knows how absurd such pejorative perceptions of salespeople are. Selling is not a sideshow, a pesky obligation apart from the real business of finance, law, or accounting. It is business in gorgeous Technicolor.

Richard Perry, the founder of Perry Capital and one of the most successful investors in America, put it very simply to me: "It's all about sales. If I have sales, I can create profit." Perry's offices are in the General Motors building on Fifth Avenue in the heart of Manhattan, a building that weaves together many strands of contemporary American business. It was completed in 1968 as an expression of the might of the U.S. car industry, sheathed in glass and white Georgia marble, and occupies an entire city block. These days, its main tenants are hedge funds, law firms, and, beneath its street-level plaza, an Apple store. In 2008, the New York developer who owned the building had to sell it because of the credit crunch to a group of investors led by Goldman Sachs and assorted Middle Eastern sovereign wealth funds. The building's evolution, from the symbol of homegrown manufacturing power to a home for hedge funds and iPhones runs parallel to that of the broader American economy.

Perry began his career at Goldman Sachs before striking out to found his own firm in 1988. Perry Capital has proved to be one of the most enduring and successful of the many hedge funds founded in New York over the past two decades, moving from investment strategy to investment strategy, from buying equities to issuing credit, fighting shareholder battles to betting big on mergers and acquisitions, making fortunes at every turn for its investors, employees, and Perry himself. During that time, he has met salespeople of every stripe, in financial services and beyond. As he sat back in one of his firm's many hypermodern conference rooms, he told me, "If you aren't selling, you aren't part of the world."

Perry possesses the supreme self-confidence required to surf the treacherous financial markets as adroitly as he does. It's a style shared among any number of successful financiers. Bruce Wasserstein, the late chief executive of the investment bank Lazard, was famously gruff and unkempt. But if you were thinking of buying or selling a company, and you could afford him, he would be the first man on your team. You were happy to ignore his brusqueness because no one knew the M&A (mergers and acquisitions) game as well as he did. His success sold his services. "The great salesmen have the facts. They're the anti-sell," says Perry. "They don't have to do anything. You just want to buy from them." It's like choosing between surgeons. Do you want the one with the tidy office and the ironed shirt? Or the rude slob who has performed 100 successful operations in a row? In some ways, this is the ideal. You have a product so irresistible that selling it is simply a question of placing it in front of the slavering prospect. No need for the artfully prepared bid, the tickets to the game, the winning smile. The salesman floats his pitch and the hungry buyer slams it over the bleachers for a home run. Everyone makes money and we all go home. But even in investing, where performance can be measured in the unforgiving digits of a risk-adjusted return, the selling goes on. Perry himself is a tall, athletic man, physically imposing and fashionably dressed. His offices are starkly white and dripping with modern art that emphasizes the firm's wealth from the moment you enter. There is no false modesty here. Even after so many years, and such an extensive track record, Perry Capital remains dressed for success.

Compare this with Warren Buffett, whose reputation is built on his gift for stock picking and his persona as the Poor Richard of our time: thrifty, hardworking, and aw-shucks despite his billions. He runs his globe-spanning firm from a threadbare office in Omaha, Nebraska, with a staff of fewer than twenty. "Successful people are very aware of what their style is, and they play it," says Perry. Success, whatever the wrapping, will attract followers.

In the United States, there are two potent and contradictory views of sales. The first was held by Benjamin Franklin and his later incarnations like Buffett and Sam Walton, the founder of Wal-Mart, and codified in the twentieth century by writers like Dale Carnegie and Norman Vincent Peale. It holds that in a properly functioning democracy, no matter the condition of your birth, if you can sell, you can slice through any obstacles of class, status, or upbringing in a way inconceivable in more hidebound societies. Great salesmen need no other prop to succeed. Selling well, in this view, is also a reflection of a healthy character. It means you are the sort of person people are drawn to—hardworking, clean living, and trustworthy— and you are likely to succeed at whatever you choose to do.

The opposing view can be found in *Death of a Salesman*, Arthur Miller's brutal portrait of a man crushed by the demands of capitalism, living out the last pathetic day of his life. Willy Loman is defeated by his work as a door-to-door salesman and by his failure to achieve the hollow dreams he has set for himself. For him, selling is a form of humiliation, an offense against human dignity perpetrated for the vile purpose of commercial gain. It is capitalism at its absolute worst. And yet year after year, high school and college students are made to read this play and perform it, and audiences pay to see it. It is the most studied play at American universities.

In his autobiography, *Timebends*, Miller describes how he wrote it. In April 1948, he drove up from his home in Brooklyn to his country house in Roxbury, Connecticut. He wanted to build a shack where he could write, and he wanted to build it himself, without the help of a professional carpenter. As he nailed and sawed, he constructed the strange architecture of his play, in which Loman, his wife, and his two sons try to understand the forces that will ultimately kill him, the awful erosion of self that Loman suffered in his pursuit of the American dream.

> I started writing one morning—the tiny studio was still unpainted and smelled of raw wood and sawdust, and the bags of nails were still stashed in a corner with my tools. The sun of April had found my windows to pour through, and the apple buds were moving on the wild trees, showing their first pale blue petals. I wrote all day until dark, and then I had dinner and went back and wrote until some hour in the darkness between midnight and four. I had skipped a few areas that I knew would give me no trouble in the writing and gone for the parts that had to be muscled into position. By the next morning I had done the first half, the first act of two. When I lay down to sleep I realized I had been weeping—my eyes still burned and my throat was sore from talking it all out and shouting and laughing. I would be stiff when I woke, aching as if I had played four hours of football or tennis and now had to face the start of another game.

It would take another six weeks for Miller to write the second act. But the sheer physical effort the first act took somehow reflects Willy Loman's own desperate trials. When Elia Kazan, who directed the first production on Broadway in 1949, read it he called Miller and said, "My God, it's so sad."

Miller hoped his play would expose the "bullshit of capitalism, this pseudo life that thought to touch the clouds by standing on top of a refrigerator, waving a paid-up mortgage at the moon, victorious at last." Thirty-five years later, attending a production of the play in Beijing, Miller described his astonishment to see the interest in Loman even in a Communist country. To the Chinese, Loman's appeal was not as a victim of capitalism, but as someone who yearned to mean something, to be anything but anonymous. "When he roared out, 'I am not a dime a dozen! I am Willy Loman, and you are Biff Loman!' it came as a nearly revolutionary declaration after what was now thirty-four years of leveling," Miller wrote of the response in China.

Both views, Franklin's sunny one and Miller's depressing one, have their adherents in culture, economics, and politics, among those who see capitalism as a cleansing fire, with competition leading to fairness and truth and a just distribution of goods, and those who see it as the cause of scorched earth and ruined lives. And then there are those who shuttle around the middle, recognizing the importance of selling as a force for economic expansion and human improvement, yet admitting to its Faustian lures. The ability to sell can be a force for extraordinary good or evil, depending on the motivation of the seller. When Hunter S. Thompson described America as a "nation of two hundred million used car salesmen," it's hard to know if he meant it as a jibe or a compliment.

To excel at sales means you possess a power over people that can easily be misused. Put a formidable salesman together with a hateful idea, and you could end up with the Nuremberg rallies. Casanova turned his persuasive talents to deflowering nuns. Mahatma Gandhi used his to argue for the principle of nonviolence. Bill Clinton sold his way into the White House and out of a sexual scandal that might have sunk a lesser persuader. The Dalai Lama is a highly conscious manipulator of his message and style, depending on which audience he wishes to win over.

But whatever your view, sales surrounds us. Many of our choices in life come down to this: sell, or be sold to. Persuade, or roll over. When I told friends the subject of this book, half of them sneered. "Salespeople? Ugh," as if they could smell the cheap cologne and hear the tiresome patter. The other half shifted eagerly in their seats, lips smacking at the idea. Selling! It makes the world go round. There is not another area of business that elicits such contrary and vigorous reactions. Accounting, marketing, law, strategy, finance all have their zealous practitioners, but they remain the province of priesthoods. An attitude to sales is shared by all of us. We have all bought and we have all sold, whether commercially, personally, or emotionally.

In my own life, there are salespeople I have loathed—the realtor who sold me my house—and those I have adored: the one who helped me buy a suit for my wedding. There are ones to whom I happily gave my money because they gave me what I needed at a particular moment. And there are those who left me feeling robbed. There are those I would recommend to every friend, and a few I wouldn't inflict on my worst enemy.

There was the man in a Hawaiian shirt who sold me a car a couple of years ago, who laughed and chatted his way through the paperwork, dispelling every mite of my buyer's suspicion, asking me about my family, talking about his, building rapport in a way so "sales-y" and yet so much more pleasant than most of my other human interactions that day or week. And then that accursed realtor, whose evasions, distortions, and delays befuddled the already torturous process of home buying to such a degree that as I crossed the finish line of closing, I wanted to leave him smeared with honey in bear-infested woods.

Even those of us not paid to be salespeople sell every day to ourselves, to our families, to our friends, and to our employers. Every morning, I sell to my children the idea that paying attention at school is worth the effort. I sell myself on the idea of writing a book. We sell ourselves into schools and organizations, and to potential mates. Waiters sell us the special and doctors sell us medication. To sell is to be human—with all that that implies.

Indeed, in the biblical view, a sale made us human. Before that sale, Adam and Eve lived in the Garden of Eden, blessed by God, naked, joyful, surrounded by abundant food and beauty. Just one thing, God said. Do not eat from the tree of knowledge. If you do, he warned, you will die. The threat could not have been much clearer. Then along came the serpent, "more subtle than any beast of the field," to persuade the man and woman to do the one thing they fear will surely kill them. In sales, this qualifies as an objection.

The serpent at this point was not the slithering creature of today but a walking, talking biped. Its purpose was to destroy the perfect equilibrium of Eden. To do away with Adam and get its scaly mitts on Eve. It did so by turning the threat of severe punishment to its advantage. How terrific must that tree be, it said to Eve, for God to make such a threat? And by the way, did he threaten you? Or just Adam? Suddenly, Eve is reeling. Well, yes, she stumbles, I suppose God did only tell Adam. Then, the serpent asks, why do you think God is so determined for you not to eat of the tree of knowledge? Because he doesn't want you knowing as much as he does. He doesn't want you knowing good and evil like he does. He doesn't want any other Gods around the place.

So go on, take a bite. Won't hurt you. Might even do you some good.

Disaster.

Eve tastes the fruit and persuades Adam to do the same. They are banished from the garden, clothed in animal skins, and forced to work the earth for food until the dreadful day when to dust they shall return. Easeful immortality forsaken for a bite of apple. But from a sales perspective, one has to admire the serpent's hustle. No longer did Eve regard the tree as deadly, but rather as the attractive bearer of tasty fruit, which had the additional effect of making her wise. The serpent was a master of the one-off sale.

On June 12, 1973, Marlon Brando, at the height of his *Godfather* majesty, appeared on the Dick Cavett show for a rare interview. He was funny, laconic, and hard to pin down, especially on the subject of his work in movies. Brando didn't want to talk about acting because, he said, there was no difference between what he did on-screen and what all of us do every day. But what he did say applies directly to sales.

"I think that we couldn't survive a second if we weren't able to act," said Brando. "Acting is a survival mechanism, it's a social unguent, a lubricant. And we act to save our lives actually every day. People lie constantly every day by not saying something that they think, saying something that they don't think, or showing something that they don't feel.

"If you're working for an ad agency on some product and you hate the idea man, the boss," Brando went on, "and you know that every time he comes in with some impossible notion, something that really makes you gag when you drive home on the freeway, you know damn well that you're not going to get a raise, or you're not going to get shifted out of the position you're in if you don't say 'Leonard, I think that's terrific. It's just beautiful.' You even lean forward, put your elbows on your knees to show enthusiasm and you do it day, after day, after day to survive in your job."

We are all selling all the time, pitching to the various Leonards in our lives to get what we want. Sales is nothing more than the purely human ordeal of rejection and acceptance. We come to know if people believe in us or find us phony. Ideally we believe in what we sell, but often we need to act, to put on a show, maybe even conceal the truth. Our ability to sell, to persuade others, to serve others, is intimately wrapped up in how we define ourselves. Could you ever say the same thing about accounting?

But what really occurs when one person faces another and persuades him to buy? How do salespeople deal with the rejection inherent in selling, the unremitting no's interspersed with the occasional, ecstatic yes? How do salespeople go from meeting to meeting making the same pitch, hearing the same depressing objections, and yet keep their spirits up? When we sell we are forced to confront the truth about ourselves. What we are willing to do for a buck: the way we present ourselves to different people in different settings to different ends; the extent to which we mix our personal with our professional relationships. There are no right or wrong answers to these questions, but whatever answers we decide upon determine much about who we are and our chances at personal success.

I am particularly fascinated by all this because on the few

occasions in my life when I have had to sell, I have hated it. No one has ever suggested I was a "natural salesman," the shiny-toothed, back-slapping hero of the car lot and backyard barbecue. I could never, as they say, sell sand to Arabs, or ice to Eskimos. Put me in front of a telephone with a list of names to call and I flinch. Tell me to ask for money, and most likely I'll disappear to the bathroom, lock the door, and not reappear until you've gone. People who are bad at sales will often use self-flattering excuses to persuade themselves that their incompetence is a virtue. "I just can't lie," they'll say. Or "I'm not enough of a bully." When in fact, like me, they're just bad at sales.

What follows is not a lesson in how to sell. It is an effort to sort through the paradoxes and difficulties of this most fascinating of professions; to confront a subject that people often try to reduce to tricks, nuggets, and ten simple steps. Selling is the single largest function in business. Millions more are employed in sales jobs in America than in manufacturing, let alone marketing, strategy, finance, or any of the other parasitic business functions. All over the world, from the most basic to the most advanced economies, selling is the horse that pulls the cart of business. It is both the most primitive and the most evolved aspect of economic life. It is ignored by business academics and is fraught with moral risk.

There are more lies told about selling than about any other aspect of business life. So I went in search of some truths. Not absolutes or answers, but honesty.

I traveled widely in my search because I wanted to be sure to think about selling not as a cultural or industry-specific problem, but as a human practice, common across peoples and businesses. The traits required to sell (resilience, conviction, persistence, and likability), are not needed just in business, but in life. I wanted to discover who can sell and how they do it. To set salespeople in their context and to ask questions that the vast sales training industry would rather not have asked at all: Is the ability to sell in fact trainable? Is the ability to sell a gift of nature or nurture? What are the personal costs a salesperson must bear?

I began with a memory from my own childhood.

Chapter 1

LOOSE ROBES

Success consists of going from failure to failure
with no loss of enthusiasm.

WINSTON CHURCHILL

asablanca in August was no place for a grumpy English twelve-year-old. The heat was tireless and the sunlight glared off the white buildings of the slumbering city. The expatriate French and English had skipped town and the remaining Moroccans had slipped down a couple of gears, escaping into the cool, tiled darkness of their homes. My father, a clergyman, had taken over duties at the local Anglican church for a month and received in return use of the vicarage and a rickety old Peugeot. It was our summer holiday.

A couple of weeks into our holiday, once my father felt confident driving the Peugeot in Moroccan traffic, we drove north to Fez, barreling along the desert roads praying that the car would hold up. There was no air-conditioning, and if I opened the window, I risked a face full of dust. The only option was to steam gently in the velour seats. One of the parishioners in Casablanca had offered us the use of his Riad in the medina of Fez. We parked on the edge of the old town and walked into its shadowy heart. At the end of an alleyway, hemmed in by shops selling bronze and silver dishes, was a heavy wooden door. My father rapped against it and we were let in. A small courtyard, cast in gray light despite the brilliant sun high above, swallowed us up. The only sound came from a small fountain in the center. After settling in, it was time for us to do what everyone who visits a Moroccan souk must do: shop.

Shopping in Morocco at the time was not a question of pushing a cart down an aisle. It was more like hand-to-hand combat. Tugging, goosing, stroking, bellowing, caressing, whispering—anything was allowed provided it brought a foreign wallet into a store. My father, who had spent many years working in India, and mother, who grew up in Burma, found it all immensely entertaining. In England, all they had was the orderly high street shops, the polite butchers and grocers ("Good morning madam, will that be all?"), and the Muzak-y hum of the supermarket. In Fez, they realized how much they had missed the hullaballoo of the Oriental bazaar.

I don't remember precisely how we ended up with three rugs, but I do remember this: Yielding to a persistent old fellow in a dark brown djellaba. Entering his narrow store, where rugs were piled high in the corners and tacked to every wall. Sitting on the floor, our backs against an itchy stack of carpets. A long, explanatory preamble, describing different rugs made by different tribes, the High Atlas tribes and the Low Atlas tribes, *Berber* pronounced as if with a shiver, "brrr-brrr." My parents talking to each other about the rooms back at our home in England and their requirements for rugs: warm, colorful, something to lift their mood and console them during chilly mornings and the frequent times when the heating system went down. Cups of sugary mint tea being brought to our feet on a bronze tray by a boy younger than me. A flurry of rugs, flicked open and drifting onto the floor around us like flocks of geese. I remember the wizened dealer producing a Fez hat, the familiar purple cylinder topped by a tassel, trying to put it on my father's head, and when he refused, placing it on mine.

Then the negotiation. My father smiling, sipping his tea, one hand resting on his knee. My mother, a far tougher proposition, scowling, shaking her head at every price, pushing the dealer lower and lower, her credit card lodged immovably in her wallet. The dealer looking up to the heavens, to the naked bulb hanging from the ceiling, and pleading with my mother, "Be fair, do not be so hard." He had mouths to feed, bills to pay, he could not be in the business of giving away these rugs, feel the quality, look at the workmanship, think of the hours invested, the bent, hardened fingers that knotted this wool. And you are offering to pay how much? Finally, settling on a price. The sigh of relief all round. The credit card swiped, the rugs taken and folded into impossibly tight bundles, and the promise that they would be sent to us in England. And then the walk home. My parents wondering if they would ever see the rugs again, their thrill at the whole performance. And then three weeks after we arrived home, the postman arriving with the packages marked "Fez." The blaze of reds and blues brightening an autumnal English day, and every day since.

Any tourist who has visited Morocco has a similar tale to tell. The haggle is as much a part of the Moroccan holiday experience as the performing monkeys in the town squares. Several people told me that they had never experienced salesmen like the ones in North Africa and Turkey. So I decided to go and see if anything had changed since I was a boy, to find out what made the country's merchants such redoubtable and renowned salesmen. An American friend who has lived for years in Morocco said the man I must meet lived in the north of the country, in Tangier.

Tangier is the most cosmopolitan city in Morocco, in the rough-and-tumble way of port cities. From much of the city, you can see clear across the Straits of Gibraltar to Spain. The white plumes of boats bustling back and forth between Africa and Europe carve up the blue of the Mediterranean, while more stately container ships move crosswise between the Mediterranean and the vast Atlantic. The cafés in the center of town feel unchanged from the 1950s when American writers like Paul Bowles came to the city in search of exotic liberation from their Western lives. All through the day, men sit at the tables drinking mint tea and coffee, smoking, watching life pass by on the street. You see a good number of older, lizard-skinned Frenchmen wearing blazers and Moroccan slippers strolling along the streets, and you feel that this remains a place of decadent escape.

Opposite the El Minzah Hotel in the center of town, where I was staying, was a doorway crammed with rugs, vases, and other decorative objects. The elderly store owner sat on a stool just inside surrounded by blue glass lanterns, orange beads, and backgammon sets. There was a large callus on his forehead from his bowing to the ground in prayer. I explained that I was in town to learn about Moroccan salesmen. He nodded and reached under the counter to produce a scruffy little white book titled *The Rogue's Guide to Tangier*. He asked me to return it when I was done.

That afternoon, I read the book, paying particular attention to the chapter "Bargaining, the Incredible Art Of." The waggish authors, Bert and Mabel Winter, wrote in the tone of nineteenth-century British colonial administrators: "The Moroccan will always let you believe you got a good bargain." He misses nothing, they warn, from the wear on a wedding band to the state of your teeth, the roughness of your hands, and the slightest display of vanity, shyness, or nerves. The Winters advise us to always seem bored during bargaining, and describe tricks the salesman will play.

He will give you lightning-fast answers to questions, and will "make the injured spaniel look" to a wife. He will say, "OK, give me a price," an attempt to elicit information that you must never answer. Instead, you should examine the object under discussion and say, "No you give *me* a price. It's not worth bargaining for." When he gives that price, just smile. His hands will fly up, he will look shocked and disappointed, but if he continues, the game is on.

They conclude:

> While Tangier tradesmen make every effort to keep prices high, it is sometimes necessary to decrease them on short notice. Two seconds later, to be precise. The speed at which the second and third price come down depends entirely on your awareness, your sense of humor, your battle prowess, and most important, your ability to counterattack with a fast answer. Don't be surprised if that makes bargaining sound like warfare. It is exactly that. A war of words which the best man will win. Him, not you.

The way to test this truth, they suggest, is to try selling back what you just bought.

So much in business is evanescent. Companies rise and fall, relationships last only as long as necessary, and technology quickly becomes obsolete. And yet travel the world, and you will always find a marketplace; whether in the ancient town squares of Europe or the souks of the Middle East, you'll find permanent structures where people gather to buy and sell. At a shadowy bend of the Rue Les Almouhades, the main artery of Tangier's Medina, is number 66, the commercial home of Abdel Majid Rais El Fenni, or Majid for short. He was the man I had come to Tangier to see. To get to his shop, you must pass dozens of others, all targeted at the cruise ship groups who come barging through the Medina's narrow streets several times a day. These stores all sell the same things: ceramic bowls, cigarette lighters, souvenir Fez hats and imitation silver daggers, tagine dishes, and models of camels. The owners sit outside badgering tourists to come in. The smarter ones cut deals with the tour guides to bring in their groups. But this is a high-volume, low-margin business. You may sell a lot of lighters, but by the time you've paid 40 percent to the guide, there isn't much left for you.

Majid's is an entirely different operation. The friend who referred me to him said that Majid had started out like every other peddler in the souk, but had figured out a way to rise above the competition. His guest book contains the signatures of Yves Saint Laurent and Jacques Chirac, and he has sold to rock stars and ritzy hoteliers. If you're rich and you want a North African feel to your home, you come to Majid. He is known to interior decorators, collectors, and antiques dealers the world over, and yet he started out a street hawker. I arrived at his store soon after he had opened for the day and he ushered me to a sofa against the back wall. He lit a chunk of sandalwood, "to change the atmosphere and create nice spirits," and settled down in a throne-like wooden chair, wreathed in smoke from the sandalwood and tobacco. Water splashed behind him in a fountain.

He is a small man with a soft, unlined face, like the inside of a calfskin purse. His eyes are nearly black and are damp, like olives bobbing in a stew. He tends to wear matching outfits: one day it's black pants, black shirt, black waistcoat, and a circular black velvet cap like an overturned soup bowl; the next day the same but in dark green. On the day I met with him, he wore a chunk of amber the size of a Ping-Pong ball on a leather string around his neck, which he fondled with his left hand as he talked. Pinched between the forefinger and second finger of his right hand was a cigarette he had rolled himself and which he was always forgetting and having to relight.

His store, he said, "is my kingdom, where I can be myself." Along the walls are cabinets, lit from inside, displaying ornate silverware, coral, and amber beads from all across North and Saharan Africa. There is a tiled fountain at the center of the main floor, surrounded by stacks of colorful blankets and rugs, silk shirts and dresses, and beautifully inlaid wooden mirrors and glass lamps. The shop has two more stories, all beautifully clean, whitewashed, tiled, and decorated with carpets and furniture, leading up to a roof garden with a view over the Medina.

Majid grew up in a village in northern Morocco. His grandfather and uncle were both tradesmen and he remembers fabric dealers coming to his house when he was a child. Typical was a portly man who would settle down beneath a tree and start to unpack his wares. Majid's grandfather and uncle would join him to look at the fabric and talk. The dealer would be invited to stay for dinner, and once they had eaten, the negotiation would begin. Within minutes, the dealer would stand up, shove his fabrics back into his truck, turn to Majid's father and uncle, break wind and waft the smell into their faces, then storm off. A few days later he would be back. There would be another dinner, more shouting, arm waving, and storming off.

The whole process could take days, but eventually there would be a deal. A few days later another salesman would arrive and the entire process would begin again.

"My uncle used to say that in business, you need three things," said Majid. "The age of Noah, hundreds of years. The money of Suleyman, who dressed his slaves in gold. And the patience of Dawud, David."

Majid's father was an artisan who made kaftans and leather goods and sold them at a stall in Fez. When the competition in Fez grew too stiff in the mid-1960s, as tourists began arriving in Morocco, he moved up to Tangier. In 1965, at the age of fourteen, Majid opened his first store, next to his father's in the Kasbah of Tangier, selling sheepskin jackets and other trinkets to the hippies passing through town. "I had this big Afro and the tourists liked to pinch my cheeks. I was a salesman kid. Every shop around me sold the same thing, so I was just another of those kids saying 'come and look at my shop, come and look at my shop' to everyone who passed by. But by today's standards, we weren't aggressive. If a tourist passed my shop, I didn't follow them and tug their sleeve. Everyone was very clear about territories."

This isn't to say he was an angel. "I looked innocent then, and I did a few tricks to make a little more money. There was this Englishman who stank of gin who wanted to buy leather. I put up with the smell of his breath because I wanted to sell. He wanted black leather. I had it in sheepskin and goatskin. If I sold him the goat, I would make only five dirham in profit. If I sold him sheep, I made twenty dirham profit. The sheep was cheaper, but had a much better margin. He wanted to buy the goat, but for the lower price of the sheep, which would have left me with nothing. So when I sold it, I just switched the goat for the sheepskin. The next day, he came back and said the leather wasn't the one he wanted. I told him that for another five dirham, he could have the goat. Then I rolled up the sheepskin and gave it back to him. The next day, he came back again and ordered two coffees and told me he was going to keep the leather, but he wanted me to show him how I fooled him. So I did. I showed him how I stashed the sheepskin behind my knee as I bent down to roll up the goatskin and then at the last minute switched them to give him the leather that made more money for me."

The more time he spent in the Kasbah, the more Majid realized he wanted to be more than just another peddler hassling tourists. So he decided to educate himself. He traveled to Mali and Mauretania to meet up with the great caravans of traders who trek through the western Sahara. He learned to buy and polish amber and taught himself about silverware and ivory. "Anywhere I heard there was something interesting, I'd go."

His travels taught him not only about objects, but also about value. "The salesman in Tangier is living in a cave," he said. "One salesman up the road sells wallets for a certain price, so you sell them for a lower one." Majid discovered that he did not have to accept this race to the bottom. With different products, he could set and manipulate prices in a very different way. After many visits to the amber traders of the Sahara, Majid came to perceive the difference between their prices and the prices acceptable to European and Middle Eastern clients. He realized he could make his own market by buying all the amber he could afford when prices were low, polishing it, storing it, and controlling supply.

"What makes me different from others is that there is a story behind every object in my window," he said. "I never studied beautiful things, but I studied the best of other people's theories about beautiful things. So I know how to deal with wealthy customers, whether it's the Rolling Stones or Catherine Deneuve or John Malkovich, Bob Dylan or Elizabeth Taylor. I remember I knew Elizabeth Taylor was coming and I brought my camera, but then I forgot to take a picture of her because I was consumed by the moment of explaining everything in my store." Through presentation and storytelling, and understanding the desires of his customers, he could create value and set prices beyond the dreams of his neighbors in the souk.

His grasp of commerce also deepened the more he bought and sold. "You judge a good salesman when he buys. The profit is not when you sell, it's when you buy. You make a profit the moment you buy. Only losers wait till they sell to make a profit. If I ask to look at something and you show it to me, 90 percent of the time, it's going to be mine. I was once in the fruit market and saw a seller wearing a beautiful embroidered jacket. It was filthy, but I could see the quality. I bought it from him and the other sellers laughed because I took his pants too. Everyone is always ready to buy or sell, it's just a question of asking. The thing that is not for sale is *haram*, forbidden by God."

Before he got married, to a Danish woman, Majid was in the habit of furnishing his home and then selling everything in it. "Now my wife gets attached to things." But if you invite him around for dinner, beware. He has been known to buy his host's carpets and roll them up and take them the moment the plates have been cleared.

Despite this apparent boldness, Majid has also developed a very stoic approach to selling. "You are like a beggar in sales, asking again and again all day. My father used to say that the salesman should have loose robes. You never get upset. Of course, sometimes you have customers and you want to kill them. But you're not allowed to."

Businesspeople often talk of the importance of humility, of serving your customers and acknowledging the fickleness of the markets. For salespeople, humility is not an option. But it is something that can be turned to their advantage.

"As a salesman, you look at everyone," Majid told me. "You pay attention. But often customers don't even look at salespeople. They treat them like dirt. But if you stand there and watch and listen, you can learn a lot about a customer. I tend to leave people alone to look at things. I turn the lights on, pay attention to what they're looking at, but I don't hassle them. The salesman who interrupts and waves his hands about has another twenty years of learning to do."

As we spoke, an Asian man entered the store, a camera hanging around his neck. Majid got up and turned on the lights in the cabinet next to where the man was standing. The man did not acknowledge him but kept walking through the store. Majid kept turning on the lights, but the man just kept walking through and out, looking just once at Majid, and only briefly, dismissively. Majid came back and sat down. Don't you mind? I asked.

"Loose robes," he said, flapping open his waistcoat. "Customers come into my store with all these stories and warnings in their heads, fears that they're going to be ripped off. There was this American man once who came in and started looking at my things. He looked at my silver and asked 'Is this silver?' I said yes, and he said 'Moroccan silver,' meaning it was a blend of metals. He looked at another piece and asked if it was antique. I said yes. He said, 'Made in the backyard, you mean.' My wife was getting very upset. But it's like fishing. When you have the fish, if you force it, you break the line. So you must let it out, bring it in, let it out, bring it in, until it gets tired. Then you just reel it in. He looked at my amber and asked 'Is this plastic?' I said no, 'It's amber.' 'Amber made in Hong Kong?' he said. He was putting me down all the time and I let him until I found the moment to push back. Finally, he picked up this beautiful ivory bowl, one that had been carved by many generations of craftsmen, and he started shaking it. So I took him by the wrist and removed the object from his hand and held it up to the light. 'You mishandled this piece,' I told him. I explained its history, and he realized how stupid he had been. He said he was sorry, and I told him it was OK. He didn't know. He felt ashamed. And that night he went to dinner with some people here in Tangier who told him of my reputation. The next day, he came by. Yesterday he was a wild horse. Today, he wants to be ridden, and I ride him. Whatever I say is now correct. He bought some impressive silver bracelets. If I hadn't had the patience, I'd have lost a good fish. I didn't use force, I used my head."

Majid's loose robes are a form of resilience, an essential trait for salespeople, and for any of us who hope to succeed in life. It is the ability to maintain an emotional equilibrium in the face of bad events. Rudyard Kipling describes it in his poem "If" as the ability to "meet with triumph and disaster / And treat those two impostors just the same." We see resilience in those who survived the Holocaust and went on to live rich, productive lives. But we also see it in anyone who survives each day hearing "no" more often than "yes."

The good news from psychologists is that resilience is far more common than previously thought, and we are starting to understand how it is developed. Early studies of soldiers who suffered from posttraumatic stress disorder (PTSD) led us to believe that certain grim events led inevitably to psychological trauma. New research, however, suggests that this was an exaggerated view. In focusing on those soldiers who did suffer PTSD, researchers had ignored the majority who did not, or who were at least capable of moving on quickly with their lives despite the appalling things they had seen and suffered. We are much more resilient than we thought. We do not all need to "work through" our problems with a psychologist or "reach closure" on every bad thing that befalls us. Many of us can put those bad events in perspective ourselves, count our blessings, and move on.

George Bonnano, a psychologist at Columbia University, has written that various factors can produce resilience: a supportive family and good friends; the experience of hardship or bad luck in childhood; and not being neurotic. Alone or in combination, these factors produce a trait that Bonnano calls "hardiness," similar to what we see in plants that can endure the traumas of harsh pruning or brutal winters and yet flower every spring. In humans, he describes resilience as "being committed to finding a meaningful purpose in life, the belief that one can influence one's surroundings and the outcome of events, and the belief that one can learn and grow from both positive and negative life experiences." Majid has this trait in spades, however blithely he flicks at his lapels, calling it just "loose robes." We will see it repeatedly among great salespeople, this acceptance of rejection and failure as essential to building the muscles necessary for eventual success. They do not avoid rejection, but see it as a vaccine that strengthens their ability to resist the personal battering inevitable in a life in sales.

All around him in the Kasbah, you used to see salesmen using force. It was the traditional way of doing things, until it reached such a pitch that tourists started to avoid Morocco. According to Majid, the low point came when a wealthy American developer visited Marrakech at the invitation of the previous king. Like every foreign arrival, he was chased in his chauffeured car from the airport by kids on motorbikes asking to be his guide. When the man's driver waved them off, one of the kids spat at the car. The American never invested and the king responded by creating a new division of tourist police whose job it is to ensure that salesmen and guides give visitors a little more space.

Nonetheless, there remains a dominant methodology to selling to tourists that hasn't changed. Most tourists arrive at a shop with a guide. The guide has learned certain details about his wards, which he will murmur to the shop owner as he arrives. They are here for an afternoon perhaps, in which they are under pressure to buy. Or they are just in from Fez or Marrakech, in which case they may be more knowledgeable. The guides use code words for speed and discretion: "plastic" means Americans; "dahanzi" means in and out; a mosque without a minaret means the customers are Jewish. Some store owners have contacts at the major hotels, which tell them how many tourists are arriving when, and how long they are staying, so they can send guides to meet them at the airports.

Once the guide has imparted his information, the sales show begins. Majid is now on his feet, dancing around his store performing the archetypal Moroccan sales pantomime. First the salesman lets you look. But the moment you express even the slightest interest, the rugs or objects are all over the floor. " Just to look, just to look," says the salesman as you shrink back. Then he says, "Tell me which one you like." It's exactly the same trick used by American life insurance salesmen, avoiding questions that might elicit the answer no. You might say, "I'm not buying," to which the salesmen will reply, "Just one you like, just tell me one." If at any point you say, "How much?" you are hooked. Then it's, "For you I give a special price. I can tell you're a good guy." If now you don't buy, the salesman ramps up the emotional pressure. It is no longer about you and him in a simple commercial transaction. As my rug seller in Marrakesh said, it was about my children, and possibly my children's children, about our duty as adults to the next generation. "You waste my time," Majid is saying, thrusting out his forearms, palms upward, elbows held to his torso. "I have to feed my children, pay bills. I thought you were my friend. Now you waste my time." Tears follow. "My family has ten kids, no room." You ask for a day to think, at which point the guide intervenes and says, "Tomorrow everything is closed." But it's Tuesday. "It's a holiday." You thought you were buying a rug. Turns out you were walking into an emotional pincer movement.

The salesmen of the Kasbah apply this method to everything they sell, and it deludes them, Majid believes. "They think they are so smart, they could sell anything. They ask for work and tell me 'I'm a knife, I'm very sharp.' And I tell them, I don't need salesmen cutting heads off in my shop. I need to protect my reputation." Majid said he had no theories about selling, just experience. He has had the same customers for more than thirty-five years. "You don't get customers like that just from having beautiful eyes." He adores what he sells, which is evident from the care with which every object in his store is presented. And he is capable of keeping the long view.

"If one of my customers brings something back because it doesn't work for them, I always take it back. And I tell them I'm happy, because the object has gained value while they've owned it." A Frenchwoman from Rabat once bought a piece of amber, then came back a few weeks later with friends from Switzerland asking for a refund. She claimed Majid had sold her plastic. He took the amber and laid out 3,000 euros, the price she had paid, and set it on the counter, then began telling stories about his jewelry to her friends. After a while, she said she didn't want the money, but rather her amber back. It will be an extra 120 euros, Majid told her, as the price of amber had gone up since she first bought the piece. She pleaded with him but eventually agreed to the higher price.

Majid's observations and techniques, which he learned entirely through experience and from growing up in a family of salesmen, hew closely to those observed in successful American salesmen, notably his use of "declarative knowledge." Declarative knowledge is knowing that something is the case, as opposed to procedural knowledge, which relates to how to do something. It is the diagnosis that precedes treatment. Salespeople in fast-moving situations must be able to assess customers and their wants before deciding how to approach them. This is one of the hardest things to teach. It requires good instincts and the ability to read people quickly. It is both the most animal skill in sales, and the most sophisticated.

Majid told me a story of a man from Texas who visited his store. He looked around at the various carpets and asked their prices. He seemed underwhelmed. He wanted a rug for his home in Houston, and he wanted the very best. Majid immediately perceived that by "best," the man meant "the most expensive." Majid decided to toy with him. He did indeed have some very expensive rugs, but he was not sure they would be what the man had in mind. The customer began to slaver. "Yes, that's exactly what I want." Appearing reluctant, Majid took him up to see a selection of rugs. He pointed out one, which, he said apologetically, was extremely expensive. "That's the one," the man said, and paid for it on the spot. Had Majid taken "best" to mean the finest, he might have wasted time treating the customer as a true rug connoisseur. But the declarative knowledge derived from his experience allowed him to cut to the chase. This customer equated quality with price and wanted more than anything to tell visitors to his home that he had bought the best rug in Morocco, at a price to prove it.

Accurately perceiving the motivations of a customer then, is just as important as understanding what product they want. A pharmaceutical rep visiting a busy doctor must know that the doctor has just a few spare minutes and doesn't want a lengthy pharmacological lecture. A realtor must be able to distinguish between the wealthy buyer wanting a beach house before Memorial Day and the young couple eager to make the down payment they scraped together go as far as possible. Often the distinctions aren't quite so obvious. Majid has spent enough time sitting in his shop watching customers come and go to know exactly when to push and when to hold back, when to turn the lights on in the jewelry cabinet and when to embarrass the husband who is showing off in front of his wife. He reads each situation correctly before deciding how to act.

The process was well described by David Szymanski, a professor of marketing at Texas A&M University, in a paper about the importance of declarative knowledge to those in personal sales. "In an environment where competition is keen and many goods can satisfy the client's product requirements, a competitive advantage may accrue to the salesperson who additionally satisfies the client's sales process requirements." In Majid's case, there is rarely time or sufficient information to decide on the perfect selling approach with every customer. So what he does is take what information he has and sort rapidly through his mental filing cabinet of experience to find the closest match. It is a system of advanced pattern recognition. "In essence," Szymanski writes, "the salesperson must engage in a qualification process at each stage. For instance, when initially confronted with a sales lead, the salesperson must decide whether the subject should be classified as a prospect or a suspect (a person or organization unlikely to purchase the good)." Once classified as a prospect, the lead must be evaluated further. Will he buy a lot or a little? Is price going to be an issue or not? Will he be able to close immediately, or will he need time to talk it over with others? At each step, the salesperson must try to maximize the return on their investment of selling effort. Their success will depend on the accuracy of their classification at every step of the sale.

Szymanski suggests that salespeople construct mental hierarchies of customer attributes. For example, a customer who wears expensive clothes and drives a Ferrari is assumed to have plenty of money and to be eager to show it off. The novice salesperson will stop there. The more experienced one might look more closely. Perhaps there's a button missing on the cuff, or the car could use a wash. Maybe this customer isn't all he's cracked up to be. A novice might quickly assume stereotypical gender roles between a husband and wife, whereas experience would tell you who really makes the buying decision. What the seasoned salesperson is looking for is the defining characteristic, the one that will identify a customer as a particular type. In the Texan rug buyer's case, it was that he equated price with quality. Majid quickly put this at the top of his mental hierarchy. The difference between effective and ineffective salespeople, then, becomes not just the accuracy of their definitions but how they rank them in their mental hierarchy. Two salespeople may see exactly the same characteristics in a customer, but the successful one will spot the characteristic that matters above all others and establish a sales strategy accordingly.

Good salespeople settle into a groove of identifying their customers' most important characteristics, selling more, trusting more in their mental hierarchies and becoming ever sharper and more successful as a result. Bad salespeople misread a few customers and then revert from specifics back to generalities. They never develop the edge we see in salespeople who are constantly adapting and refining their approach for each and every sale. Majid is a master at categorizing sales leads (the people who walk through his door) and tailoring his approach accordingly. He compared the different modes of selling to gears in a car. "You change because the gear needs changing," he said. Sometimes you need to be patient. At other times, you must treat the customer as a king, to make them feel powerful and inclined to exercise that power by buying. Sometimes you need to teach, to establish your authority with customers who take you for a mere peddler. Majid watches, listens, and adapts, keeping his emotions in check so he can read the cues of his customers correctly. Stress, greed, or any other kind of excitement would inhibit his ability to work at speed, to process the information he absorbs to create the perfect blend of product, message, and sales process. Time and again, he sees customers come into his store, as he puts it, like wild horses. He gives up his time, he keeps his robes loose. He lets them go to other stores to compare prices and products. He does not compromise or grovel. And five out of ten come back. "When they come back, they're not the wild horse anymore." Majid rose from his seat as he said this, bent his knees a little, and settled into the posture of a man riding a horse, one hand out front gripping the reins, the other tapping gently with a crop. "Now you just ride them in."

Majid's approach marks him as an expert in the art of the personal sale. But it's worth noting that his abilities are useful to anyone, regardless of their profession, in myriad life situations. The skills that distinguish the best salesmen are also those that can allow us all to thrive anywhere in the social world, where success so often comes from "reading" others and adjusting our own actions and strategies accordingly to achieve our ends. But if sales acumen opens a window on life's broader possibilities, the challenges salespeople face—the stresses of anxiety, rejection, and outright failure—are a concentrated dose of the punishments life inflicts on us all.

Chapter 2

THE PITCH

The successful showman must have a
decided taste for catering for the public;
prominent perceptive faculties; tact; a
thorough knowledge of human nature;
great suavity; and plenty of "soft soap."

P. T. BARNUM

ajid's education in selling was purely experiential. He
grew up in a family of salesmen and then spent his
adult life in the souk. He is resilient, funny, keenly
insightful into the unspoken desires of his customers, and masterly
at categorizing them. And he doesn't get hung up on the ethical
quandaries of what he does. He regards commerce as a delightful
game. But while Majid honed his skills in the ancient alleyways of
the Tangier Medina, his qualities appear in equal doses in Tony Sullivan, another self-taught salesman who operates in a very different
and much newer galaxy of the sales universe: TV infomercials.

A good infomercial is often more entertaining than the television shows that surround it. There are the rudimentary displays of
choppers, mops, and devices that work wonders on your abs; the

constant repetition of benefits and price; the exhortations to "call now" to receive "not one, not two, but three" extra items! And then there are the hosts themselves, an exotic collection of carnival barkers and soapbox seducers, the night owls of cable television. Watching infomercials, like walking through the souk or into Majid's shop, is entertainment enough, whether you buy or not.

I first came across Sullivan late one night when he was pitching the Smart Mop. What grabbed my bleary-eyed attention was not the mop itself, but the fact that he was a fellow Englishman, pitching on American television. And he wasn't doing the traditional aristocratic Grey Poupon routine. Rather, he reminded me of the men who would pitch their wares in the open-air market in Northampton, the English town where I grew up, smiling and cracking jokes even as the cold wind rubbed their cheeks raw.

"What do you do if you get a spill like this all over your kitchen floor? This is a whole can of soda," Sullivan barks, as he pours a can of Diet Coke on the floor. "I'll tell you, you reach for the Smart Mop. Watch this. To wring it out, you lift and you twist. You never bend your back and you never touch the dirty water. Unwind it, drop it down, and you're ready to go." Cut to a shot of the mop soaking up the mess. "Now, it's made of synthetic chamois and it will hold and absorb up to twenty times its own weight in liquid. And the best part is it doesn't drip. To prove it, I'll hold it over my head. You can see, no drips. And in these tough times, wring it back into the glass and it's ready to drink all over. Sand on a kitchen floor, ketchup to make it worse, even mustard to make it really bad. You could just push it under the fridge, or pick it up with the Smart Mop. Watch as it picks up the sand, the dirt, the dust, the ketchup, the mustard—no sweeping and no vacuuming. It cuts your cleaning time in half." Every one of Sullivan's staccato directions and boasts is accompanied by images of the Smart Mop in action. "You shimmy the chamois and look, this mop is as thirsty as a camel in the Sahara desert." It is an extraordinary piece of instruction and persuasion that left me wishing that children could be taught science this way.

I met Sullivan at the offices of his company, Sullivan Productions, on the ground floor of a condo building just south of Tampa's downtown, close to the water. He lives just a five-minute drive away on Davis Island—twelve houses down from the Yankees' shortstop Derek Jeter. Parked at a dock in Sullivan's backyard is a colossal speedboat, which he likes to take on spins down to Miami. Sullivan is a tall man with broad shoulders and cropped gray hair who seems to be constantly fighting the urge to laugh. He talks and walks quickly, and the moment he mentions any of the many products he has sold, he drops effortlessly into his pitch. The amazing Washmatic? "It makes water run uphill. You give your car a shower not a bath." The Fluoroscope? "See things twice as bright and twice as clear." The Turbo Snake "gets your flow to go. You ever take a shower and end up taking a bath? Dog hair, cat hair, long hair, short hair, your hair, my hair, the Turbo Snake gets it all." The Hard Water Wand "turns a toilet that looks like poo into a toilet that looks like new."

Since 2004, Sullivan has taught a class at Princeton University, at the invitation of Dan Nosenchuck, a professor of mechanical and aerospace engineering. The class is part of an undergraduate course called Entrepreneurial Engineering, which aims to teach students how to bring their goods and services into the marketplace. "Many classes which try to teach this use case studies and panels of judges who look at various products," Nosenchuck told me. "But the problem remains this: does the market want or care about what these engineers are producing? And how do you find out?" Nosenchuck turned for answers to a local New Jersey company, Telebrands, which creates products, tests them with infomercials, and then tries to distribute them through retailers like Wal-Mart and CVS. Telebrands put him in touch with Sullivan, who makes and stars in many of its infomercials. "What Sully does is give students the confidence that they can create an effective solution for bringing their product to market. He comes and lectures and gives students specific tools and techniques, storyboards and scripts, a lot of real-world advice. He merges the worlds of test marketing and selling. He'd make a very effective professor of business."

Sullivan gleefully describes himself as a "pitchman." And while that is certainly how he began his professional life, he is now something considerably more, a vital piece of a highly evolved chain of inventors, manufacturers, and distributors. While he appears to be selling on television, he is also fulfilling a more important purpose, testing the response to products. The real money in infomercials these days is not in actually moving merchandise, but in proving concepts and testing markets for products so they have a chance at the real jackpot: shelf space in Wal-Mart. Infomercials are a kind of highly targeted focus group, by which you can test products and the methods of selling them. They are a way to develop the declarative knowledge required to sell a product. What matters to consumers, and how do they wish to be sold to?

"Many professors will get up and talk about sales only in passing," says Nosenchuck. "They'll give some acknowledgment to the fact that it's important ultimately to sell the product. But selling is not met face-on at universities. Sully backfills that very nicely for us. His isn't a course in developing direct-response products, but in imbuing students with the knowledge that markets are comprised of constituents in multiple venues"—who need to be approached and have their responses tested. "Sully melds the elements which go into these infomercial productions. He melds the notion of marketing, testing, and sales very well."

Sullivan grew up in northwest Devon, an idyllic corner of England, where his father ran a successful business renting one-armed bandits to pubs. "From the age of four, I would go on the rounds with my dad, so I grew up in the company of publicans, these flamboyant, joke-telling, storytelling characters." His father, he says, was a terrific salesman, a storyteller who would tell him that in life and business he should "never let anyone tell you no." The first sale Sully recalls closing was on his parents' house. He was nine years old. "The estate agent came round with these prospective buyers, but my parents weren't in, so I showed them around." There was a narrow flight of stairs up to the playroom which he urged his visitors to climb. He took them out to see the tree house. It turned out they had young children too. "I took them all around the yard and showed them everything I loved about the house. I remember telling them I didn't want to move because it was such a great house, but my parents had to move." The couple bought the house and the real estate agent told Sullivan's parents, "Your son sold your house for you."

When Sullivan was in his teens, his father started sending him out on collection calls. "I was quite nervous about it, but I remember Angie, the assistant in my dad's office, telling me, 'Don't ever be afraid to ask for what people owe you.' I still think of that." He would have to pursue payments for fruit machines and pool tables, and on several occasions was chased from pubs by angry landlords.

Sullivan's path to infomercials began one summer when he was twenty-one, when a friend called Phil Clamp failed to pay a parking ticket. Clamp was running a T-shirt stall at Bideford market, held during the summer on the grounds of the local soccer club. One day he had to go to court to dispute the ticket, and he asked Sullivan to look after his stand. Sullivan arrived early in the morning and spent a couple of hours erecting the metal stand and laying out the stacks of T-shirts. Then, shortly before the market opened, a man pulled up opposite him in a brown Volvo wagon. He took out a folding table and a few small contraptions. After drinking a cup of tea, he began his pitch for the amazing Washmatic: "It gives your car a shower rather than a bath!" Sullivan sat at Clamp's stand and sold a few T-shirts all day. The man opposite him was drawing in crowds and selling four or five Washmatics every seven or eight minutes. "He had no different sizes, one color, one SKU [stock-keeping unit code]," says Sullivan. "And he did it all from one folding table. He made £500 in a day. I made £50. The difference was he was pitching, and I was just sitting there waiting for customers."

At the end of the day, Sullivan went up to him and said he wanted to learn. The man brushed him off. When Clamp finally returned from Barnstaple County Court, he gave Sullivan £10 in commission and thanked him. "But I told him that if he ever saw the Washmatics man again, he should tell him I'm serious about learning his business."

The following week, the salesman called. His said his name was Mark Bingham, and he told Sullivan to meet him the following weekend at Croyde Bay market and bring a tape recorder. He told him to record his pitch and then learn it word for word. The week after that, Bingham said he'd give him an hour over lunch to sell the amazing Washmatic. Sully would park his car at the house he was renting and recite the pitch and perform the display in the reflection of the front window. "My brother and my friends would see me and they thought I'd lost the plot." Two weeks later he got his hour.

"I was a nervous wreck," he says. But then the first person approached him and asked how the Washmatic worked. "So I began talking like Bingham had told me to, sticking to the script, word for word. 'It's like giving your car a shower instead of a bath. The faster you go, the faster it flows. As soon as you stop, it stops.' The first guy bought one, and suddenly I had a crowd—two, four, eight, sixteen people. I didn't fail and I worked the whole hour, getting a little more confident all the time. I ended up selling seven units in an hour. Bingham was floored. He spat his tea out." He told Sullivan to come back the next week to work Bideford while he worked another town. The next week, Sullivan sold sixty Washmatics. "I remember that summer very clearly. I wore a straw hat, had £1,000 in my pocket and got paid £200 in cold hard cash for a day's work. I realized I was good at it."

Sullivan quickly joined the cast of vendors who toured markets around the country. "In the UK, the pitchmen are lovable rogues, wide boys. People would come to the market, buy a hot dog, a cup of tea and watch the pitches. It's part stand-up, part sales, part entertainment. People would say, 'go and see the kid with the Washmatic.'" He enjoyed the minor celebrity it brought him, the affection of the market crowds. At night, Sullivan would go around to pubs and clubs organizing karaoke evenings, often playing second fiddle to stand-up comics. "I'd pick up their one-liners and add them to my pitch."

The purpose of the pitch is to put a crowd "under the ether,"

Sullivan explains. It is about telling an irresistible story. "Ray Charles used to say that people like country music because of the stories. It's the same with products." You want your audience so enraptured that when you say, "Who wants one?" there is simply no other possible answer besides "I do." It all begins with a seemingly casual, friendly conversation with the first person who approaches you. "Good morning, mate, where have you come from? Bristol? I was just up there . . ." Then the moment the person looks at your product, you slide into the pitch. "You want me to show you how it works? You got a minute? Well you take your bucket of water . . ." This first person is your "number one." Number one has to stand there for the length of the pitch. You've got to keep number one. But then as number two approaches, you can make eye contact and perhaps slip in a personal question. "Where you from? Bristol as well? How about that? This? You want to know about this? It's like giving your car a shower instead of a bath."

As he talks, Sullivan moves his hands like a man directing traffic. "It's a hypnotic thing you do with your hands, so their eyes follow them around. You also do a lot of nodding. I get people to agree with me a lot. 'That's pretty good! I'd say so!' " His head is going up and down like an oil derrick. "And then you say 'Watch this!' or 'Listen,' it's the same as when a teacher shouts 'Listen!' in class—everyone listens. Sometimes I'll just shout out in the middle of the pitch, 'Look,' 'Listen,' 'Watch.' " However long or short the pitch, its basic rhythms never change. "You keep bringing it back. Let's just recap. You never put your hands down." Then once he has everyone under the ether, it's time to close, by creating a sense of great value and scarcity. "Come on in," he'll say, taking a step backward, which makes his audience step toward him. "Not $40, not $30, but just $19.95 for one mop and three extra heads. I can do this for five people. Who'll be number one?" He puts his own hand up first and others quickly follow. He never uses the word "buy." Sullivan says he has had fights break out for his $20 mops.

"All there is to selling is to be likable, to share a joke, be a good storyteller. It's like when you've been on a great holiday and you're talking to a friend and you tell them 'You've got to go to Vail. And when you do, you have to go to Russell's and Terra Bistro and there's a bartender who'll set you up.' It's the same thing."

Around the time Sullivan began selling the amazing Washmatic, satellite television began airing in Britain, introducing scores of new channels to British homes, and with them, infomercials. "I was mesmerized," says Sullivan. He recalls an advertisement for Auri car polish, in which a man fried a hamburger on his car and then cleaned off the mess with Auri. "I wanted to know how they did it. I bought everything I saw in those infomercials. I lit my dad's car on fire trying to do the hamburger and Auri test. I tried this stain remover called Didi Seven on my mum's wedding dress. Didn't work. But even if the products didn't always work, it didn't mean it wasn't worth buying them for the story. I'd be disappointed when things didn't work, but at least I hadn't bought a piece of land or the Eiffel Tower."

As the hot summer days in Devon turned to winter nights selling on London street corners, the harsher realities of selling set in. "What helped me through were the characters. I remember once getting in early to the Arndale Centre in Wandsworth and having a cup of tea with Charlie Kray," the brother of London's most famous gangsters, the Kray Twins. "I remember thinking, this is great." He also kept at it for the "red" days, those when every pitch seemed to result in dozens of sales. But more typical were long, cold days hawking gadgets and trinkets. "I was standing on a corner in London in December with this girl called Samantha and we were selling Blinkie Badges. My hands were numb. That's when I realized I had to get into TV. The transition took two years."

The product that brought him to America was the Smart Mop. It caught his eye when he was selling rolling rulers at the Ideal Home Exhibition in London. Growing up in Devon, Sullivan had always been an enthusiastic surfer. In his late teens, he'd rustled up a plane fare to Hawaii and spent a summer working for $4 an hour as a janitor in a youth hostel. "It was enough for me to eat, buy beer, and surf." He remembers the worst part of his work was cleaning the sand-encrusted floors. He couldn't just mop them. He had to scrape them, sweep them, and then mop them. "The Smart Mop would have been a godsend."

Sullivan discovered that the people selling the Smart Mop were based in Los Angeles, so out he flew and got a job selling mops up and down the West Coast. He had six months before his tourist visa expired, and his friends and family told him he'd be back before then. "But I knew that by coming to the States, I'd end up on TV. All the programming was in the U.S." He rented an apartment on Santa Monica pier, which he inherited from a woman who was marrying Mick Hastie, the pitchman for the Magic Bullet, a mini-blender they called "the personal, versatile, countertop magician." Sullivan kept the cash he made from selling the Smart Mop in VHS cases, first one, then eventually an entire library. "I just hoped no one came round to watch *Gone with the Wind*."

Sullivan quickly moderated his London street pitch, adapting it for the West Coast. "It was warm all the time, so people weren't in such a hurry. They weren't so interested in the hard sell. If they liked something, they'd hand over $30 in mid pitch." Even though he couldn't speak Spanish, he had his pitch translated and learned to pitch a mop in Spanish.

In March 1993, the day after a hurricane called the No-Name Storm had blown through Florida, Sullivan arrived in Clearwater Beach, home of the Home Shopping Network. He had heard from his bosses that the network was interested in the Smart Mop. While the other mop salesmen were heading back to Los Angeles, Sullivan decided to stay in Clearwater Beach, sleeping with his merchandise in the back of his van. He figured that if HSN did want someone to pitch Smart Mops, if he was right there, he would get the gig. And so it came to pass. It was usual for HSN to use its own hosts to pitch products. But Sullivan pitched the head producer so effectively, he was allowed to go on to demonstrate the product. "We sold 5,000 units in the first eighteen minutes," Sullivan recalls, like an athlete recalling his greatest game. "HSN was really stale back then. They were selling cubic zirconia and Capodimonte figurines with guests like Ivana Trump and Barbara Mandrell. Jackie Collins was flying in on a Gulfstream, and I came in with a mop and bucket and blew the doors off." Television got Sullivan off the road.

HSN also gave Sullivan his first insight into the entire value chain of his industry. When he was selling at fairs in England and the United States, he would pick up the merchandise, go to a certain spot, and sell. The most powerful people seemed to be the people who owned the real estate in the fairgrounds and markets. There was also a dodgy whiff about the business. He recalls being in Boston and making $35,000 in cash. The owner of the merchandise then insisted he drive around town buying $3,000 mail orders so that the money could be sent back without trace.

At HSN, he began to meet the manufacturers and retailers, the people who actually went to China and commissioned products as well as the retail buyers who were always looking for sellable products. "There were the products on the street, television shopping and infomercials, and the guys doing print ads and mainstream TV. I remember thinking there's got to be a way to do all of that." What emerged over the next decade were companies like Telebrands, licensing products from inventors, having Sullivan test them with infomercials, and letting Wal-Mart bring them to the mass market.

For many years, Sullivan's business partner was Billy Mays, who earned his spurs like Sullivan, selling Amazing Washmatics at fairs. Whereas Sullivan talks to his audience like a cheeky plumber, the heavily bearded Mays would shout at his viewers and thrust products at the camera. His exuberant rants turned him into a cult figure. But Mays died in 2009, and Sullivan took up much of the slack, doing many of Mays's old pitches. Sullivan became sole star of the reality television show *PitchMen*, which he did for one season with Mays. In it, he selects products brought to him by inventors and decides how best to pitch them. The experience of meeting so many inventors and discovering what they go through to bring their products to market has been fascinating for Sullivan. "Billy and I were just very hungry sales guys, but in this show, we became dream merchants. We realized we could change people's lives."

Sullivan is a strong believer in the "natural ability" theory of sales. "I have people who work with me who know everything about sales, but they still couldn't sell. They don't have what it takes. And then I've watched kids on YouTube who make fake infomercials and they're getting millions of views." He has read *The Seven Habits of Highly Effective People* and attended a Tony Robbins convention, but finds them superficial. "They get you all fired up, but you fall back into your old ways pretty soon. When you get into a bar fight, you revert to what comes naturally, the old-fashioned tactics."

At sunset, we drove back to Sullivan's house in his black Range Rover, over a bridge spanning the water, and I asked him the same question I had asked Majid El Fenni in the souk in Tangier. Could you sell ice to eskimos? His answer was startlingly similar. "I find that idea insulting. I don't want to sell ice to eskimos. They've got enough ice. I'd rather sell them an igloo, or a beach holiday in Florida. I don't want to sell sand to Arabs. I want to sell them some water. Or air-conditioning." It's curious to hear it from a man who sells Smart Mops and Turbo Snakes for a living, but Sullivan is down on consumerism. "It scares me that the basic health of the economy is measured in terms of consumer spending. On Black Friday, you have people driving into Wal-Mart to buy things they don't need. We've become obsessed with stuff. You get these young salesmen who think they can sell anything, and in sectors like financial services they're selling things with a very negative impact on people's lives. They're selling crappy product with no accountability." But, come on. The Turbo Snake? "I've been called a huckster, a snake-oil salesman, everything. But now more than ever, if a product doesn't work, or people don't think they're getting value, they can destroy your reputation online. It's easy. If that happened to me, I wouldn't still be in business."

The strange thing is, he's right. Sullivan is exposed as a salesman in a way the salesmen of Wall Street are not. Institutions and governments protect the latter when things go wrong. Sullivan may only be dealing in toilet cleaners and mops, but his reputation is constantly exposed to the bleaching sunlight of consumer scrutiny and market response. His professional safety net when selling gadgets is far smaller than for those selling products that can sink an entire economy.

When he's traveling, Sullivan says, people come up to him in airports, show him a gadget, and say "Pitch this." "With any product, I need to go home, use it, think about it. It takes me quite a long time to come up with a pitch. I don't just dream it up on the spot." For all his on-screen enthusiasm, Sullivan says he is not a salesman in every aspect of his life. He makes an effort to turn it off when he's not working. When he shops, he's not a haggler. "I don't like to be sold. It makes me feel uncomfortable. If I go to a car dealership, I'm already there to buy, so I just want to be closed. I like hearing a good pitch, but I'm not a good buyer."

Soon after Billy Mays died, Sullivan was out running on Davis Island close to his home. A ten-year-old boy rode up to him on his bike and said, "Are you the *PitchMen* guy? Sorry about your friend." Then he peeled off again on his bike. Sullivan kept running, his spirits, beaten down since his friend's death, suddenly lifted. Soon after he got home, he heard a rap at the door. It was the boy on the bike. "Mr. Sullivan," he said. "We've got this competition going at school to sell magazines. I'm number two right now, and I've really got to beat my friend who's number one. Can you help?" Sullivan bought $300 worth of subscriptions. It was expensive, he remembers thinking. But whatever, it's for the boy's school. Two hours later, the boy came back and handed over $180. "He said to me, 'I'm sorry, Mr. Sullivan. I totally ripped you off.' But the thing is, I didn't mind. I wanted to buy from this kid. He didn't oversell me and he had a big smile on his face."

It frustrates Sullivan that sales remains, as he put it, a "dirty word" in business. He resents the fact that when people hear the word *salesman* they think of the fast-talking closer, "the guy who didn't go to law school or medical school, who took a job at the car dealership because he had to." Much more respect is given to marketers. "Marketing people have a degree in marketing, but they're the worst black-suit-wearing, namby-pamby . . ." Sully's voice trailed off before he got to the expletives. "You give them something to sell, you know they're going to come back and tell you why it was the wrong color, the packaging wasn't right, and the price was wrong." Such thinking has led to a dreary homogeneity in how things are sold. "Everything's so compartmentalized these days. Newscasters all look the same. Cars look the same. We get bombarded by the norm—so the question is how do you break through? I don't care if you don't like my message, just don't ignore it."

Given Sully's ubiquity, it *is* hard to ignore him. The moment Prince William and Kate Middleton announced their engagement, his mind was whirring. They were engaged on a Wednesday; Sully called a partner on Thursday. They ordered cheap replicas of the engagement ring on Friday, received a sample on Saturday, and shot the commercial on Sunday. Within days, you could buy the Royal Heirloom Ring from the Sterlington Collection for "the low price of $19.90." Even Sully cannot resist laughing at the absurdity of it all. But as he said, he's not selling you land or a dodgy mortgage.

Like Majid, he is the closest you find in sales to a natural, an irresistible enthusiast who creates value out of thin air and is never afraid to ask for your money. "We unblock drains, make your whites whiter, make your car a little bit cleaner. We're the good-news guys, amidst all this doom and gloom." As he pitched me on the value of salesmen, he was waving a small, square black-and-orange packet at me. "Come on! Ten dollars for a Turbo Snake!"

. . .

Stories serve two purposes in sales. They enable a salesperson to sell to a customer, and they enable salespeople to sell themselves on the value of their work. A good story works in three stages, which resemble those of the sales process itself. The first involves getting your audience's attention with an event or challenge that throws them off balance. Their everyday routines are upended and a problem now stands in their way. You make the audience feel a sense of crisis and crave an answer. The second stage consists of the struggle to solve the problem or overcome the enemy—human, emotional, or practical. The last step is resolution, a galvanizing moment that compels your audience to take action. These are the same stages Aristotle prescribed for tragedy in the *Poetics*: an inciting incident, a climactic struggle, and, finally, a resolution.

Sullivan's Smart Mop pitch may not be *Oedipus Rex*, but it contains the three stages of storytelling. Your kitchen floor is suddenly covered in filth, ketchup, dirt, soda. The usual cleaning methods don't work. You struggle but fail. Enter the Smart Mop, and with a shimmy of the chamois, your problems are solved. But don't just sit there and watch. Call now. Make your own life easier and be the hero in your family. Buy a Smart Mop, or two or three.

The key to galvanizing your audience with a good story is to make listeners feel that they can be heroic. When good salespeople prospect and pitch, they must be alert to the stories running through their customers' minds. What is their internal hero story? What do they wish to achieve through this sale? Whom do they wish to impress? What kind of person do they hope this sale will help them become? A sales manager seeking to motivate his salespeople must ask similar questions. What do salespeople really want from their work? And how can you enable them to live their heroic fantasy?

In the spring of 2008, I received a call from a friend, a British hedge fund manager, who was attending the Milken Institute Global Conference in Los Angeles. "I've just heard the greatest business speech in my life," he told me. "Bar none." The man he had heard was Steve Wynn, a billionaire hotel and casino owner. The way my friend described it, Wynn had walked unsteadily to a microphone onstage. His eyesight was failing and he needed to be guided to his spot. He had then begun talking quietly, so everyone in the audience had to lean forward to hear. "I'm going to discuss something publicly that I've never discussed in my career," he began. He called it the "most profound business lesson I have ever learned." Now he had everyone's attention.

Wynn has thrived in one of the toughest, most competitive businesses in the world: Las Vegas gambling and hospitality. He has been a key figure in the rapid growth of Las Vegas over three decades. Financed by junk bonds issued by Michael Milken of Drexel Burnham Lambert in the 1980s, Wynn was able to build the Mirage, his first great casino resort. Then came Treasure Island, the Bellagio, and ultimately his eponymous Wynn Las Vegas and Wynn Macau. When a man like that promises to reveal a business secret, you listen.

A few years ago, he had dropped his wife and adult daughter off in Paris and then flown on to Singapore. They were staying at a Four Seasons Hotel Georges V, just off the Champs-Élysées. One morning, they ordered breakfast in their room. Wynn's daughter Gillian ordered a croissant. It was delicious and rich, and she could eat only half of it. She wrapped the rest in plastic wrap and left it on the refrigerator so she could eat it when she returned from her day of meetings.

But when Gillian and her mother returned to their room, the croissant was gone. Ah well, they thought. Fair enough. Housekeeping must have assumed it was left to be thrown away. Then they noticed the message light was flashing on their phone. Wynn's wife, Elaine, called the reception desk. The housekeeper wanted a word. "Thank you for calling," the housekeeper said. "We wanted to know when you got back so we could bring you a fresh croissant. The one you left out would have gone dry by now." So impressed was Elaine that she called her husband on the other side of the world. He in turn was so impressed that he called his friend Issy Sharp, the founder and chairman of the Four Seasons, in Canada. "He lit up over the phone," said Wynn. "He said 'Oh boy, isn't that great?'" As he told his story, Wynn himself, who has a broad, white smile, was grinning at the memory.

If he could have one professional wish come true, he said, it would be this: "that my employees would relate to people not as a customer with an employee, but as two human beings talking to one another. Not Mr. Black Jack Dealer to Black Jack player, but as Louise with Mr. Jones. If somehow we could harness that energy, we could change the history of the enterprise and achieve total market dominance in any service business in the world." Is it actually possible to scale up the attentiveness of that one housekeeper to an entire organization employing thousands? Could you, as he put it, create a situation where your employees, left alone with a customer, with no management supervision, could find a way to deliver service that made them feel instantly gratified? Threatening punishment or offering financial incentives in a systematic way was difficult without an impossibly high level of monitoring. The only way would be to make an employee want to deliver this extraordinary level of service for reasons that they found personally fulfilling. That, said Wynn, would be "the answer to a sailor's dream."

The dream turned out to be a system called "storytelling." At the Wynn Resorts, before each eight-hour shift, groups of twelve to eighteen employees meet up with their supervisor. Maids meet their inspector, dealers meet their pit bosses. These are the lowest ranks in the firm, the staff who deal with customers, and their immediate supervisors. The supervisors begin the meetings with the question "Anything happen yesterday that's interesting?" Slowly, the hands go up. As Wynn describes it, one man mentions that he saw a woman drop something from her purse as she went into her room. He saw it was her credit card, picked it up, knocked on her door, and returned it to her. Another man was helping a couple who had just arrived and realized they had left their medication at home in Encino, just outside Los Angeles, a five-hour drive away. They were panicking and thought they were going to have to cancel their vacation and go home. No problem, the man said. Is there anyone at your house? A housekeeper, the couple said. Fine, said the Wynn employee. His brother, Mr. Ramirez, lived not far away. He told the couple to instruct their housekeeper that a man named Ramirez would be coming to pick up their medication, and that the Wynn employee would then retrieve it from his brother. He told his supervisor about the situation, who told him to set off right away. The medication was with the couple before morning. And their loyalty to Wynn Resorts was likely guaranteed forever.

Each of these stories is published on the Wynn intranet and printed up and posted on the walls of the service areas in the back of the house. Now, says Wynn, every member of staff wants their story on the wall. "Everyone goes to work looking for a goddamn story the next day," said Wynn. "It is pristine, it is simple, it is profoundly effective, and it has changed the history of my enterprise." For Wynn, storytelling as a means of getting employees to feel good about themselves through their work and provide superlative customer service as a result is "like splitting the atom."

Clotaire Rapaille, a French psychologist who has worked for many of the world's largest corporations, describes successful salespeople as "happy losers." They see each rejection as a step on the way to a win. They yearn to see themselves on a classic hero's journey, using rejection as a means to personal transformation. This mind-set usually stems from a childhood experience of selling, a mental reference point that remains with them the rest of their life. Perhaps it was a lemonade stand, or an attempt to persuade their parents to let them stay home from school. That first "no" can go two ways. In some it leads to fear and a dislike of the activity in question. In the future salesmen, it makes them want to find a way to "yes."

At several of the companies Rapaille has worked with, he has held weekly meetings with salespeople and asked them how many no's they received that week. He found that the more no's a salesperson received the more money they made. The no's were an indication of effort and creativity. The salespeople with more no's were making more calls, trying new things, making more mistakes. Not only did it indicate resilience in the face of rejection, it showed willingness to take each acceptance to its absolute limit. Even at the point where the customer had already been sold on two dresses, a belt, a sweater, and a top, the great salesperson kept pressing: "A pair of shoes with that?" Each sale, by this standard, has to end with a "no," though it may be preceded by a dozen yeses.

When firms hire salespeople, Rapaille recommends, they should be looking for this willingness to fail rather than a track record of successful selling. They should ask, "How many things did you try in your life that you failed at?" If someone says they have only ever tasted success, it suggests they have lived a very sheltered life and will soon crumple under the personal assault inevitable in any sales job. He has compared the thrill of sales to the thrill of foxhunting. Scores set off in pursuit of the fox, many fall and injure themselves, and the fox may even escape. But the thrill of the chase is what excites the hunters. At sales meetings, he suggests awarding "the gold medal of rejection: Jonathan sold 500,000 computers last month, but he was rejected 5 million times! It may sound ludicrous, but this is the way to get fire in the belly of your sales force—particularly in America, where beating the odds is highly prized."

The reason Donald Trump is so admired by salesmen, Rapaille says, is not that he has been successful, but that he has succeeded, failed, and risen again. He is an object of ridicule to many, but a hero to many more. He has flirted with bankruptcy and gotten wealthy again; people laugh at his hair, but he has a beautiful wife. It is his response to adversity that has made him a salesman's icon, with an endlessly retold and inspiring story.

No one in the history of American selling cut a wider swath than Phineas Taylor Barnum, the nineteenth-century showman and storyteller. He mixed the qualities of righteousness and cheerful deceit, or "humbug," as he liked to call it, that came to define later generations of salesmen. He preached the virtues of abstinence and hard work, piety, and fidelity, all the while duping his audiences and calling it entertainment. As one of his biographers wrote, "When act and ideal clashed, Barnum didn't make a choice. He reviewed the ideals. He lived the dream of many Americans who understood that the former codes of human behavior were breaking down, but dared not overstep them like he did."

Selling for him was a game for people to master and enjoy, whether they won or lost. Others worried about whether to call him a liar, huckster, or cheat. Herman Melville's final novel, before he abandoned writing to become a customs inspector, was a moral and philosophical inquiry into the likes of Barnum called *The Confidence-Man*. While Melville the depressed, penniless writer plumbed the swampy ethics of selling and persuasion, Barnum skittered gleefully across the surface to ever greater fortune.

For his critics, Barnum's success represented an unjust fact of life, that it is frequently the most tawdry, deceitful, and brassy people who succeed, while restraint, honesty, and diligence go unrewarded.

In 1846, Benjamin Robert Haydon, an English painter, opened an exhibition of his historical canvases in the Egyptian Hall in central London. Unfortunately, in another part of the hall, Barnum was showing a dwarf, Charles Sherwood Stratton, who performed under the name General Tom Thumb. The despondent Haydon wrote in his diary: "They rush by thousands to see Tom Thumb. They push, they fight, they scream, they faint, they cry 'Help!' and 'Murder!' They see my bills and caravan, but do not read them; their eyes are on them, but their sense is gone. It is an insanity, a rabies furor, a dream, of which I would not have believed England could have been guilty." A few weeks later, a financially and emotionally ruined Haydon killed himself with a shot to the head, and when that didn't finish him off, by slitting his own throat. Barnum's success could do this to people.

Barnum was born in 1810 and grew up in a time when the young United States was still figuring itself out, wrestling out of the tight clothes of British tradition toward a more expansive and liberal set of ideas. Barnum was well suited for a time when ambition and the pursuit of personal gain came to be seen as the ideal means for inciting human progress. Like so many great salesmen, his commercial gifts were honed in childhood. At the age of twelve, he began working as a clerk in a country store in Bethel, Connecticut. Many of his customers worked as hatmakers. Barnum later wrote of them: "The customers cheated on us in their fabrics. We cheated the customers with our goods. Each party expected to be cheated, if it was possible. Our eyes, and not our ears, had to be our masters. We must believe little that we saw, and less that we heard."

He tried various schemes, including newspapering, running a lottery, and selling Bibles door-to-door, before moving to New York City in 1834 and embarking on a life as an impresario, running a variety troupe, and later acquiring a museum in lower Manhattan, for the exhibition of freaks and curios. In 1842, he agreed to pay a rival showman $12.50 a week, around $340 today, to lease the "Feejee Mermaid," an ugly, dried-up specimen three feet long, which had the body of a fish and the head and hands of a monkey. He promised exclusive woodcuts of the mermaid to newspapers that wrote about it, though somehow every newspaper in the city received the exclusive. He set up a dispute between scientists and doctors on his payroll, who argued over the authenticity of the mermaid. As they bickered, Barnum released a new advertising campaign admitting to the doubt and yet using it to stoke interest in his object: "Who is to decide when doctors disagree?" he wrote.

Whether it was a "work of nature or art" it was "decidedly the most stupendous curiosity ever submitted to the public for inspection."

That same year, he met Charles Stratton, a five-year-old who had gained just six pounds since birth and stood just two feet one inch tall. He had a variety of dwarfism that left him tiny, but he was perfectly proportioned. Barnum saw in him the story of perpetual youth, dressed him in costumes, and taught him to perform songs and skits. He claimed Stratton was eleven years old, to make his size seem more outlandish, and said he was born in England rather than Connecticut. Stratton became General Tom Thumb, one of the greatest attractions of the time, a classic Barnum humbug. When he took Tom Thumb to London, Barnum decided that the way into British hearts was to appeal to their snobbery. He rented a mansion in Mayfair, surrounded by the homes of the British aristocracy. He invited the aristocrats one by one to visit his young protégé, and eventually received the invitation he had been waiting for. Queen Victoria wanted to see Tom Thumb perform. He was a huge hit at the palace, fighting with the royal poodle and running and falling backward out of the royal presence. Thumb's later appearances in the Egypt Hall were a commercial smash. Barnum had successfully used the approval of Britain's aristocrats and royal family to sell his act.

Social scientists would later say Barnum exploited the idea of "social proof," selling an item by appealing to people's desire to be part of a larger, better group. If Tom Thumb is good enough to entertain Queen Victoria, then he is good enough for me and my family. It is the same idea behind the modern celebrity endorsement. If a handbag is good enough for Gwyneth Paltrow, or a pair of sneakers for LeBron James, then they are good enough for me. Perhaps they will allow me to float awhile in these celebrities' exalted orbit.

But just as today there are those who abhor such vigorous peddling, so there were in Barnum's time. Reading Melville's *The Confidence-Man*, you feel as though the once swaggering author of *Moby-Dick* has been undone by having to think through the implications of Barnum. The Confidence Man of the title is a satanic figure who adopts various guises to sell everything from herbal medicines to coal to an Indian charity. He promises the medicine will heal, that the coal stock will soar, and that the poor Seminoles will be helped. None of it, of course, is true. But in his conversations with passengers aboard a steamship, the Confidence Man lays out the structure of the debate about selling. To live life as a cynic, watchful and leery of every human wile, is to be a misanthrope. And yet to be too gullible is to risk being cheated. Where is each of us going to settle? As players in this dangerous game, fully socialized, ready to play, and thus exposed, or fearful and suspicious and thus alone?

Melville's heart is clearly opposed to men like Barnum, but the back-and-forth in his book suggests a wearied acceptance of our need for them. One critic wrote of *The Confidence-Man* that it "exposes all that was wrong with the liberalism of Melville's day: its commercialism, its superficiality, its philistinism, its spurious optimism, its glad-handed self-congratulation, its wishful vagueness, its fondness for uplifting rhetoric, its betrayal of all tragic or exalted human and natural values, its easy belief in automatic progress."

A few years earlier, Timothy Dwight, a president of Yale College, had taken similar aim at the culture of "peddling" that had taken root in the United States and even among his students. "Men who begin life with bargaining for small wares will almost invariably become sharpers. The commanding aim of every such man will soon be to make a good bargain, and he will speedily consider every gainful bargain as a good one. The tricks of fraud will assume in his mind the same place which commercial skill and an honorable system of dealing hold in the mind of the merchant."

Our view of salesmanship, then, becomes an issue of belief. Do we side with the puritans like Dwight, who equate selling with "sharping," a lesser, unethical form of business than that practiced by the elevated merchant class? Or do we embrace Barnum in all his contradictory exuberance? Do we scowl at Barnum's humbugs or celebrate them?

Barnum tried to answer this question himself in his memoir. He argued that every "humbug" he inflicted on his audiences was more than justified by the genuine curiosities he brought before them. "If I have exhibited a questionable dead mermaid in my Museum, it should not be overlooked that I have also exhibited cameloleopards, a rhinoceros, grisly bears, orang-outangs, great serpents, etc., about which there could be no mistake because they were alive; and I should hope that a little 'clap-trap' occasionally, in the way of transparencies, flags with exaggerated pictures, and puffing advertisements might find an offset in a wilderness of wonderful, instructive, and amusing realities. . . . The titles of 'humbug' and the 'prince of humbugs' were first applied to me by myself. I made these titles a part of my 'stock in trade.'"

Barnum's memoir became the second-bestselling book in nineteenth-century America, after the New Testament. He wrote that he saw nothing wrong with humbug or hype, but opposed outright fraudulence of the kind he described in another book, *The Humbugs of the World*. He vigorously opposed slavery and racism. He argued for abstinence and invested in the improvement of Bridgeport, Connecticut, where he eventually settled. This personal morality was in certain ways rigorrus and upstanding. Just not always in selling.

There is evidently a line here somewhere between humbug and deception, between Barnumesque hype and outright lies, between reading your customers to give them what they need and exploiting their weakness to your own advantage. But it can easily get lost in the heat of commerce, as became clear in my conversations with the head of retail operations at one of the world's top jewelry chains. David is not his real name, as he asked to remain anonymous. For David, selling is all about manipulation, about coercing a customer into buying. As a man with a bottom line to manage, he is not inclined to ponder the moral philosophy of sales. Rather, he says, "there's an intimidation factor in selling. Someone entrusts you to help them make a decision, so your job is to get that decision made, to go after the sell. Salespeople are good at manipulation. They're like therapists in general. Many buyers are lonely people who need to feel validated. Our job is to help them feel validated through shopping." His gift is understanding the stories running through the minds of those who step into his store and providing a resolution with a sale.

David, like Majid, Sullivan, and Barnum, grew up around selling. His father was a camera salesman. But David always wondered what it would be like to go from selling tens of thousands of dollars' worth of cameras to millions of dollars in jewelry. He studied art and antiques and then decided to apply for a job at Cartier in Beverly Hills. Before the interview, he spent most of his savings on a Cartier wallet, pen, and watch. When he arrived at the interview, he took out his Cartier wallet to extract his business card. Halfway through, he asked if he could make a few notes and produced his Cartier pen, shooting his cuff so his Cartier watch was visible. "It showed I had a passion for the brand. I had taken the time to study how people in the store dressed and presented themselves, and I was hired on the spot."

His war stories are all about his ability to persuade, to turn a failing situation around, to pull one over, to close. He loves turning a hesitation, even an outright rejection, into a sale. He sees himself as a hero. "This older woman once came in. She was very well dressed, and she took off her gloves," he said. "As she did so, I spotted the label on the inside of her bag. It was Christian Dior. She was a reluctant customer, but we talked, and after a while, I said, 'Obviously, you have great style ma'am. You're carrying a beautiful, vintage Dior bag.' She looked stunned and said to me, 'How do you know that?' I said, 'Well, ma'am, we're about the finer things in life.' Boom. I had her right there. Now she trusted me."

Another time, a couple were hemming and hawing over an expensive piece of jewelry. "I talked to the husband. I told him to stop worrying so much about the price. I told him that I lost my mother at a young age. Then I said, 'I'm sure you know that at the end of the day, it's not the price that matters. Look at your wife. She's smiling. Isn't that what this is all about? Now, all you need to say is "I'll buy it for you."' And then I turned to the wife and said, 'Now, all you need to say is "Thank you, dear."'"

Sometimes, he says, women who usually shop with their husbands come into the store alone. If they come across a piece and like it, David will try to trigger the sale by saying, "Isn't it liberating sometimes to buy something on your own? To make your own decision?" He turns the act of buying jewelry into a story of escaping the tiresome obligations of marriage and doing something for yourself for once. It is an extreme form of the sales truism that you sell the benefits, not the features, of your product. Forget about the carats, for a moment, and think of what spending $20,000 without your husband's approval will feel like.

If a woman walks in holding an expensive bag, and then winces at the price of a necklace, he might try to embarrass her into buying. "Ma'am, you're carrying a $15,000 Birkin bag," he will say, proving he has identified her bag and thus her buying habits. "Why are you hesitating about buying a piece of jewelry?"

The best salespeople, he says, are seductive in different ways with different clients, tapping a range of dramatic story lines in their pitch, eliciting one emotional response after another, much like an actor with an audience. "First they ask a few key questions to touch one emotion or another," he says. "Is this a businessman buying for his wife, or his girlfriend? Is he feeling giddy or thinking how much it will cost to keep someone silent or happy? You get women who come in every day, shopaholics for whom buying is their drug. With them, it's about feeding and babysitting. These are the kinds of people who invite salespeople to their parties because they actually think they're their friends."

David is a keen reader of people's underlying fears and wants, who applies his dramatist's gift to closing jewelry sales. But such a gift comes with a price. Like the ability to seduce, it is both empowering and corrupting. I once read of Bill Clinton that his self-destructive behaviors were driven in part by a need to test his own powers of recovery, his ability to charm people into forgiving even his most unforgivable flaws. To see people succumb so easily to your humdrum charms becomes boring after a while. The great salesman wants to see just how potent his gifts are. What is the deepest hole I can dig myself out of? What story can I tell to gloss the truth or earn forgiveness? A great storyteller or pitchman's powers can be highly combustible. "We hire people who seem effervescent and bubbly," says David, "but salespeople in general tend to suffer from a lot of mood swings. Their drug is to make the sale. You'd like to have salespeople who are stable, but the truth is that the best are extremely emotional and dramatic. They are often the hardest to manage. One of my managers has a sign outside his office which says WAIT ON THE COUCH. Managing a team of them is extremely difficult." He says that you should never trust a salesperson. "They are always stealing from other sales associates, putting their names on sales they didn't make. Their job is to sell customers on their integrity, yet behind the scenes there is no integrity."

The head trader at a now defunct British bank once told me that whenever he hired people, he asked what they would do if they suddenly had an extra £100,000. Some people said they would pay off some debt or put down 20 percent on a house and put the rest in a savings or retirement account. A few said they would go out and buy a very expensive car. These were the ones who were hired. The trader's rationale was this: "I want people who want to make a lot of money because they want to buy a lot of things. I don't want cautious savers on my floor."

In luxury goods sales, a similar mind-set applies. The best sales-people, says David, crave the lives of their clients, and live vicariously through their work. They have to realize that ultimately their clients are very different, but to make their pitch, they need to understand what is driving them. "They have to want the same $15,000 pair of shoes their client wants. They have to understand that when a rich man comes in, he wants to bejewel his wife as a mark of having succeeded. They need to know that most women buy jewels to impress other women and that women want diamonds to sparkle at night, not as an investment. They want what even their other rich friends can't have." The salesperson has to empathize to sell.

Chapter 3

THE SOUL OF A SALESMAN

We have a better product than soap or
automobiles. We have eternal life.

JIM BAKKER, AMERICAN TELEVANGELIST

At its most basic and technical, selling is about understanding a customer's needs and delivering a product to meet them. There are three pieces to this. The first is economic: what the customer is willing to pay and the price at which you are willing to sell. The second is structural, to do with the process of selling. A quick, one-off sale in a store is very different from a months-long sale to a company, where you have to deal with numerous people in various stages. The final piece is psychological: the battle of wits, personality, and emotion between the seller and buyer. In every sale, these three elements are tightly interwoven. In most retail stores, for example, the salesperson must make quick judgments about who the customer is, what they need from both the product and the sales process, and what they're willing to pay, before he handles their objections and tries to close them on a sale. One classic formulation of this process is AIDA: attention, interest, desire, and action. It was first proposed in 1898 by E. St. Elmo Lewis, a writer and early proponent of the educational benefits of advertising. The salesperson stokes up the customer, gets their attention, then turns their interest into desire, and finally gets them to buy. In a longer sales cycle, the same process is drawn out over weeks and months. Instead of having to make quick judgments, salespeople can ask questions and try to elicit and develop the customer's needs. "If you need this," they might say, "then you'll also be needing this!"

The big organizational sale is an expansion of these basic steps. Benson Shapiro and Ronald Posner broke the big corporate sale into eight separate tasks. The first is to open the process by learning there's a potential sale. Leads can emerge from cold-calling, referrals, or more sophisticated profiling. Next, you must qualify your prospect and define the extent of their potential. Is it a long shot or a slam dunk? Who needs to be sold and how? Do I even have what they need? Then comes the sales strategy, in which you plan your campaign, listing your contacts, your meetings, your information and to-dos. Are you targeting the right people? Do they have control over the checkbook? What will you need from your own organization to make this happen? Then you organize the justification for the sale by imagining yourself in the buyer's shoes and figuring out how they can explain this purchase to themselves and their colleagues. With the planning over, you move into the trenches by pitching your potential client. By this time, you should have all the relevant decision makers in the room, fully briefed on what this sale is all about. You take any feedback and return to your own company to gather the resources and people it will take to satisfy the customer. And then you close. By this time, it should not be a surprise if the sale is made or not, because you will have lived the process for months. The eighth and final phase is nurturing the account relationship, making sure the customer is happy and keeps buying for years to come.

Described like this, selling seems largely a matter of organization, in which case the only inhibitors to success should be disorganization and laziness. Yet it is an occupation awash in feelings of fear and insecurity, which explains why sales as a subject is so enticing to playwrights. Beyond the technical demands of selling lie a complex set of nontechnical demands that can make or break a salesperson's spirit. Academic studies of selling, such as Shapiro and Posner's, are most successful when they focus on the processes of identifying the various types of buyers and the sales processes best suited to them. Where studies tend to flounder is in understanding the mind of the successful salesperson.

In 1985, four academics, Gilbert Churchill, Neil Ford, Steven Hartley, and Orville Walker, published the most important academic article on sales of the twentieth century, as voted by their academic peers. "The Determinants of Salesperson Performance: A Meta-Analysis" was their attempt to summarize all the published research into what makes some salespeople more effective than others. They crunched the numbers on what are considered the major determinants of sales performance: aptitude, skills levels, motivation, role perception, and other personal, organizational, and environmental factors. It was a beast of a task. What they found was that success in different sales settings depended on very different sets of factors.

Motivation most affects performance, they found, when you must deal with the long, punishing sales cycles involved in selling industrial goods. Aptitude, or inherent ability, matters more in the highly transactional sale of products where there is little prospect of a long-term relationship; what matters is one's knack for closing one sale after another in quick succession. More important than either, however, were personal variables, a ragbag of factors including age, sex, height, weight, race, education, marital status, even club membership. These differ from aptitude in the same way talent differs from physical gifts. A tall basketball player is not necessarily a talented one, but he may be better equipped to make dunks. Being a member of a country club may not mean you can sell to your fellow members, but it does at least gain you access to them. The research into personal variables showed dramatic variations across different studies. In some fields of selling, they mattered a great deal in terms of predicting performance, in others hardly at all. In high-end real estate, club memberships matter. Not in selling asphalt to road builders. When selling drugs to doctors, it helps to be an attractive young woman. Not so much in telephone sales, where no one sees you.

But across the board, the most significant predictor of performance, the academics found, was role perception. How a salesperson felt about what they did tended to have the largest effect on performance. If they knew what they were doing and why, if it was clear what they would be rewarded for and whom they needed to impress, they thrived. The more ambiguity and conflict surrounded their job, the more poorly they performed. If they felt lost or purposeless they could not sell. Selling, like many other human activities, can easily lead to all kinds of personal and ethical conflicts. Letting salespeople thrash around these issues without clear and honest guidance is the surest way to ensure that they fail. If there is no company or manager to provide this guidance, the salesperson must figure it out alone. To understand what you are doing and why, and how far you are prepared to go in doing it, is the most important thing you can do if you want to succeed as a salesperson.

. . .

In 1961, the *Harvard Business Review* published an article by Robert McMurry, an industrial psychologist from Chicago, titled
"The Mystique of Super-Salesmanship." McMurry was an academic
psychologist trained at the universities of Chicago and Vienna, and
was among the first to apply the tools of his field to understanding
business, notably marketing and sales. His advice was keenly sought
by CEOs across America. Though his writing may still smack of its
time, and his conclusions owe more to the psychologist's casebook
than the social scientist's academic rigor, it prompted much more
serious examination of sales. He helped establish a unique position
for the study of sales, somewhere between economics and psychology, where it has remained to this day.

McMurry wrote that for all the advances in modern industry,
from automation to organizational theory, "salesmanship—as an art
applied at a face-to-face level—remains just as primitive today as it
was 100 years ago. It works, but no one seems to understand why."
Even the very best salesmen are hard-pressed to explain why they
can do what they do. He was among the first to lay out the very different types of sales tasks, from basic to complex. The very simplest
sales role is that of the deliveryman, whose job is to provide good
service with a pleasant manner. He is the face of the organization
whose product he delivers to the customer, like a postal worker. The
most complex is the person who sells intangibles—advertising or
education services, for example—where the product is not easily
demonstrated and must be conjured up in the prospect's imagination. In between are five more levels: the in-store order taker, working behind the counter in a store, whose customers already know
what they want but might be persuaded to upgrade or buy a few

extras; the order taker who also gets out into the field, serving an established network of customers who don't require a hard sell but do need efficient, pleasant service in order to keep placing orders; the ambassador salesman, who must go out and drum up interest in a product without necessarily closing sales; the technical salesman, who provides consultative services to a client buying a complex product; and then the creative salesman of tangible products—cars or refrigerators, for example—who must persuade customers that their existing product is unsatisfactory, then close them on his own.

The salesmen at the complex end of McMurry's spectrum are the most highly compensated. Without them a business would cease to exist. Investment bankers, for example, are constantly seeking to persuade companies that they need to merge or issue stock or debt. If these salesmen fail, there is no business. A postal worker does not affect the survival of the U.S. Postal Service in the same way.

McMurry argued that the good salesman does three things. First he seduces the prospect, sifting quickly through the prospect's emotions and fantasies to arouse the particular one that will be satisfied by his product. Then he provides the logical justifications for buying the product, which the prospect may neither need nor be able to afford—"It's a twelve-month payment plan, Mrs. Johnson, just $75 a month, and this offer ends tomorrow." Finally, he applies the pressure to close, to relieve the prospect of their cash. Those three steps of seduction, rationalization, and closing may require very different talents. The seducer may not have the authority or dominance to close. The rationalizer may depend too much on logic and fail to make an emotional connection. The closer may be too much of a bully to seduce.

McMurry suggested that the single most important trait in a salesperson is "the wooing instinct." The habitual wooer is "an individual who has a compulsive need to win and hold the affection of others." This trait is the product of their early environment; the wooer is "characterized by the conviction that he is really unloved and unwanted" so must use every means at his disposal—charm, flattery, even deception—to win others over. He has a high degree of empathy, which makes him compatible with whomever he is selling to. But there is an underlying hostility to everything he does. He uses people and ends up despising those who fall for his tricks. "Wooing in a sales context is as difficult to teach as wooing in a boudoir," McMurry writes. "And if the student is not a wooer by nature, to try to make him one is comparable to trying to make a Don Juan out of a John Calvin." The wooers can come in very different packages, of course. One can be a noisy brute, the other a whispering cad. But the trait remains consistent.

McMurry identified five lesser characteristics useful for the successful salesperson: boundless energy and optimism; plenty of self-confidence in order to brush off rejection; a "chronic hunger for money"; self-discipline and a capacity for hard work; and finally a "state of mind which regards each rejection or obstacle as a challenge." The big problem for companies, McMurry wrote, was that not only are all these traits hard to find in the same person, but they are also not trainable. What can be trained are the procedural aspects of selling: product details, time management, identifying particular groups of customers, and a set of techniques akin to acting. Salespeople can be drilled in endless selling scenarios, down to the phrases they must use. It is a way of minimizing the personal by turning each salesperson into a rote performer. In the absence of thousands of salespeople with those rare wooer traits, the best a company can do is to create platoons of highly trained actors.

McMurry's description of salesmen is unsettling. Of the best of them, he wrote: "They tend to be confidence men first and sales-men second. Since they are, first of all, completely selfish, they are incapable of loyalty to anyone—employer, associates, supervisors, or prospects. They are, almost without exception, 'lone wolves' of the first order. Again, the primary motivation of many 'star' salesmen is, in my observation, an amalgam of greed and hostility." Their charm has often rendered them immature, spoiled by always getting what they want. "Few are happy and relaxed." Instead they are commer-cial Hannibal Lecters, highly attuned to other people's needs and yet vicious in exploiting them.

Empathy is a two-step process of understanding another person's feelings and then sharing them. Psychopaths understand other peo-ple extraordinarily well, but unlike the rest of us are not restrained by sharing what their victims feel. Instead they revel in causing pain, targeted at the very weaknesses they have perceived. This is one def-inition of evil, an acute understanding of others coupled with a ruthless willingness to exploit that understanding, regardless of the victim's feelings. In McMurry's estimation, the successful salesman is not so different, empathizing to the point of understanding, but then taking advantage of what he sees to make a sale.

In 1964, three years after McMurry fired his salvo against the sales industry, two young academics, David Mayer and Herbert Greenberg, refined his ideas. On the basis of seven years of field research, much of it among insurance agents, they wrote that suc-cessful salesmen must have two qualities, empathy and ego drive: enough empathy to listen and understand what is in the customer's head, and enough ego to close the sale.

They compared good and bad salespeople to old and new

missiles. Old missiles were fired off into the air, where they either hit or missed their target. Modern heat-seeking missiles approached the target and tracked its evasions before eventually hitting home. Empathy served as a sophisticated tracking system enabling salespeople to be more creative in uncovering and meeting the customer's wants.

The ego drive they describe arises from a salesperson's need to make the sale to enhance their own sense of self-worth. To sell for the money is not enough. Each sale must feel like a struggle to forge one's identity. Mayer and Greenberg write: "Because of the nature of all selling, salespeople will fail more often than they will succeed. Thus, since failure tends to diminish their self-pictures, their egos cannot be so weak that the poor self-picture continues for too long a time. Rather, the failure must act as a trigger—as a motivation toward greater effort—which with success will bring the ego enhancement they seek. A subtle balance must be found between (a) an ego partially weakened in precisely the right way to need a great deal of enhancement (the sale) and (b) an ego sufficiently strong to be motivated by failure but not to be shattered by it."

Here lies the challenge in finding good salespeople. You need excellent empathizers who aren't so empathetic they can't close a sale. And you need people with strong ego needs who can still take a moment to figure out what another person wants. They must be aggressive enough to close, but not so aggressive they put people off. Too much empathy and you'll be a nice guy finishing last. Too much ego drive and you'll be scorching earth everywhere you go. Not enough of either and you shouldn't be in sales at all. It's a miracle anyone can do this job.

Indeed, Mayer and Greenberg found that despite decades of research, insurance companies were still having trouble finding good salespeople. Fifty percent of their new hires quit in their first year, and 80 percent within three years, with all the attendant costs of training, hiring, firing, and mishandled accounts. Mayer and Greenberg believed that companies' hiring policies favored the kind of failing salespeople they already had, rather than those they actually needed. The companies would ask potential hires if they were interested in selling, which of course they were. They would apply tests that were easily passed by anyone who could spot the right answer to a question like "Would you rather be with people or at home with a good book?" The tests were good at identifying lots of similar people, conventional, standardized types, rather than those with a wide range of talents. But worst of all, they looked for isolated traits, sociability or diligence, for example, without seeking the most important factors of all: empathy and ego drive.

Ironically, given the benefits that have accrued to someone like Majid through his experience, Mayer and Greenberg found that one of the worst traps companies could fall into was hiring according to experience. While it is natural, especially in more technically complex businesses, to want to hire people who already understand the product and market, hiring on professional experience alone means you ignore the early developmental factors that create the right personality types for sales. The tendency among sales managers is to hire salespeople like themselves, and this leads to what Mayer and Greenberg called the "inbreeding of mediocrity." If you went out and interviewed butchers, coal miners, steelworkers, even the unemployed, they argued, 10 percent of them would have the stuff to be top-producing salespeople, and 20 percent would be rated B or better for most kinds of selling. "Many of these are potentially far better salespeople than some who have accumulated many years of experience," they wrote.

They described the case of "Big Jim," a man who had come

in seeking work in a car dealership that was participating in their research. He had taken both the standard salesman's tests and Mayer and Greenberg's test designed to identify ego and empathy. He had flunked the standard tests but aced Mayer and Greenberg's. When the researchers came to the car dealership to ask more about him, the salespeople looked sheepish. They had passed his tests on to them as a joke, they said. He was a rube who came in wearing denim overalls and tattered sneakers. He had never sold anything before, but he took a look around the showroom and said, "I do hanker to sell them there cars." Mayer and Greenberg told the dealership to hire him. Sure enough, he turned out to be a crack salesman. "Soon after he started working, he 'hankered to see that there Seattle World's Fair,' and sold enough cars in the first week of the month to earn the money to get there and spend two weeks. On his return he made enough money in the last week of the month to equal the staff's monthly average."

Experience, the researchers concluded, was a trivial predictor of success at selling, as was a "good front," or fine appearance. Much more important were these "inner dynamics" of empathy and ego. People with these attributes could be made into even better salespeople through training. But those without them would always struggle, no matter how many training courses they went through.

Studies of emotional intelligence suggest that whatever patterns of brain activity we inherit, our temperaments evolve over time depending on environmental effects. Professor Jerome Kagan at Harvard has identified four temperamental types—timid, bold, upbeat, and melancholy—which are dictated by the wiring of our amygdala, a part of the brain that processes emotion and the memories that ensue. In shy people, the amygdala is easily and quickly aroused, which leads them to suffer anxiety and take measures to avoid uncertainty. In the more outgoing, the amygdala is less easily aroused, so they are less easily frightened and more willing to take risks. Experience can moderate the effects of this neural hard-wiring, especially in childhood and adolescence, when the brain is more plastic. But later on, the pathways are set. Temperaments calcify. This notion jibes with what McMurry said about selling. By adulthood, you either have the inner dynamics to succeed or you don't.

Psychologists make another distinction, between fluid and crystallized intelligence, that buttresses the notion that salesmen are born rather than made. The psychologists Raymond Cattell and John Horn have argued that intelligence is composed of various different abilities, which interact and reinforce each other. Cattell describes fluid intelligence as "the ability to perceive relationships independent of previous specific practice or instruction concerning those relationships." It is the ability to think and reason quickly through new problems in a way independent of education and experience. Crystallized intelligence is what you develop through study and experience, facts, book smarts, and wisdom. Fluid intelligence is what you use when you don't already know what to do. It is nature to the nurture of crystallized intelligence. These two forms frequently interact.

Majid has a vast body of crystallized intelligence made up of his experience in selling, but he also draws on a formidable fluid intelligence, a well-stocked working memory, which allows him to make fast and accurate assessments of his customers. Of the two, fluid intelligence is less specific to products or customer, and so is more easily applied to many different kinds of selling. When we talk of a salesperson being a "natural," we are referring to their fluid intelligence. Their instincts and native wit are like big lungs in a cyclist, a physiological gift that most of us, however hard we study and practice, can never compete against.

I could have stayed in America to meet insurance agents; there is no shortage of them here. But instead I went to Japan. The Japanese, I had been told, dislike commission-based selling, because they believe that salespeople deserve a living wage each month, the same as people working in accounting. They also have their own set of formal, interpersonal codes, heavy on social deference and respect, which seem at odds with the pushy ways of American insurance sales. Here is a country as economically developed as any in the world, and yet it operates in sales, as in so much else, by its own set of rules. I wanted to know whether my assumptions about selling were relevant in a very different, but economically equal, culture.

The headquarters of Japan's life insurance companies curl northward along the eastern side of the Imperial Palace in Tokyo, a row of corporate megaliths keeping watch over the city. For decades now, they have been their country's principal hoarders and distributors of capital, sucking in monthly premiums and reinvesting them in stocks, bonds, and property. Since the end of World War II, there have been no more important financial institutions in Japan, or perhaps all Asia, than the life insurance giants of Tokyo.

As with every Japanese business, the senior executives are men. What makes the life insurance industry unusual in Japan is the crucial role played by women. In the wake of World War II, the insurance companies hired war widows to go door-to-door selling their products. And to this day, the practice continues. In a still male-dominated Japanese business world, life insurance remains an area where a good saleswoman can thrive. None more so than Mrs. Shibata of the Dai-ichi Life Insurance Company.

When General MacArthur was looking for an office from which to run postwar Japan, he chose the sixth floor of the Dai-ichi Life building, reportedly because it was one of the few places that looked down on the Imperial Palace, the home of the defeated Emperor Hirohito. Walking up the building's wide granite steps into a vast, echoing atrium, you would never guess that Japan had ever been in a long economic slump. Dai-ichi's home oozes a sense of stability, and vast reserves of wealth. The reception desk looks shrunken against the intimidating acres of gray stone that surround it. Once you ascend one of the narrow escalators, which rise steeply from the ground floor as if to some distant heaven, you find yourself in a corporate anywhere, floors of anonymous cubicles full of silent, unmoving heads. But far off in one corner, in a conference room overlooking the palace gardens, where a summer drizzle is beating against the floor-to-ceiling glass walls, is a short but splendid-looking figure in a neck-to-ankle purple dress covered in white flowers, with a circular purple hat perched on the back of her head. Mrs. Shibata wears practical, flat-soled shoes, large diamond-and-ruby earrings, a huge pearl ring on her wedding finger, and a necklace threaded with pearls the size of gumballs. Her vibrant purple eye shadow matches her dress and hat.

She is the top insurance salesperson at Dai-ichi Life and, depending on the year, in all Japan. She is a popular writer and authority on the subject of selling, and her two daughters have followed her into the business. As Donald Trump and his children are to New York real estate, the Shibatas are to Japanese life insurance: rich, ubiquitous, and relentlessly chatty on the subject of business success.

When she was in her twenties, Mrs. Shibata and her husband

worked at the same clothing manufacturer. When their boss told them it was inappropriate to have a married couple at the firm, Mrs. Shibata left and worked for a few years at a computer tech support business. She was competent and well paid, but frustrated by the lack of opportunity. She wanted more control than an office job allowed. So at the age of thirty-one, after her daughters were born, she began working in life insurance, on the bottom rung of Dai-ichi's vast sales force. The first challenge was to make a list of three hundred people she knew and sell them life insurance. "I didn't know 300 people," she says. "I went to every one of my relatives and neighbors and eventually got a list of 181 people." Then she had to hit them up, going door-to-door, inquiring about their lives, sending follow-up notes, and slowly persuading them that buying life insurance was better than frittering their money away on petty luxuries. "You have to want to sell insurance, because it's hard work. At first, no one wants to talk to you. Life insurance is not a product people like to discuss. It's about death. The person who pays sees no reward while they're alive. So when you pay, you have to believe it's going to reward your family after you are dead. Life insurance won't save your life, it won't bring you any cash. But you buy it out of love for your family."

The rejections almost overwhelmed her. "I often thought I couldn't make it. There were times when I couldn't get a contract and I wept in front of a prospective client. But if you're rejected three times, you have to go back and figure out what you're doing wrong. Even when you're in a devastated situation, it's a step forward to what has to be a better time. I came to learn to have an objective view on my own performance. To enjoy the hard situations. Later on, when I was trying to cold-call banks, I was rejected ninety-eight times in a row. I just wasn't getting it. But when your motivation is down, that's just another excuse. I kept coming to work because the passion was in me."

During those early days, she persuaded herself that what she was doing was for her clients, for their security and welfare. She told herself that it wasn't about what she needed for herself, but what the client needed. Not just any salaried stooge, she was going to fight for her present and future clients' best interest. They needed life insurance and she was going to give it to them.

"This is how I contribute to society. If it's just about the money, I have more than I can ever spend. But families need the backup provided by insurance. This is about me and how I can help people." Salespeople tell themselves this story all the time, that they're in it for the client, that by selling their product they are doing society a service, that if they were their client, they'd buy their product in a heartbeat. It's not always convincing. But Mrs. Shibata says all this with such a sincere smile and playfulness that it's impossible not to believe her.

After the early hell of calling on friends and relatives, Mrs. Shibata began to expand her network, to collect more and more references. It was not so different from any business start-up. To achieve scale, you need credibility, but to achieve credibility you need scale, or at least a track record, which salespeople at the outset don't have. What carried her through this period was her doggedness and a focus on self-improvement and process.

It's during these early days that most people embarking on a career in selling fail, and understandably so. It's brutal on the ego and the wallet to endure so much rejection and financial uncertainty. It reminds me of the scene in *Cast Away* when Tom Hanks's character tries repeatedly to sail his raft over the swells battering the island where he has been washed up alone. If only he could get past them, he would be in clear water and able to escape. But time and again, he is swept back to shore, back to the beginning. It takes patience and a titanic force of will to carry him through to the open ocean, where life is just as hard, but at least more fluid.

The event that took Mrs. Shibata across the waves and out into the ocean was a meeting with the then president of Nissan, Yutaka Kume. "I was referred to him by a well-known writer who told him that I had a very pure heart and a very pretty face. When I went in to see Kume-san, he told me I wasn't so pretty. 'But Kume-san,' I told him, 'you look like the sleeve of a kimono.' And he laughed and we broke the ice." It was a spontaneous remark, and could have got her thrown out. Instead, it opened the doors to the biggest accounts in Japan. It made her realize that there was a virtue to being Mrs. Shibata, a chatty, short, avowedly unglamorous pistol of a woman. She lost any fear of simply being herself because it turned out that Japanese executives, surrounded every day by obedient men and servile women, enjoyed swapping jokes with a woman who reminded them of a favorite aunt.

Through Kume, she was invited to attend a dinner party held weekly for Japanese CEOs. She prowled the room looking at the name cards on the dinner table and committed every one to memory. Thirty minutes into the dinner, one of the CEOs turned to her and said, "You're the saleswoman, what are our names?" She rattled off every single one. "They said, that's why you're number one."

Sales, she says, is all about referrals. When she wanted more corporate clients, she started by asking the few she had to refer her to bigger companies. When they refused, she said small company referrals would be fine. Sure enough, many of those leads became sales. "None of this is easy," she says, "but when you get the referrals rolling, you keep meeting people and you keep learning and that way, you keep selling. All those young men I cold-called at companies are now senior management. I grew up with them. As my career evolved, so did theirs."

Today, Mrs. Shibata calls herself "the woman who has never been beaten." In her first month at Dai-ichi Life, she looked around and saw the men she was competing against, and she became determined to sell more than them. It took her just eight years to become the company's top salesperson, and she credits that to her genes. "My daughters are now top salespeople because they have inherited what I inherited, motivation and a great spirit."

She still pushes hard for sales. When a corporate vice president told her recently that he was ready to spend 300 million yen ($3 million) on life insurance for his company but then cut the number to 200 million, she drove him back up to the original number. "I never say thank you until I have what I think the person should be spending." Courses and books can take you to a middling position in sales, she says, but to get to the top, it comes down to personality. "Selling is very hard to teach, because it's about what exists in your head and what goes on in your whole life. If you keep your friends and respect your parents, the benefits of that come back to you in this life. It comes back as income you can see. The objective in sales becomes the same as that in the rest of your life, to respect others and do the best for them. Then you don't have to be a salesperson about what you do. Selling becomes an activity consistent with who you are."

In 1990, an American professor, Guy Oakes, published a book called *The Soul of the Salesman: The Moral Ethos of Personal Sales.* It evolved from his research into companies and individuals who sold products as varied as life insurance, cosmetics, vacuum cleaners, and mutual funds. He described two basic views of sales. The first, a strategic interaction between buyer and seller, in which the seller's goal is to maximize their commission using the buyer as a means. The second, sales as service. The problem, he wrote, was "How can the ruthless gamester also qualify as the caring services professional?"

Drawing on interviews with life insurance agents and data from the Life Insurance Marketing and Research Association, Oakes worked his way disgustedly through the evidence. "My limited experience in exploring the occupational lives of life insurance agents suggests that although they live off the trust they inspire in others, they are extremely parsimonious in the investment of their own trust. As one agent put it, with an excess that is typical of the industry: 'In this business, you don't trust anybody.' Everyone, it seems, has an angle, a hidden agenda, and ulterior motives that are probably base, indefensible and calculated to thwart the agent's own interests."

The original sin of this industry, Oakes argued, lay in its training methods. It does not simply teach product knowledge and the classic five steps of prospecting, approaching, interviewing, closing, and servicing. It also demands that trainees evolve through habit into different people. "The training program requires agents to exercise a systematic surveillance and control over the conduct of life as a whole and all of its details." They must rise early and dress sharply, keep detailed records of their activity and immerse themselves in their products. In the evening, they must not waste their time on frivolous entertainment, but read the great books and serve as pillars of the community. Oakes found that agents were encouraged to develop a "twenty-four-hour awareness of what makes an individual a potential customer." As they become "connoisseurs of the flotsam and jetsam of trivial conversations and the informational effluvia of life," they become subject to a "rage for connectedness." No parent–teacher association, sports club, or Rotary Club is free of the trolling salesperson, veiling their commercial interest behind inquiries about your family. They are encouraged to have no boundaries.

For example, a single issue of *Life Association News* published in April 1989 contained articles on how to sell life insurance on children to parents who have just lost a child and how to talk to someone in mourning. Parents are often loath to buy insurance against the death of their own children, the magazine explained. So, one solution is to target working-class parents of more than one child soon after the death of one of their children. Most likely they will be paying off the funeral in installments and reliving the child's death with every check, so may now be susceptible to a plan to free them of such an obligation if another child were to die. In the case of someone in mourning, the magazine suggested that if agents don't know the deceased, they should try to become acquainted by using the tiniest shards of personal information. Try saying something like this: "I know you will miss going to the theater with her. Maybe you and I can do that together soon in honor of her." This may sound like weaseling your way into the life of a grieving widower just to sell them insurance, but think of it this way, the article suggests: you are making a friend and helping them out.

Professors Oakes, Mayer, or Greenberg would recognize Norman Levine as an archetypal American life insurance salesman of the old school. He has written numerous get-up-and-go books, including *Yes You Can, Selling with Silk Gloves—Not Brass Knuckles*, and a series of tapes titled *If You Sell Well—There Are No Impossible Dreams*. In his author photographs, he sits with his chin resting on his hands, a meditative millionaire. He is part of a tradition of salesmen going back to Dale Carnegie who develop a thriving parallel career as a sales and life philosopher. He lives in Palm Springs, and when he answered the telephone he sounded more brass knuckles than silk gloves. He let me know quickly that the notion that a nonsalesman should be writing a book about sales offended him. "A real expert doesn't need to ask other people," he scolded me. Fortunately, his enthusiasm for his subject swiftly carried him away. Levine, his official biography reports, is the only person to have won the top four accolades in the life insurance sales profession: Top of the Table, for selling personal life insurance; the Master Agency Award, for managing his own company; the Managers' Hall of Fame; and the life industry's John Newton Russell Memorial Award, named after a fabled life insurance salesman who worked in the early decades of the twentieth century. He is an apostle of Ben Feldman, reputedly the greatest life insurance salesman of all time.

Feldman lived and worked in eastern Ohio, selling insurance to small factories, mills, and businesses. Over the course of his fifty-year career, he sold over $1 billion in life insurance on behalf of the New York Life Insurance Company. Feldman's approach was to soft sell customers by appealing to their better instincts, rather than to terrorize them with the fear of what might happen to their families if they died without a policy. Feldman believed that study and technical knowledge were the key to success in sales. He boasted that he would spend two hours every night from ten to midnight studying life insurance, sales, persuasion, financial planning, and anything else that might stand him in better stead with his customers. "Read!" he would advise fellow salesmen. "Study never stops, because publications never stop coming in. It's read and study. And think about what you're studying. Take it apart and put it together. Ask 'why?' And know the answers." Study, plus the right attitude and a proclivity to work would rocket you past the great majority of your rivals. He liked to articulate his philosophy in what became known as "power phrases": "Doing something costs something. Doing nothing costs something. And, quite often, doing nothing costs a lot more"; "If you've got a problem, make it a procedure and it won't be a problem anymore"; "The key to a sale is an interview, and the key to an interview is a disturbing question"; "Don't sell life insurance, sell what life insurance can do."

When he visited a prospective client, Feldman liked to say to them: "You'll have the same problems when I walk out as you had when I walked in . . . unless you let me take your problems with me." Though the life insurance packages he sold rarely differed from customer to customer, his pitch did, as he decided what problem the customer most wanted solved. If the customer had children, Feldman would sell life insurance as a means to paying for a college education. If the customer had a thriving business, he sold it as a way to ensure the business could pass down in a healthy state to the next generation.

Levine believes firmly that the ability to sell, the skill he shares with Feldman, doesn't correlate with one's formal education or knowledge of the more academic science of marketing. "Most sales-people who come out of the higher educational institutions are incompetent in the field," he says. "There is no difference between being a marketing expert and someone with no sales credentials at all." He is also leery of people who call themselves salespeople and yet work for well-established firms. "People go to Macy's because it's Macy's, because of the credibility of Macy's. If I worked for IBM,

I would get sent off for training and then go out with IBM's reputation behind me. The true salesperson starts out naked as a jaybird, with no product and no people." For Levine, selling is not just his job. It determines who he is. He wakes up a salesman, goes to bed a salesman, and dreams a salesman. If you want to be enthusiastic, he believes, act enthusiastic. To be successful, act successful. "To act to be requires a lot of discipline," says Levine. "All my life, I've been presumed to be highly enthusiastic and positive. And now I am. But in my early days, when I was taking my lumps, I had to act that way. I did the things I had to do even when I didn't feel like doing them."

Levine's approach to human relations is summed up in a method he calls the "non-interview." The idea is that selling is basically about selling oneself rather than any particular product. What people buy is not your cheese grater, but you as a credible, trustworthy person with something to offer. To sell, you have to be an effective means for people to achieve what they want. To know what they want, however, you must first get inside their heads. You must, in other words, have empathy. For Levine, this has meant embedding himself in his community, joining school boards, parent–teacher associations, clubs, community organizations—any group where he might find customers. He is consumed by Oakes's "rage for connectedness." Every human contact for him becomes an act of prospecting. A casual chat at the school gates or at the church coffee morning is a non-interview. "I may have to do the non-interview ten times at the PTA before I develop an interpersonal relationship. It can take ten years before I can make a move." Levine has no problem with blurring the line between personal and business friendships. "Most of my friends are clients and most of my clients are friends," he says. What Oakes abhorred, Levine and Mrs. Shibata describe with pride.

. . .

This blurring of the personal and professional can have tremendous economic consequences. In Japan, life insurance costs two to three times what it costs in the United States and Europe, because it is still sold through antiquated networks of door-to-door salespeople who show up once a month to inquire after your health. In the Internet age, there is simply no need for them. But Japanese customers hate to terminate an existing arrangement, to end a relationship with a salesperson. Japanese life insurance companies continue to be so profitable because Japanese consumers cannot say no.

One of the few disruptive forces in the Japanese insurance world has been Prudential, the American financial services firm, which swept into Japan in the late 1980s offering salespeople the chance to make commissions far and above those offered by Japanese companies. Every Japanese salesperson I met claimed to have been approached by Prudential at some point with a gold-plated offer. Mrs. Shibata said she was offered seven times her Dai-ichi base salary to move, but she refused. For her, the stability, status, and camaraderie of a Japanese corporation outweighed the potential gold rush offered by the new American arrival.

Someone who did take Prudential's offer was a burly former university rugby player called Oka. I've changed his name at his request. Oka is in his early thirties and in his sixth year at Prudential. He comes from an eminent academic family, with university professors on his mother's and father's side. When he graduated from university, he joined a large advertising agency, where he managed an account for a carmaker. He found the work stultifying. "Japanese companies do not pay for performance, so I found I was rated the same as the people who did the same job, regardless of how much better I did it," he said. "I thought I needed to have more respect for myself. I went into life insurance sales to change my life."

Of course, that's the propaganda a company like Prudential puts forth to its potential employees, so it was intriguing to hear it spoken with such conviction. Before Prudential hired him, Oka underwent several rounds of interviews. At the first, he was asked what a professional salesperson did. All salarymen with college educations, he says, talk about meeting targets and contributing to a team. Oka told the interviewer what he wanted to hear: that selling was like hitting in baseball. If you can't hit, you make nothing.

In the second interview, he and the interviewer discussed the fulfillment of a career in sales. The questions were all about his life up to then. There were no questions about what he might do in the future, because that was considered irrelevant. "The firm believes that human beings obey patterns, especially at moments of dramatic change. By understanding their past, you can predict their future. Saying you want to do something in the future is meaningless if it has no link to the past. It's like saying you want to play rugby, but you've never done a bench press. Prudential says it can train you to build muscles, but only if there's some indication you really want to. You have to appear trainable."

He recalls one question in particular that jolted him. When in your life do you remember feeling that you were firing on all cylinders? He knew immediately when it was: in his fourth year at university, his graduating year, when he was playing on the rugby team. Nothing in six years of corporate life had come close. "I realized in that interview how wrong that job in advertising was for me. I took it because I thought I was good at convincing people, but I never got the opportunity to convince anyone. And here at Prudential was a company that in two hours looked so deeply into me that I saw what was wrong." His interviewer told him that if he was interested, the firm could train him. It would be tough. Two years with no holidays or days off. His base salary would sustain him for the first three months, but then shrink to zero over twenty-four months. If he could suck it up, he could change his life.

"My father always told me that the purpose of life is to learn. We are born to study. From rugby, I learned how to speak to other people. I chose advertising because I thought it would be about communicating. I chose sales for the same reason, and because I thought I could excel against the competition." Oka studied hard. He memorized the fat manual of Prudential sales pitches, tailored to meet every possible twist and objection a client might present. He learned how to hold a pen, how to record himself on video and dissect his own performance. "It's like baseball, where you perform and then sit down with your coaches and go over how you did. Even the best salespeople do videos and try to improve."

Like Mrs. Shibata, he began by trying to sell life insurance to his friends. "I couldn't sell at all. I approached sixty people at my old advertising agency and they all said no. But then several people at my rugby club signed up, they referred others, and that's how I grew my pie." I asked him to give me his pitch. He looked at me squarely. With his gelled mohawk, wide, thick-featured face, and broad shoulders shifting under a well-cut dark suit, Oka is a fearsome-looking man, a Queequeg of sales.

Life insurance is about dealing with two dreams, he begins. The first is a nightmare. That when you die, your family will be in trouble. Maybe your children won't be able to go to university. Your wife will be cast out onto the street. You have insurance on other things of value—your cars, your houses—why not your own life? As a father, don't you feel you have as much value as your house? The other dream is a positive one, that by putting your money in life insurance, you are preserving your capital. When you reach a point in your life when your family is secure and you no longer need the insurance, you can cash in your policy and get back 70 to 90 percent of what you put in. That lump sum will be good to have in old age. "The first sale I made was to my parents and my wife's parents," he told me. "Because I would never sell anything that the most important people in my life would not buy."

As I listened to his pitch, I feared that if I looked away, he would reach over and swat me back into the moment. "Most life insurance people beg," said Oka. "I beg for time, but then I tell the client to assess for themselves if what I have is valuable. If they think it's a good buy, then I ask them to refer their friends." He is a very hard man to say no to, which may explain why he now earns over $1 million a year. His least favorite pitches are to people who he can tell regard his line of work with contempt. "They act as if they are better than me. They tell me they've only got a couple of minutes. So I tell them right at the start, why did you bother meeting me today? I asked for ten minutes. Then they say they're not interested in life insurance, and I tell them that most people already have it, so there must be some reason they offered to see me. I'm doing all this from a script, reading them, watching them, seeing how they react, and adjusting my own performance."

Selling, Oka claims, transformed his very nature. "Work has enabled me to change. Few people find their calling in their first job. But then at some point, there comes a time when you are bored, you want more excitement, satisfaction, or money. Then you turn to selling. But to do it well, you must believe the work will change you. You must expect it. Our founder says that if your way of thinking changes, your actions change, if your actions change, your habits change, if your habits change, your personality changes, and if your personality changes your self changes. And once your self is changed, your whole life is different." Perhaps it's true that greater experience doesn't make one a better salesman in the narrow sense, but for Oka, Mrs. Shibata, and others whose natures predispose them to sales, the sustained act of selling can transform their behavior and character.

Every morning now, Oka cleans his own toilet bowl, a huge man in a tiny bathroom scrubbing away as a gesture of self-sufficiency and humility. He does it to prepare his mind for the day. Standing in the shower, he runs through a list of his clients, thanking them for their business. Hanging inside the front door of his apartment is a sign that reads GRATITUDE EVERY DAY. He and his wife look at it then bow their heads and give thanks. It's like a religion, I said. "Yes," he replied, smiling. "A religion for sportsmen turned salesmen."

From Professor Oakes's perspective, Oka's behavior and language are evidence of self-deception. By reciting scripts, Oka relieves himself of the duty of analyzing the ethics of his work. He becomes an actor, and as such is no more responsible for his actions than an actor playing Macduff is responsible for murdering Macbeth. Oakes wrote that "a belief in the legitimacy of their vocation would be compromised, perhaps even destroyed, if agents saw themselves as crass opportunists, attempting to trick and deceive the public and reducing all their human relationships to the cash nexus." Instead, they develop a "will to ignorance." They con themselves into thinking that commerce and service need not be in conflict. They develop a belief system that does not admit to doubt. It *is* a form of religion, but one that Oka seemed more than happy to adhere to. What to Oakes might seem a cult, to Oka and thousands of others seems a better way of living.

. . .

Self-deception is not the only risk salespeople must run in the course of their work. They must also beware of companies and entire industries that seem to regard sales as an excuse for dubious conduct. Car dealers have an especially bad reputation, based on tricks like the Hull-Dobbs system, also known as the System or the Drill. Jimmy Dobbs and Horace Hull ran a Ford dealership in Memphis at the start of World War II. As business slumped, they developed a four-stage selling strategy to sell more cars. In the first stage, their salesmen would ask customers arriving at the dealership for their driver's license for "identification" and their car keys, so the garage could take a look under the hood and assess their old car's trade-in value. Next, the customer was detained at the dealership. If they asked for their keys or license, they were told they couldn't be found, or distracted by the promise of a great trade-in deal. After this came pressure. The salesman kept coming up with prices and offers, adjustments, extra features and payment plans, popping out every few minutes to "see what I can do" with the manager. In the toughest situations, the manager himself, normally the top salesman, would come in to close the deal. The final step was the release, when the buyer, exhausted by hours at the dealership, capitulated and bought. The salesman was then warned to check any celebrations until the buyer had driven off the lot. The System helped the Hull-Dobbs dealerships thrive and expand, and variants on the practice became widespread in the industry.

The pharmaceutical industry, despite its supposed responsibility to care for patients, is no better. Rather than simply developing cures and selling them to those who need them, pharmaceutical companies are constantly trying to expand the boundaries of treatable illness.

A major part of their sales strategy has been "disease mongering"—convincing healthy people they are sick and encouraging doctors to prescribe their drugs for ever more ailments. They hire marketing firms to define new diseases in the public mind, consumer groups to come up with "victims," and PR firms to unveil their breakthrough "treatment," clearing the path for their salespeople. The public is led to think of mild symptoms as more serious than they are and to interpret personal problems as medical ones.

The long commercials we see on television, showing couples walking on beaches and throwing sticks for dogs while a fast-talking narrator tears through the side-effects of a sleeping pill or erectile dysfunction treatment, are the subject of easy jokes. Jerry Seinfeld said of them: "They show people climbing rocks, they give you the name of the drug, and you have to figure out if you need it or not." But this is more than harmless commerce. It heightens public anxiety and diverts vital medical resources from real problems. Hair loss, for example, used to be just hair loss. Now it is a medical problem. The *British Medical Journal* reported in 2002 that in order to sell its hair-loss treatment, finasteride, in Australia, Merck hired the public relations firm Edelman to arrange for experts to contribute articles on the dire consequences of hair loss. These experts explained that when losing their hair, men underwent all kinds of emotional problems. Their job prospects and mental well-being collapsed. Newspapers reported that an International Hair Study Institute had been set up to consider this awful epidemic. Few mentioned that the institute was being funded by Merck.

Pharmaceutical companies regularly hire ex-cheerleaders to sell their drugs. The logic is simple and crude. Most doctors are men. To get in to see them, it helps to be a peppy, attractive young woman. The overprescription of drugs often correlates with this sexual dynamic. Doctors buy more and prescribe more to please ex-cheerleaders than they do for salesmen who look like themselves. Hence the saying goes in sales that you'll never meet an ugly drug rep. As the cheerleading adviser at the University of Kentucky said of the pharmaceutical companies that badger him for sales recruits, "They don't ask what the major is. Exaggerated motions, exaggerated smiles, exaggerated enthusiasm—they learn those things, and they can get people to do what they want." It would take a very honest pharmaceutical company CEO to admit that the key to his business's success was exaggerating the need for his drugs and then sending attractive women to sell them to bored, busy men. Once again, sales proves to be a concentrated version of life itself, in which moral standards must compete against everyday practice and the urge to achieve financial success.

An especially ghoulish case of dubious sales practice is revealed in the Federal Trade Commission's guidelines for consumers planning a funeral. The Funeral Rule prohibits specific misrepresentations, which have evidently been tried by funeral companies. You cannot tell consumers that embalming is legally required when state or local law does not require it. Refrigeration is a cheaper option and must be offered. You cannot tell them they must buy a casket for a cremation, if an "alternative container" such as an unfinished wooden box meets legal requirements. You cannot tell consumers that anything you do to the body will delay natural decomposition. These prohibitions attempt to protect the bereaved from the lies and commercial gouging of funeral salesmen, and they spotlight another reason why an instinctive antipathy to sales is so widespread in our culture.

. . .

In his memoir *The Salesman of the Century*, Ron Popeil, the legendary infomercial pitchman for products such as the Veg-O-Matic, the Popeil Automatic Pasta Maker, and the Popeil Pocket Fisherman, made his own peace with this subject. Popeil grew up selling at state and county fairs before making his fortune in infomercials. He wrote about selling not as a stand-alone business activity, but as one piece in a process that begins with great ideas and includes patents, design, packaging, pricing, manufacturing, advertising, and publicity. The greatest salesman, by Popeil's definition, understands how all these steps are integrated because he is the inventor, manager, and seller. The moment selling becomes a separate business function, you are sunk. But Popeil is also highly attuned to the ethical challenges of selling and how to deal with them in practice. He tells a story of visiting an army general to pitch a new spray-on boot polish for the National Guard. Popeil went in with his business partner and offered to demonstrate the spray on the fearsome officer's boots. As he sprayed, the boots turned white. Desperate, Popeil invited the general to pick another can of spray to try on another pair of boots. The same thing happened. The boots turned white. Popeil was devastated. But he gathered his nerve, looked the general in the eye, and said, "Well, General, can we sell the National Guard?" To his astonishment, the general replied, "Well, if it's okay with Colonel Kane, it's okay with me." It turned out the general thought Popeil had a connection with this highly connected Colonel Kane, and was ready to say yes to anything he thought Kane wanted. "How could I do what I did to the general's boots and then look the general in the eye and have the nerve to say what I did?" wrote Popeil. "When something is all lost, you might as well go for it. Don't just fall down and play dead. I think the ability to do something like that gives you some insight into a good salesperson. Not giving up. I could have apologized and said I was sorry and tried to figure out later what happened. But that wouldn't have created a sale."

In that statement, we see the salesman's mind dancing around ethical questions that might flummox the rest of us. His product was evidently a bust; it turned out that a chemical in the spray reacted badly to humidity. But he didn't just admit that. He lunged for the sale. The ethical question reared its head only once Popeil had triumphed in the practical battle of winning the sale. Later, he decided not to sell the defective product because, he wrote, doing so would "hurt my reputation." Ultimately, he made the right choice in moral terms, but for practical reasons

Popeil also described how he sold one of his most successful products, the Chop-O-Matic, with a "valuable recipe book—fifty secret recipes by world famous chefs" thrown in "at no additional charge." As an aside, he noted, "In all candor, I don't really remember where all those world famous chefs came from." In almost every paragraph of his book, Popeil ricochets from homilies on the importance of selling a good product at a good price to glib asides about how it's all a tremendous lark and maybe a bit of a scam.

You can find countless other examples of common, yet unpleasant, selling practices. Investment banks pitch IPOs they don't believe in, or credit derivatives they know are going to blow up. Restaurants sell the special, which consists of food about to turn bad. It is not always the salesperson making the decision to sell like this, but rather a manager who never has to meet the customer or say the words that might make him feel uncomfortable.

What separates the successful from the unsuccessful salesperson is the ability to believe that what you do is consistent with who you are. Internal and external conflicts are inevitable in sales. To succeed, you must manage them to the point where you feel, like Mrs. Shibata or Oka or Norm Levine, that your life and your business are intertwined. However we might judge their balance between ego and empathy, they do not appear to suffer from any personal conflicts about what they do. To succeed, you cannot fear that every pitch is a fight that risks forcing you into depression or destroying an important relationship. You need to set limits for your own behavior, which you can live with and explain to yourself. You need to love the battle itself, to revel in playing the odds. Nature might endow you with a sensitive amygdala and low fluid intelligence, which makes you highly sensitive and less quick at sizing up situations. But if you can nurture a clear understanding of your role as a salesperson, and all that it entails, you will ultimately have the edge over the lazy natural who prefers willful ignorance to self-knowledge.

Chapter 4

I BELIEVE

I don't want a salesperson looking at your
wallet. I want them looking at your heart.

RON JOHNSON, SENIOR VICE PRESIDENT OF RETAIL, APPLE

A senior manager at Apple told me the following story. He was up for a promotion and his boss told him there was a chance he might have to meet Steve Jobs, the company's late CEO. If that happened, he'd better make sure he was wearing the uniform. The manager was relatively new at Apple, so he asked what he meant. He was startled by the specificity of the response. The uniform consisted of jeans, but nothing designer. Levi's, Gap, or Wrangler would do. A plain white shirt, sleeves rolled up, to give a sense of informality, but only one button undone at the top, and a T-shirt underneath. The watch must be modest and functional. Shoes should be slip-ons, or sneakers, preferably not leather and definitely not dressy. Socks or no socks, but nothing garish. Any eyeglasses should be unmemorable; no jewelry and no overpowering scents. The only item you should carry in to the meeting was the latest MacBook. "The idea is that you should convey no strong identity," the manager told me, "so that Steve can imagine you just the way he wants to." The manager kept his uniform in a gym bag in the trunk of his car for six weeks so he could slip into it at a moment's notice. Sadly, he never got the chance—he got the promotion but never the meeting with Jobs.

When people talk of Apple as a cult, they are referring in part to this kind of behavior, the slavish abandonment of self to a cause of questionable value.

Apple thinks and behaves in crucial ways like many of history's greatest evangelical organizations. It was founded and was run for many years by a highly charismatic leader in Jobs, who referred to his own achievements as "magical" and "revolutionary." Its advertising describes its products as possessing miraculous powers. A video celebrating the first year of the iPad featured a mother of an autistic child saying, "I define a miracle as something that comes in and changes your life for the better in ways you did not expect." The miracle was the iPad and her son's enthusiastic engagement with it. In the same film, Ron Johnson, who oversaw Apple's stores at the time, says, "The iPad has to be held, has to be touched to truly understand how magical it is"—as if it were the Turin Shroud.

Apple's stores act as churches, dedicated spaces for gathering the faithful and attracting new converts. When Apple was planning its first stores, in 2000–2001, it emphasized the importance of putting them in central, urban locations to attract passersby, and letting visitors use the products. The company's intention was to increase the number of "switchers," people ready to abandon their PCs to become Apple users. The difficulty of converting millions to Apple demanded soaring spaces, latter-day cathedrals like Apple's glass cube on Fifth Avenue, and a selling method akin to missionary work. The stores were laid out with the new products up front, so customers who had never owned an Apple product could try them out; next was a Red Zone, abuzz with staff and energy, where the conversion could take place in the form of a sale; and then a Family Room, where customers would be called by name and helped with service, support, and lessons. As Johnson said of the stores, "We invest here to build promoters for Apple," fresh armies of consumer evangelists who can go out and preach Apple's gospel. The symbol Johnson used to describe the earliest days of the Apple stores was an Evian bottle, because the company gave out three thousand of them to people waiting in line for the first store to open. The first Genius Bar gave away water to connect with customers, to show Apple cared. At a time when its rivals were trying to sell $2,000 computers in soulless big-box stores using cutthroat sales tactics, Apple went in the opposite direction. Johnson said that while others were hiring sharks to sell PCs, Apple sought "not sharks, but . . . teachers, photographers and filmmakers," converts themselves who sold out of enthusiasm, not just for commission. Today, school groups can book Apple stores for night and summer camps held for children to spend time learning about technology. Visit an Apple store day or night in many locations, and you realize it has become a secular church hall.

The most favorable interpretation of Apple's sales tactics is that they reflect a genuine desire to improve the lives of their customers. An iPad can be a wonderful thing, just as miraculous and transformational as its evangelists claim. The ugly interpretation is that the company is exploiting its customers' desire for meaning, significance, belonging, and inspiration for commercial ends, with no concern for its adherents beyond what they are willing to spend. As an Apple customer milling through the stores, I've felt both sensations myself, that of exhilarated devotee and powerless commercial mark.

Part of the genius of Apple's approach is that under the ultramodern skin, by conflating commerce with religious forms of organization and behavior, the company has joined a long, successful selling tradition. Chaucer's *Canterbury Tales*, written in England at the end of the fourteenth century, contains "The Pardoner's Tale," about a rotten Catholic cleric who travels the country displaying fake relics and persuading simpleminded crowds to buy them in return for holy indulgence. He drunkenly admits to the devious nature of his scam, but performs it anyway, and then tells a morality tale to dissuade people from his own vice of greed. He is a liar, a cynic, a successful businessman, and a moralist, all in one. As one modern literary critic wrote, "His kind is ubiquitous, and his inheritors are all around us, in our own day, in salesmen and politicians and all the other public traffickers in words for profit." The Pardoner was an extreme case, a religious crook trafficking in fakery; Apple delivers goods with real benefits. But the essence of its pitch is about more than touch screens and processing speed. It goes back centuries.

The sociologist Thorstein Veblen wrote in 1923 that commercial salesmanship had its roots in evangelism. He called the Roman Catholic Church "quite the largest, oldest, most magnificent, most unabashed, and most lucrative enterprise in sales-publicity in all Christendom." In nineteenth-century America, organized armies of salespeople were sent out to sell books and other products, replacing independent peddlers. These new sales forces were organized using the model of Methodist and other proselytizing religious groups that abounded in the country at the time. The instructions issued to salespeople retained an evangelical flavor, emphasizing the importance of faith and a sense of duty in overcoming the loneliness and many rejections of life on the road. Asa Candler, who turned Coca-Cola into a major enterprise in the late nineteenth century, was a devout Methodist who would lead his salesmen in singing "Onward, Christian Soldiers." He was also vice president of the American Bible Society, one of the most successful door-to-door sales organizations ever.

In 1925, Bruce Barton, an advertising executive and the son of a Congregational minister, fused selling and religion in his book *The Man Nobody Knows*, in which he depicted Jesus Christ as a heroically successful salesman. "Let us forget all creed for the time being, and take the story just as the simple narratives give it," he wrote, "a poor boy, growing up in a peasant family, working in a carpenter shop; gradually feeling his powers expanding, beginning to have an influence over his neighbors, recruiting a few followers, suffering disappointments and reverses, finally death. Yet building so solidly and well that death was only the beginning of his influence! Stripped of all dogma this is the grandest achievement story of all! . . . Success is always exciting; we never grow tired of asking what and how." He listed three reasons for Christ's success as a salesman. First, he had a magnetic voice and manner, supported by an "overwhelming sincerity." Second, he hired well, recognizing the hidden talents in the ragtag group who became his disciples. Third, and most important, he possessed "unending patience," which he used to train his organization. He was empathetic, yet he had enough resolve, or ego drive, to succeed. John the Baptist could draw a crowd, but he had "no program for them after their repentance." John could close; Christ could maintain the relationship. Or to put it in contemporary sales terms, John was the hunter, Christ the farmer. "Because of his marvelous instinct for discovering their latent powers, and because of his unwavering faith and patience, he molded them into an organization which carried on victoriously," Barton wrote of Christ.

Barton was widely lampooned for his brazen conflation of sales and the sacred, but his book sold over 750,000 copies and propelled him to a seat in Congress. He was hardly the only one to describe sales as a quasi-mystical means to self-discovery and personal transformation. Og Mandino came to America from Italy with his family in the early 1930s and settled in Natick, Massachusetts. His plans to attend journalism school were foiled by the death of his mother. Instead, he worked in a factory and flew bombers during World War II. On his return home, the only job he could find was selling life insurance. He loathed the work, ran his family into debt, and became an alcoholic, often sleeping on the street.

Then one snowy night in Cleveland, he stared at a gun in the window of a pawnshop and considered suicide. But he couldn't even muster the courage for that. Instead, he kept walking and found himself in the local library, standing in front of a row of self-help and motivational books. He took a few off the shelf and began to read. One was W. Clement Stone's *Success Through a Positive Attitude*. Stone was a successful insurance salesman and Mandino found a job on the bottom rung of his company. Inspired by Stone's philosophy, Mandino was soon managing the top sales team in the firm. He then took a week off work and rented a typewriter and wrote a handbook to selling insurance in rural areas. Stone moved him up to the sales promotion department and eventually made him editor of a national magazine called *Success Unlimited*.

In 1968, Mandino published what would become one of the bestselling sales books of all time, *The Greatest Salesman in the World*.

It is a story set in Jerusalem just before the birth of Christ. A young man named Hafid asks a dying trader the secrets of his success. The trader tells him that when he was young, he was given ten scrolls by a rich man, which allowed him to become the greatest salesman in the world. Subsequent chapters describe the contents of each scroll, and Mandino advises that you should read each one three times a day for thirty days before going on to the next. The themes contained in the scrolls are commitment, love, persistence, miracles, time, emotion, laughter, value, action, and guidance. But Mandino's overarching message is that the fulfilled person is the one who takes action today—the salesman who fights off exhaustion and despair and acts instead with generosity and hope. Barton's and Mandino's books have a biblical ring of authority, and their extraordinary success suggests that sales really is a unique business function, in terms of how its practitioners are motivated and organized, and how they must think of their work.

To this day, many direct-selling companies, such as Mary Kay cosmetics and Amway, hew closely to religious organization and rhetoric. Mary Kay lists its priorities as God first, family second, career third, as it flogs its salespeople to move more inventory. The Southwestern Company, which employs fleets of college students to sell textbooks door-to-door over their summer breaks, uses prayer and religious readings to help their salespeople accept rejection and to persevere. Omnilife, a Mexican direct seller of health products, hosts recruitment events at which audience members come onstage and testify to the products' miraculous powers. Prospective salespeople are then welcomed onstage to raucous cheers from current employees, in a mood similar to that when evangelical Christians surge up the aisle of a stadium church to be saved. Tupperware used to go even further, "baptizing" its top distributors at an artificial lake at its headquarters in Kissimmee, Florida, called Poly Pond, after Poly-T, the plastic originally used to make Tupperware products.

Apple is more subtle than this but, in essential ways, no different. It flatters its customers by telling them that by buying Apple, they "think different." In the words of one of the company's most famous advertisements, Apple and its buyers are among "The crazy ones. The misfits. The rebels. The troublemakers. The round pegs in the square holes. The ones who see things differently. They're not fond of rules. And they have no respect for the status quo." These words were intoned over images of Einstein, Amelia Earhart, Muhammad Ali, Gandhi, Maria Callas, and Martin Luther King Jr., among others. And yet the difference is not the feeling you have when visiting an Apple store, where crowds venerate holy relics laid out on pale wooden altars, conceived by the quasi-divine Jobs. Through its stores, Apple, like Barnum, exploits the principle of social proof—the more people do something, the more likely it's a reasonable thing for me to do. Its selling methods successfully erode its customers' will to do the very thing that as a company it claims to do best: think different.

The psychologist Robert Cialdini wrote that "no leader can hope to persuade, regularly and single-handedly, all the members of the group. A forceful leader can reasonably expect, however, to persuade some sizable proportion of group members. Then the raw information that a substantial number of group members has been convinced can, by itself, convince the rest. Thus the most influential leaders are those who know how to arrange group conditions to allow the principle of social proof to work maximally in their favor." In Steve Jobs, Apple had a charismatic leader, comparable to a religious guru. He inspired not just customer loyalty but faith. When he presented new products, he did so in front of a clapping, adoring audience who rose to their feet at significant moments. Long before he died in October 2011, the financial markets fretted over his health and succession the way Catholics worry about the next pope.

The definition of a charismatic leader is one who inspires absolute devotion, who insists that followers become converts and devotees and approach the world with a philosophy consonant with his own. Such a leader proves his or her abilities through miracles or repeated success, and convinces others they have the power to bring order out of chaos and thus to shape the world for the better. All these definitions applied to Jobs. He wanted people to abandon his rivals and live their digital lives through Apple. He boasted of his products' magical qualities and Apple's unprecedented growth and commercial success. He articulated a broader philosophy of making the complex simple and living rich lives at the intersection of art and technology. And his followers mobbed his stores every time he released a new product, displaying obsessive behaviors hard to understand for those who see only the utilitarian value of Apple's devices. Once part of Apple's tribe, devotees tend to exhibit the zeal of converts, displaying a sense of superiority and a willingness to sing Apple's praises to the heathen. The tribe aren't just using a different smartphone or tablet, they are living a better life.

The Harvard academic Rosabeth Moss Kanter wrote of utopian groups that "members were distinguished on spiritual or moral grounds, according to how well they exemplified ideal traits of membership or how thoroughly they were committed to the community, with the more spiritual, moral or zealous members receiving greater deference." What applies to utopian groups, religious congregations, and to Mary Kay and Amway also helps explain how Apple became the greatest corporate success story of our times. It inspires more than a commercial relationship. It inspires faith.

. . .

In the course of a best-of-seven game series in April 2010, the Washington Capitals ice hockey team fell apart. Having taken the first three games, they needed to win just one more to go through to the next round of the Stanley Cup play-offs. They were overwhelming favorites, having played an excellent season behind the most exciting player in the league, Alexander Ovechkin. Their opponents were the much lower rated Montreal Canadiens. But the Capitals lost four games in a row, and that was it. Earlier than they had imagined, they were out. The morning after the final defeat, Ted Leonsis, the owner of the Capitals, wrote a blog post titled "If It Doesn't Kill You—It Makes You Stronger." He described the defeat as "deeply personal and deeply agonizing." He felt he had let a lot of people down. "But," he wrote, "my personality and outlook on life is thus 'if it doesn't kill you—it will make you stronger.'" He vowed to sort through the reasons for the defeat, to adjust, and to keep building. He affirmed his commitment to making the club "just right." He wrote, "As I have said . . . we have miles to go before we sleep. The woods are dark and deep. We are committed to improvement and we will be better next season. Onward. Thank you."

Leonsis is a large man in every way. His body is large; his head, framed by a wave of dark hair and a beard, is large; and his achievements are outsize. Stick a gold hoop in one ear and a cutlass between his teeth and he would make a convincing pirate. He made his name as the president of AOL during its glory days of the 1990s. Today, he invests hundreds of millions of dollars of his own money in everything from technology start-ups to sports teams. He is one of those rare, very successful men about whom no one has a bad word to say.

And as he said when I met him, "I consider being called a salesman a compliment." His explanation following the Capitals' defeat showed a good salesman recovering from a setback. He felt the defeat personally, but was not crushed by it. He acknowledged his own fault, but saw that success would depend on the work of many people. He wallowed for a moment to ensure that he had learned all he could, but then moved on, confident that this defeat would guide him toward a better tomorrow. He demonstrated a profound faith in the future.

This is an attitude consistent with successful selling, according to the work of Martin Seligman, a professor of psychology at the University of Pennsylvania. In 1986, Seligman sent out eleven hundred questionnaires to the entire sales force of the Pennsylvania region of the Metropolitan Life Insurance Company. The questionnaires were designed to elicit the salespeople's "attributional style," or the way in which they interpreted the reasons for their successes and failures. Were they optimists or pessimists? Did they think the sun would come up tomorrow or that the world was set against them?

Seligman's Attributional Style Questionnaire (ASQ) evolved out of his study of depressives. He found that many of them suffered from "learned helplessness," a state of mind caused by uncontrollable bad events. When we experience such events, our interpretation of them, and how they affect our behavior in the future, tends to fall into three categories. First, we see the bad event as either internal, caused by us, or external, caused by a particular situation. "I lost my wallet because I'm an absentminded fool" would be internal. "I lost it because we were in a mad rush to get to the airport and the children were screaming" would be external. Second, we attribute the event either to stable or unstable factors. My losing the wallet is typical of how we travel, always leavings things to the last minute. Or, this was a one-off event, which is unlikely to happen again. The final category contains global versus specific attributions. "The lost wallet symbolizes my life of incessant failure, disorganization, and futility" is a global attribution. Specific would be "Really, it's just a lost wallet and once I've called my credit card companies and gotten a new driver's license, life will go on as before—no big deal." Depressives tend toward internal, stable, and global attributions, tying themselves up in self-flagellating, persistent, and pervasive gloom. Whereas optimists prefer external, unstable, and specific situations, sloughing off the worst as stuff that just happens. The ideal is someone like Leonsis, not a la-la land optimist, but able to attribute the reasons for success or failure correctly and to remain positive about the future.

The ASQ is made up of twelve hypothetical events, six good and six bad. In each category, three deal with achievements and three with one's relationships to others. An event in the bad achievement category is that you have been looking for a job unsuccessfully for some time. You are asked to write down one reason for that. Then you are given a seven-point scale to rate yourself on the internal-external, stable-unstable, and global-specific spectrum, in which 1 is your fault, 7 is other people's. Is your failure to find a job entirely your fault or the fault of other people and circumstances? Is this a one-off, or is it always like this for you? Is your failure specific to job hunting or does it seep into every aspect of your life? Other bad events include an audience reacting poorly to a talk you have given, your struggling to do the work others expect of you, a friend being hostile toward you, a date going badly, or your failing to respond to a friend's request for help. The good events are that you become very rich, you get a raise, a friend compliments you on your appearance, your work is praised, you get a job you badly want, or your partner is being more loving toward you. The ASQ seeks to find out why you think any of this happens.

The first questionnaire was completed in 1978 by fifty male and thirty female undergraduates studying psychology at SUNY Stony Brook. When matched up with explanations and attributions gleaned from therapy, the ASQ turned out to be excellent at predicting depression. Seligman then turned to life insurance salesmen. Few professions require such frequent acceptance of failure. Those who take every rejection personally risk letting the swell of no's overwhelm their entire sense of self. Of the 1,100 questionnaires Seligman sent out to the salespeople of Metropolitan Life, 169 were returned completed. Ninety-four of these came from salespeople with established track records, which could be used to test the validity of the ASQ in predicting performance. Despite the small data set, the results turned out to be compelling. Agents who scored in the optimistic half of the explanatory style scale sold 37 percent more insurance than those in the pessimistic half. Those in the top decile sold 88 percent more than those in the bottom decile. A positive attitude turned out to make you a much better salesperson. It is the attitude reflected in Leonsis's e-mail to fans of his ice hockey team. In defeat, wounds will be licked and lessons learned, but nothing will stop the forward momentum.

Leonsis's office is above the Washington Capitals' practice facility atop a multistory parking structure in Arlington, Virginia, just west of Washington, D.C. Draped along the front of the building are banners showing the great Ovechkin in full flight. As I entered, I heard the sound of children on the team's practice rink. Leonsis believes in the importance of opening up his team and its facilities to the local community. He grew up in a Greek household in

Brooklyn, New York, before moving to the working-class town of Lowell, Massachusetts, at the age of eight. His large extended family believed ardently in the immigrant American dream. "They'd always tell me you can be anything you want. And I'd think, what were they smoking?" His father was a waiter and his mother a secretary. Despite being short, he was a fierce and dogged high school basketball player. He was also smart enough to skip eighth grade and head to college at just seventeen years old, to Georgetown, in Washington, D.C., where he felt socially out of place. "I remember going to a party there early on and a girl asking me 'Where do you summer?' And everyone was saying they summered in Nantucket and Martha's Vineyard. I said Lowell, Massachusetts."

Like Majid, Sullivan, Warren Buffett, and others, he started in business early, with a company called SnocoLoco, which he ran during his college vacations. "We sold red, white, and blue snow cones. Our slogan was: 'Be a patriot. Give your tongue a sleigh ride.'" He graduated at twenty, and for the next few years knocked around Washington, D.C., searching for a good business idea. It came to him standing in line at the supermarket. He was looking through the magazines at the checkout and saw a copy of *TV Guide*. On the cover was a sticker announcing that here was America's top-selling magazine. Since his family had never owned a television, he'd never bothered reading it. As he flicked through, he found brief interviews with celebrities followed by pages of television listings. "I could not believe this was the number-one-selling magazine in America," he told me.

He went home and stared at his Apple IIGS computer and said to himself that one day the PC would become as ubiquitous as the TV. "I realized that the television and computer business would be one and the same. That was my 'aha!'" So he set about creating a *TV Guide* for computers, which he named *LIST*, the Leonsis Index to Software Technology. For the front half of the magazine, he interviewed leading figures in the still-nascent PC industry, like Bill Gates. In the back he listed all the hardware and software on the market. To fund the business, he wrote up a business plan and through a friend secured a meeting with the CEO and senior officers of E. F. Hutton & Co., a stock brokerage firm. "I wrote this big presentation and talked about the returns, the forecasts, and at the end the CEO said, 'Young man, none of us in this room could appreciate nor had a clue what you were talking about. But we know that what you are forecasting will happen. And we want a piece of it. We think you can sell snow to Eskimos.' And he gave me $1 million on the spot. I knew then I could sell."

His basic pitch has not changed over the years. Leonsis likes to sell and invest in businesses with multiple bottom lines. "My pitch back then wasn't just the magazine. That offered a really good investment in itself. But what made it even better was that they were investing early in an unbelievably rapidly growing field and that they would learn a lot while they were making money. I told them that they'd meet a lot of people, learn a lot about this industry, and make a lot of money." The company he started in his bedroom grew into Redgate Communications, a new-media company that was acquired by America Online in 1994.

At AOL, Leonsis's main role was battling Microsoft, a job he relished. He had to motivate a large group of people by stimulating both their intellect and their emotions. "I had to identify the enemy, Microsoft, and then conceptualize it." One of the ways he did this was to hire an enormous inflatable dinosaur and float it in the air above AOL's offices to symbolize the aged, creaking Micro-soft. "I told them that this was like Pearl Harbor. My father grew up and fought in World War II, and I used to sit in his lap and ask him 'What did you do in the war?' I told the people at AOL, that it was the same situation, to the victor the spoils. People didn't debate whether or not to fight after Pearl Harbor. You got up and fought."

Sales was at the heart of AOL's business, and Leonsis made sure that whatever his other responsibilities, he went on sales calls. "No payroll gets met unless you make a sale," he says emphatically. "You get all these marketing people who've never sold anything, senior marketing people who because they've never been in sales will make the big miss and get fired. They'll launch a product and the dealers will know they've never been in the showroom. They'll try to sell a car on sex appeal when all consumers want is miles per gallon." He told me a story about Benjamin Franklin, who in addition to his many other achievements is credited with introducing advertising to newspapers. One day, Franklin was sitting in the offices of the *Pennsylvania Gazette* when a local shoemaker came in and explained that his business was growing, along with the city of Philadelphia, and that he was planning to open a second shoe store on the other side of town. Was there any way he could pay Franklin to inform his customers, through his newspaper, about the new store? "The man didn't come to buy advertising," says Leonsis. "He came because he wanted to inform people that they no longer had to cross town to use his service. Instead they could use this second store. No one wakes up in the morning and thinks 'I want to buy an advertise-ment.' They think, 'I have a perception to change. How do I best do that?'" Franklin hired his son-in-law, a drunk, to go around Phila-delphia knocking on doors to see if anyone else had anything they wanted to tell the rest of the town about. And thus grew classified advertising.

Selling for Leonsis is not an emotional battle in which buyer and seller deal personal blows until one triumphs and the other crumples back into drudgery. It is simply a means to an end. He pointed up at a painting hanging over his desk, showing a beautiful, elegant blond woman. "I'm married to a spectacularly beautiful woman who grew up wealthy. Other men were intimidated by her. But I figured that unless you ask, you never know. So I asked her, you want to go to dinner? She said Sure, I'm not doing anything. Everyone assumed she had lots of dates. So I always ask people, what's the worst that can happen?"

He believes it applies to business as much as it does to one's personal life. "I remember being at an account and I was with a friend and we'd got fired from this account and they weren't going to pay us. They said in the meeting that the guy who did the deal wasn't authorized to do it and so they weren't going to pay what we'd already spent. We were going to lose millions of dollars. So we get outside and my friend is devastated. He says he's going to resign. And we stand there outside the office and I look across to these woods, and the wind is blowing and the trees are changing color. So my friend says to me, 'Why aren't you freaking out?' And I told him, Well, what's the worst that can happen? We lost an account. My wife still loves me. The trees look beautiful. We'll go and look at our accounts and you'll find another account in thirty days which will be double what we just lost." Leonsis looked at the problem as a Stoic philosopher might, with equanimity and without fear. In the grand scheme of things, like all human triumphs and failures, it did not matter at all. This is not to say that he didn't care. Rather he saw the loss as past, and that an eventual gain was still entirely within his control.

· · ·

One stubborn question that remained from Seligman's research was whether optimism predicted good performance or whether it developed as a result of successful selling. Was it easier for Leonsis to say "What's the worst that can happen?" because years of success had given him the confidence to think that way? The way he tells the story of his own life, this fearless attitude was there from an early age. To better understand this, Seligman conducted a second study involving new sales agents hired by Metropolitan Life in the Pennsylvania region in the spring of 1983. All took the ASQ immediately after they were hired, and after a year, the results were compared with their first four quarters of sales performance. The optimists were found to be more likely to stick at the job, and their performance over the second half of the year was found to be significantly better. Of the 101 agents profiled, 42 were still with the firm at the end of the year and 59 had dropped out, a quite typical ratio at insurance firms. Of the 42 survivors, two-thirds had scored in the optimism half of the ASQ. And the higher up on the optimism scores, the more likely it was agents would stick with the work. The ASQ also predicted the productivity of workers. In the second half of the year, once the agents had had a chance to absorb their training and develop some specific skills and knowledge, the optimists sold 20 percent more than the pessimists.

The crucial finding here was that pessimists, who believe that bad things happen for internal, stable, and global reasons, will be destroyed by failure. They simply cannot cope with rejection, and the sense of failure it engenders will only lead to more failure and the state of learned helplessness observed in depressives.

By contrast, optimists succeed in sales, which leads to more optimism and more success. They feel the opposite of learned helplessness: learned optimism. Optimism and pessimism turn out to have a compounding effect on success in sales. It is what many salespeople had been saying all along, just not in a way academics cared to believe.

Closely linked to optimism and pessimism in selling are confidence and fear. Fear of selling is much like any other social phobia. Whenever we engage in a social situation, all of us make certain assumptions about how we will be perceived. The confident believe people will like them and all will go well. The socially phobic are seized by three paralyzing assumptions. First, they believe they must perform to an impossibly high standard. They worry that they must know everything, speak at the right moment, and rivet their audience. Second, they believe that dire consequences will ensue if they fail in any way to live up this standard. If someone disagrees with them, they will feel foolish. If they stammer or say too little, people will think they are boring and incoherent. Third, they assume that they really are as bad as they fear they are. They don't just worry that they will look foolish, they believe they really are foolish, and so any social situation is bound to lead to disaster.

Going into a sale, the socially phobic are already racked with fear. This fear is then aggravated by a set of interlinked patterns of behavior. The first pattern involves an acute focus on their own discomfort, which leads to exaggerated fears of what others are seeing. Their minds fill with images of their most frightened selves, so they assume this is how they look. Where an observer might notice a slight tremble, a pause in speech, and a bead of sweat, the socially phobic imagine they are shaking violently, stuttering uncontrollably, and sweating bullets. They become so wrapped up in this exaggerated self-image that they can't process any external cues, which would tell them things aren't nearly so bad. They begin to see themselves as social outcasts, even while people are treating them quite normally. In their minds, the merely ambiguous comment—"Would you mind moving your car? It's blocking the driveway"—becomes negative—"You blundering fool, don't you know there are other people here?"—while the negative—"That's an ugly tie you're wearing"—becomes catastrophic—"You are ugly and unappealing in every way."

Phobics then perform "safety behaviors" to minimize the feared social disaster. People afraid of having nothing to say memorize stories and jokes; if they worry about blushing, they wear a scarf to cover their neck and part of their face; if they fear sweating, they keep their arms folded to conceal any wet patches. Such behaviors make them especially conscious of the perceived problem, and may end up worsening it. Keeping your arms tightly folded makes you sweat even more. The more you fear blushing, the likelier you are to blush. Watching too closely what you say will likely stiffen you up and make you seem aloof, the opposite of what you want. But then there is the compounding danger that the phobic will wrongly credit these behaviors with preventing the feared social disaster. Rather than simply going through a social situation and discovering how easy it can be, the safety behavior becomes a crutch. When the feared disaster does not occur, the phobics thank the behavior for saving them, and never break free of their fear. They become prisoners of their defensive behavior.

Finally, all this stress means the phobics cannot process social cues that might ease their anxiety. They are so consumed by a negative internal perception of themselves that, rather than letting external cues put them at ease, they tend to seek out confirming evidence of their direst fears. Speaking in public, they will interpret a quiet audience as disapproving rather than pensive. If they see someone checking his e-mail, they will assume their speech must be atrociously dull, rather than perhaps that the person is glancing at the results of a child's doctor's appointment. Before a social situation, the socially phobic work themselves into a highly anxious state that leads them either to avoid the situation altogether or to underperform. And afterward, they rehash everything with a negative focus on themselves. Details that might have gone entirely unnoticed by anyone else leave them staring at the ceiling at 2 A.M. embarrassed and bubbling over with hatred toward the world.

Sales is to the socially phobic what the subway car is to the claustrophobic. Researchers estimate that anxiety about sales calls affects 40 percent of salespeople in the course of their careers. I suspect that this is a conservative estimate. Anxiety about selling can take several forms: fear of criticism from your manager or peers, or the even more dire fear that if you fail to meet quota, your bills won't get paid this month or your health insurance will lapse. There might be a conflict between your work and family life, the demand from your employer to sell to family and friends, to present yourself to them as something other than what you have been in the past. This creates cognitive dissonance, the jarring sense that who you are and who you must be to sell are two incompatible people. Perhaps there are moral compromises you are afraid to make. Maybe you don't believe in your product, for good reason, but must gloss over its failings in order to make a sale. Once again, we see sales as a concentrated version of life itself.

As with any form of social phobia, failure and the fear of failure in selling diminishes self-esteem, leads to false reasoning about the causes of failure, and causes a downward spiral of motivation and emotion. Willem Verbeke and Richard Bagozzi, scholars of sales-call anxiety, have written that "personal selling seems to contain inordinate opportunities for social anxiety because of its very nature, which includes the possibility of multiple rejections and failures on a daily basis and the effects of this potential on feelings and thoughts about the self." Sales anxiety emerges most often in the contexts of cold-calling and closing. These are the two areas where the most intense personal dramas unfold. Cold-calling is hard because of all the unknowns. It's like going to a party where you know no one. But at least at a party, all you might hope for is to create a favorable impression. As a salesperson, you must try to convert that impression into a financial commitment. You might be cold-calling people of higher social or economic status, in which case, do you grovel in order to ingratiate yourself or stick to who you are and refuse to defer? Navigating any new set of social or cultural cues is exhausting. Canvassing for clients is vague, and ambiguous, leaves you vulnerable to rejection, and hence induces anxiety.

The anxiety about closing is also based on the anticipation of rejection. When you ask for commitment, you are giving others the chance to say no. Not only might you feel personally rejected, but you must then go back to the office or your family and explain why you didn't make the sale. The no sends you skittering back to the beginning of the sales process. Furthermore, once you're near the close, you cannot escape. Social anxiety makes people want to flee, to get out of the hellish nightclub or cocktail party or Thanksgiving dinner. The salesperson cannot run. He is trapped until the sale is resolved one way or another.

What we know of other forms of social phobia applies equally to anxiety about sales. The good news is that it tends to be highly specific, and treatments can reason people away from their irrational fears. Sales anxiety is not an enduring pathology but rather an error in our normal functioning. If we can dissect our fears, then we can overcome them. If we can identify the situational triggers, we can manage them.

For example, if you think a customer does not like you, explain to yourself in detail why you think that. Then imagine you are someone else looking at your explanation. Would you still think the customer disliked you? Do your assumptions about their behavior make sense? What other reasons might they have for seeming distracted? Might their company be imploding or is their child in trouble at school? Their behavior might not entirely be explained by their feelings about you. If you applied your own biases and prejudices to your own behavior, would they make sense? Or would they lead to wild misinterpretations of the truth? If you stammer, are you stupid? If not, why would you assume anyone else thought that of you? But to understand all this, you must be able to disconnect from the immediate situation and to analyze it objectively, in a state of what Verbeke and Bagozzi call "disconnected mindfulness."

This strategy points to a notion we encounter again and again throughout this book: sales success entails the ability to step away from one's ego. Majid does so with his resilient "loose robes" approach, which prevents him from letting a perceived slight impede a deal. And the phobic salesman blocks a deal by wrongly obsessing over his own perceived shortcomings and others' reactions to them.

Another means to this ideal state of disconnected mindfulness is to abandon safety behaviors entirely. Some of the very greatest salesmen illustrate the kind of extreme behavior that can prove effective. Larry Goodman, the head of sales at CNN during its finest years, in the 1980s and 1990s, told me about working for Ted Turner, the network's founder. "His passion was contagious. He had this pure conviction that the cable business was the future of television. He could walk into a room and even if you had your back to him, he had that dynamism that comes from innate greatness and charisma. People wanted to see him, touch him, say they shook his hand." But tapping Turner's charisma to sell advertising could be a hair-raising experience. By 1987, only one of the top twenty-five advertising agencies in America was still not buying airtime on Turner's channels. Larry decided to take Turner in to see them the next time he was in New York. A breakfast meeting was arranged.

"So we show up with Ted and the eight top people are there, in a conference room," said Larry. "Ted greets everyone and turns to Bob, the head of the agency, and says, 'Thanks for seeing me.' Bob says, 'My pleasure, Ted.' Then Bob says to Ted, 'Would you like to bring everyone up-to-date on Turner Broadcasting?' And Ted says, 'Any other day, that's exactly what I'd do. But today, I want to listen. Perhaps we can go around the room and ask everyone to give me their perception of Turner Broadcasting.' Then Ted turns to this big young Irishman with red hair and pale skin and says, 'Why don't you lead off?' So the young man starts saying the broadcast networks have a lot of fresh, original programming that the cable networks don't have. He goes on for five minutes and uses these words *fresh* and *original* maybe thirty times. It was painful.

"When the guy had finished, the head of the agency said, 'Ted, shall we carry on round the room?' But Ted says, 'No. I'd like to comment now.' And then he starts talking in this very low, slow voice. 'You know, every day, I wake up in my bed. I stretch. I get out of bed and walk to the window and look out over Atlanta. If it's sunny or raining, it doesn't really matter. It just feels good to be alive. I look back, and there's usually a beautiful woman in my bed. Sometimes two. Then I go to the kitchen and make myself a cup of coffee, pour a glass of orange juice. Then, you know what I do? I go to the bathroom and I take a fresh, original shit. Every morning. And you know what's in the bowl? That's what you're buying from the networks. Murder of the Week. What do I have that's fresh and original? Jacques Cousteau, National Geographic, twenty-four-hour news on CNN. Fresh and original? I beg to differ. What you're buying is a bunch of shit.' By this time, Ted is talking so loud, his tie is vibrating. I can't even capture the violence of the way he was speaking. Then he just gets up and leaves. I wait for a moment, then go running out of the room and catch him by the elevator. We're standing face-to-face, and Ted leans right into me with a huge smile and says, 'So, Goodman. How do you think it went?'"

Two weeks later Turner Broadcasting received its first major order from the agency. Not that Turner was always like this. "When we took him on sales calls for a whole day, he'd ask for one index card per client, describing their background, their needs, and their buying history. He then had an uncanny instinct for when to be traditional in his approach and when to be outrageous."

Modeling Ted Turner may not be for everyone. But it is worth considering his behavior as you try to do what psychologists call "widening the bandwidth." Rather than feel inhibited by strict but murky social rules, you must try to discover that there is in fact a wide range of acceptable behaviors for any social situation. You don't need to be the same as everyone else to succeed. You need not be ruled by your fears. Video feedback, which allows an individual to work slowly through each step of a sales interaction, is useful in unpacking anxiety and restoring self-image by closing the gap between misguided fears and reality.

Peter Schulman, one of Martin Seligman's research associates, carried on Seligman's work to explain how exactly optimism can be learned. His advice resonated with that offered in the popular sales literature. He argued that in any industry where persistence is required to overcome adversity, a sense of optimism is vital. It is more than just blithering happy talk to say that optimism is necessary to succeed in high-stress roles like sales. It is true. Schulman laid out several ways by which the salesperson can learn to banish pessimism, irrational assumptions, and errors in logic on the path to optimism. Pessimism we have already defined as the result of excessively internal, stable, and global attributions. Irrational assumptions would include "I need to close every sale," or "I cannot risk making a mistake." Errors in logic, Schulman wrote, include "personalization," or assuming everything is about you. Your boss passes you in the hall without acknowledging you and you immediately assume you have done something wrong, when in fact he may have just learned his dog has died.

Other common errors include the magnification of negatives, such as a mild criticism in a quarterly review, and minimization of positives, such as an otherwise excellent quarter of sales. So many of us focus on what is wrong in our lives rather than on what is right, and in sales, where so much more will go wrong than right, this attitude can be corrosive.

To correct these problems, Schulman laid out a four-stage plan. The first stage is to identify the self-defeating thinking and the events that prompt it. Each of us will be stopped dead by a particular work chore. For some it is public speaking, for others cold-calling. The mere prospect of it slows us down, until our day becomes a heavy slog through the molasses of inertia.

The next stage is to gather evidence to support or undermine the fear inhibiting us. Are we really so terrible at public speaking? Is the person who says no to my cold call really saying no to me? If not, why do I take it so personally? The essential step here is to challenge one's fears and assumptions and, as Schulman puts it, to "de-catastrophize" them, or put them in perspective. For example, if the nature of cold calls is to be rejected forty-nine times out of fifty, then why sweat twenty no's in a row? If one in fifty is the hit rate, then the fact that I've already made forty failed calls can only mean I'm closer to a success.

These are the kinds of arguments that we often recommend to friends, but find harder to deploy on ourselves. It is always so much easier to tell a despondent friend to look on the bright side and count their blessings than it is to do so oneself. Schulman recommends distraction techniques to snap us to our senses before we enter the nose-dive of negativity. Snap a rubber band around your wrist. Write down your bothersome thoughts. Count backward from one hundred in increments of seven. Recall a success. "We believe the criticisms of inadequacy that we launch at ourselves," he wrote, "criticisms that we would never just swallow from others. The training teaches people how to treat these internal criticisms as if they had been uttered by an external rival, whose mission in life is to make you miserable, and to dispute that rival."

Go too far toward optimism and you risk becoming naive and reckless. Succumb to pessimism and you endanger your career and mental health. What the good salesman needs, like all of us, is something in between, an attitude of cheerful realism. You need

Ted Leonsis on your arm after each disastrous pitch, telling you to look at the fall leaves swirling in the wind. Think of your family, your children, your friends, the good things in your life. Come back to work tomorrow, put your head down and try again. Have faith. Really, what's the worst that can happen?

No one in the twentieth century had a greater influence on selling than Dale Carnegie. Born in 1889, the son of a poor Missouri farmer, he sold bacon, soap, and lard to midwestern ranchers before attending drama school in New York. When he could not make it as an actor, he tried teaching public speaking at the YMCA in Harlem. His courses caught on. He changed his name from Carnagey to Carnegie, to give the false impression that he was somehow connected to the steel tycoon Andrew Carnegie. At the age of forty-six, he published *How to Win Friends and Influence People*, which became one of the bestselling books of all time. Its advice is simple enough, the kind a parent might give a child: be nice, smile, maintain a tidy appearance, be on time, look people in the eye, do what you say you are going to do. But for some reason, Carnegie's formulation of these home truths caught people's imagination.

Warren Buffett, the investor, credits Carnegie with changing his life. One of Buffett's biographers wrote: "Unlike most people who read Carnegie's book and thought, gee, that makes sense, then set the book aside and forgot about it, Warren worked at this project with unusual concentration; he kept coming back to these ideas and using them. Even when he failed and forgot and went for long stretches without applying himself to the system, he returned and resumed practicing in the end. By high school, he had accumulated a few more friends, joined the golf team, and managed to make himself inoffensive if not popular. Dale Carnegie had honed his natural wit; above all, it enhanced his persuasiveness, his flair for salesmanship." To this day, Buffett calls Carnegie's *How to Win Friends and Influence People* one of the two most influential books he has read. (The other was Benjamin Graham's book on valuing stocks, *Security Analysis*.)

Carnegie died in 1955, but Dale Carnegie Training, which he founded, continues to thrive. Its chief executive is Peter Handel, a soft-spoken veteran of the fashion business. We met in the company's New York offices, a basement warren on Third Avenue in Midtown. The recession was biting as much in New York as in the rest of the United States, but the meeting rooms and corridors here were bustling with people on training courses, learning the twenty-first-century iteration of a timeless set of principles. Dale Carnegie is not a company taken seriously by academic students of business. But corporations and eminent business leaders seem to adore it. Wal-Mart has been a major client for years. I asked Handel to explain why Carnegie's unremarkable message bore so much repeating over so many years. The reason, he said, was that common sense is rarely common practice.

"The key is to be yourself," he said. "Don't change who you are." In a very few words, Handel has crystallized the antidote to sales phobia. Fortunately for his business, this antidote is much harder to apply than it is to prescribe. Even Dale Carnegie himself struggled. On the occasion of his second marriage at the age of fifty-six, he joked: "Even after I wrote the book, it took me eight years to persuade a woman to marry me." In a speech to a group of editors, publishers, and advertisers in New York, he said: "I know there's considerable criticism of my book. People say I'm not profound and there's nothing in it new to psychology and human relations. This is true. Gentlemen, I've never claimed to have a new idea.

Of course I deal with the obvious. I present, reiterate, and glorify the obvious—because the obvious is what people need to be told. The greatest need of people is to know how to deal with other people. This should come naturally to them, but it doesn't."

By 2010, when I met Peter Handel, eight million people had completed a Dale Carnegie course, in twenty-eight languages and two hundred offices around the world. "It's just about being friendly and getting the customer to say yes," said Handel. All over the world, the courses delivered by Dale Carnegie Training convey the same commonsensical message, with just a little local seasoning provided by local franchisees. "People are always surprised to hear that France is one of our most successful countries," Handel said. "We have French people teaching what we teach in Indianapolis. In Poland, we would teach one of the key Dale Carnegie principles, to smile at people. But in Polish culture, if you smile at someone to whom you haven't been introduced, people think you are nuts—stark, staring nuts." In Kuwait, the firm had to abandon a classic team-building exercise in which participants throw a soccer ball to each other because it is considered deeply offensive for a man to throw a soccer ball at a woman. In Saudi Arabia, no women take the course at all. The Indian government hired Dale Carnegie because it was concerned that its top schools were producing brilliant engineers with no idea how to communicate. Just when you think there can be no more use for the home truths of Carnegie, Handel explained, modern life throws up another one. "We do a lot of training with IT companies where we find people aren't used to dealing with people. They are afraid of it. In the digital world, they lose their ability to connect with others. We can help them with that." In China, Dale Carnegie's approach to letting everyone feel they win in a transaction resonates strongly in a business culture where the idea of "saving face" is paramount.

Listening to Handel, it struck me that the experience of a Dale Carnegie course was no different from attending church or practicing any mental or spiritual discipline. You don't go to learn. You go to repeat and reinforce, to be reminded of what life causes you to forget. You go to turn common sense into common practice. Sales people are so buffeted by rejection and lies, by people promising and then reneging, by targets and quotas, by management who treat them with disdain and yet depend on them to generate revenue, by the loneliness of endless travel, that they need to be reminded to smile, to stay upbeat, to wear "loose robes."

Part of the reason for academic suspicion of selling is the cultlike success of men like Jeffrey Gitomer. From the moment I started thinking about selling, his presence loomed everywhere, in airport bookstores, where his works are piled high and sell by the bucket load, and online where his "Git Bit" aphorisms and jokes are enthusiastically shared. Talk to a hundred salespeople, and you can bet sixty of them will be Gitomer devotees. His success drives other sales teachers crazy. They call him a snake oil peddler, an oversimplifier. He travels the world rousing crowds with his 7.5 or 12.5 rules of success, firing off jokes, reducing sales to a problem of attitude and basic but overlooked behaviors. His *Little Red Book of Selling* has sold more than two million copies worldwide, promising "12.5 Principles of Sales Greatness. How to make sales FOREVER." He publishes a syndicated newspaper column, produces videos and online sales tools, and makes a fortune ginning up sales forces all around the world.

If academics fail to understand selling because it does not submit to their scientific methods, Gitomer seems to go too far the other way, dumbing down the subject to the point of idiocy. The day before attending his seminar, I visited his website. There was his mantra, "People don't like to be sold. But they love to buy!" and a YouTube video Gitomer posted in September 2010, "The Pizza Philosophy. What toppings do you offer?" in which he said that everyone loves pizza because they can customize it. You can choose your own toppings. And even have it delivered to your home. He challenged his viewers: "Can you say this of your own business? Do you give clients what they want, or just what's easiest for you?"

One overcast day I joined six hundred people at the Marriott Hotel in downtown Hartford, Connecticut, to hear Gitomer speak. The rock song "Spirit in the Sky" blared out over speakers in the conference room while Gitomer fussed over his presentation at the front. He is a crotchety-looking man, with a shaved head, a large nose, and hangdog eyes. His features look as if they're about to slide right off his face. He wore black jeans and a red work shirt with his name on one breast pocket and SALES ATTITUDE DEPARTMENT written on the other.

"Here's what I'm going to talk about," he said to start his talk. "The origin of swine flu." Up came a slide of a child kissing a pig. Then he told a story about going to a Chinese restaurant, the House of Nanking in San Francisco. He said he eats out a thousand times a year, so he knows what he wants to eat before he sits down. He asked for a cup of tea. The waitress said, "No, you can't have that. We don't do that." He imitated her thick Chinese accent. All they had was a glass of tea for $5.95. So, reluctantly, he ordered it. The tea came in a beer stein with a ball of tea, looking like twine, in the bottom. After a couple of minutes the tea ball burst into flower. "I bought two," said Gitomer. "If you surprise your customers with quality, the price won't matter."

The next few slides were about football. "I hate the New England

Patriots," he said. "I hate the New York Giants. You know the only difference between Peyton and Eli Manning? One of them sucks." He also hates the Dallas Cowboys because he's from Philadelphia, where they have real fans and real players, not showboaters. "In Philly, we got fans. You go to the men's room and you just pee. Sink, trash can, doesn't matter." The next slide showed a young boy, his face smeared with Eagles green, raising his middle finger. The caption: "Cowboys Suck."

He asked the audience if they thought Pete Rose would ever get into the Hall of Fame. Did it really matter what players do after they played? Did it matter that Babe Ruth was drunk the whole time even when he was playing baseball? Leave Pete Rose alone, was his opinion. He cracked a few jokes about Tiger Woods, but then interspersed them with pictures of his grandchildren. He was building rapport, setting himself up as the funniest guy in the office, the sports-loving family guy, shouting obscenities at the game one minute, cuddling his granddaughter the next. He was doing what he advises salespeople to do, making himself a character with whom we could all identify. Within just a few minutes, we all had a few Git Bits to take back with us. A few one-liners to cash in with a fellow salesman at the airport bar.

He told us he listened to rock and roll before sales meetings because it got him in the right mood. He didn't listen to the angry voices of talk radio, or the weather. "While you're watching *Good Morning America*, I'm making money. You're watching the weather? Let me tell you, the weather is for shit up here. All winter long, it's freezing. The weatherman says 'Let's turn to the map.' Why not turn to the window?" After every few slides about sales, he slipped in a couple more of his children and grandchildren, because after all, it's not all about business. It's about family too.

Gitomer was born in Florida and grew up in Brooklyn. His parents, he said, made the "Jewish migration," from Manhattan north into the suburbs, to Mount Vernon and New Rochelle. He attended Temple University from 1963 until he dropped out, in 1969. It was a period during which he says he listened to a lot of music and smoked a lot of weed. He spent the next two decades in various sales jobs, from selling bean bag chairs to department stores to flogging his own sales and marketing seminars, long before his books took off and made him famous.

His sales epiphany came in 1972, when he was twenty-six, while listening to a tape recording of J. Douglas Edwards, an old-school sales instructor, talking about turning a question into a close. Edwards explained that if a customer asks "Does this come in green?" the correct response is not "yes" but "Would you like it in green?" "I thought 'Ahhh,'" said Gitomer, and he began reading up on sales. He read Napoleon Hill and P. T. Barnum and Dale Carnegie, and in 1992, at the age of forty-six, began writing himself. Two years after that, he began offering his own talks on selling, eventually becoming one of the most coveted business speakers around. He is a caustic everyman. And on a gray morning in May, he made sales seem fun again. He complained about everything salespeople hate: airlines, bosses, selling systems. During the breaks, people flocked up to have their books signed and to have their photographs taken with him. He looked everyone in the eye, and not one person left without a big smile.

Gitomer's basic message is a familiar one. That the power to sell is within us, but unleashing it is a problem of attitude. Fixing that attitude in order to attract rather than repel customers is a question of rectifying one's thoughts and behaviors in the simplest ways, but being disciplined about it. It is the same message contained in all the bestselling sales books of the past century, that a positive attitude plus hard work cures all.

Critics of this approach say it imbues American culture with a mindless optimism. It recalls Albert Teetsel, the Fuller Brush Company's top salesman in the years before World War II, who started the Fine and Dandy club. The idea was that no matter how you felt, it was important to answer the question "How are you?" with the words "Fine and dandy." Teetsel explained: "The psychosocial effect of the words 'fine and dandy' or 'I'm fine and dandy, how are you?' is to impress the party spoken to with the enthusiasm and cheerful outlook of the speaker." A more irritating club is hard to imagine. But from CEOs to the humblest mortgage borrower, there are those who think the worst can just be "thought" away. Gitomer, however, does not say that you can think your way to riches. He says you must get off the couch, build your social network, and make yourself noticeable and likable. He exhorts his audiences not to be half-baked about their lives.

In this he is echoing one of his personal heroes, Earl Nightingale, a radio announcer and insurance salesman. In 1956, Nightingale recorded "The Strangest Secret," an eighteen-minute speech still regarded as one of the touchstones of the positive-thinking movement. Like Gitomer, Nightingale maintained that the key to success in life and sales is a deep-seated self-belief, a willingness to establish one's own goals and pursue them regardless of convention. "The opposite of courage in our society is not cowardice," Nightingale intoned in his rich, leathery voice. "It is conformity." Nightingale described an existential crisis in America. Experts, he said, claimed that most of us use just 5 percent of our potential. That's not just 5 percent of our working potential, but also 5 percent of the fun and joy. "In each of us, there are deep reservoirs of genius that we habitually refuse to use." One symptom of this was the way so many of us followed others rather than made our own choices in life. From our earliest days at school, we are encouraged to conform, to be liked, to do as others do and follow the herd. We take jobs because other people take them and we are taught not to make a fuss. We make fools of ourselves by adhering to corporate and social norms rather than having the courage to buck them. And then at the end of the day, we slouch home, flick on the television, and passively consume the lives of others instead of living our own. So we drift through life toward death, only to realize far too late that we wish we had done things differently.

Success, according to Nightingale's definition, is "really nothing more than the progressive realization of a worthy ideal." The successful person is the one who wakes up in the morning and knows what they are doing, why, and where their actions are leading. It could be anything from studying for an exam, teaching, to running a small business or a very large one. The ideal itself does not matter. The sense of purpose and action with which you pursue it does. Nightingale claimed that only one in twenty of us achieves this broad definition of success. Most of us are just drifting, composites of others we don't particularly admire but by whom we would rather be liked than not. He argued, like Gitomer, that convention is an ass. "Whatever the great majority is doing in any circumstance, if you do exactly the opposite, you'll probably never make a mistake as long as you live." The tragedy, Nightingale said, is that people die without ever making full use of their abilities and lie on their death-beds consumed by regret.

To avoid this pitiful state, Nightingale recommended using a checklist, "like an airplane pilot uses." His version contained seven items necessary for living a full life. The first is a goal, because without it a man is no better than a "starfish or amoeba" living hour to hour, day to day, always reacting, never setting his own course. The second is attitude, because it determines others' attitude toward us. A positive attitude begets a healthy life. The third item is thinking, "deliberately and with a purpose," not being buffeted by circumstance and biddable by others, but thinking for oneself. Fourth is the "Law of Laws," the notion that we get what we give. Fifth is truth, because it will be reciprocated. Sixth is investing in one's own development, just as a company invests in research and development, in order to grow. And seventh is that strangest secret: We become what we think about most of the time. Our thoughts determine our fate. Whether we become dictators or gas station attendants, it is what we think of most of the time that leads to these outcomes. It is why, Nightingale says, that thinking and having a goal are so important. Without them, we are nothing.

Gitomer has taken Nightingale's encouragement to think for oneself to heart. He adores assailing the petty conventions of selling. He asked his audience in Hartford, "When you're with a customer, who's the most important person?" "The customer," the audience yelled back. Gitomer replied: "There's two people left on the planet. You and a big customer. Who do you want to die?" The customer is important, was his message, but never as important as you. He reserved special scorn for marketing brochures. "What do you think happens to brochures? You think people frame them, send them home to their mothers?" He said that salespeople make the mistake of "vomiting" information all over their customers, then waved around one of those plastic sheets of fake vomit you can buy from a novelty store. He said you were better off taking the brochure and putting it in a trash can, then presenting it to the customer in the trash can to show that you are willing to save them the time of throwing it away themselves. The audience, who had clearly spent too long lugging around the latest marketing publications, lapped it all up. For one hour of his three-hour presentation, Gitomer answered questions, riffing about his life and sales. He told us that he was a member of New York's Museum of Modern Art, that he collected vintage sports memorabilia and books, notably the works of the African American poet Langston Hughes. He likes to buy art that makes him laugh and showed us a painting he owns of a group of dogs laughing at a cat dressed up to look like a fire hydrant. The caption read: "Bad choice of costume."

The first question from the audience was, How do I get my customers to return my calls? "What I do is this," he said, holding his hand to his ear as if it were a telephone. "I call and I say, 'Hi, I'm Jeffrey. I was talking to a couple of your biggest customers yesterday and they said . . .' Then I hang up." He said a friend told him this was unprofessional. Gitomer told him that if these people weren't calling him back anyway, what did it matter?

Another question was about qualifying sales leads. Gitomer's advice was not to qualify people, but simply to like them. He talked about realtors. When you go and ask to see a few houses, their first reaction is to ask if you're selling or whether you have a mortgage, questions to ascertain your budget and likelihood of buying. The last thing they do is actually show you a house. "People who qualify are looking at people for their wallets. Make a friend and they'll give you their wallet."

Gitomer is a savage leveler of the business landscape, boosting the rank and file and demeaning those on top. The key to sales, Gitomer repeated, is not a process or a science. It is about being friendly and responsive. Sales specialists often overcomplicate it, he said, offering up hard-to-follow, multistep methods. "I've given you permission to be yourself," he said. "Don't you think you're smarter than the training department?" The sales trainers, he said, are part of a world that consistently sells us untruth. They are like the television networks that airbrush every wrinkle from images of their elderly anchors. Or the movie stars with perfect bodies parading around on E! news. We are surrounded by lies, he said, none more potent than those that say sales can be solved by science rather than attitude.

Watching Gitomer's audience was like watching a tightly wound piece of cloth unwind, slowly, then faster and faster, the salespeople shrugging off the mental cages and crude business processes that inhibit them all day and relaxing into Gitomer's seductive message of "just be yourself." After all, if this unprepossessing-looking man slouching around the room telling sports jokes can be America's top sales guru, there is hope for us all.

Gitomer showed us a slide from a garage in Coos Bay, Oregon: "We can't change the world, but we can change your oil." It was a rejection of all those high-minded slogans we hear in business. A reminder of what businesses can do when they're honest about themselves. Gitomer argued repeatedly for the individual's capacity to change his or her life. His message was that we are not just cogs in the machine, victims of whichever company or product we happen to serve. Each of us has the power to differentiate ourselves, to build those relationships that lead to sales and financial success. He recommended that his audience of salespeople find out from their customers why they bought from them, or not. He told them to build relationships that aren't about pitches, proposals, and yeses or no's, but about friendship and rapport. "Friendliness begets friendliness," he said, and if that doesn't interest you, you should not be in sales. "Make a sale, earn a commission," goes one of his Git Bits. "Make a friend, earn a fortune."

He told us he had no time for people who agonized over work-life balance. "You don't need balance, you need money," he said. Balance is not a problem for people with money. Cut to more photographs of Gitomer with his family. He spoofed that perennial question asked by pious interviewers of business leaders: What keeps you up at night? "What if the guy says hot sex? What are you going to do with that?"

He encouraged his audience to be completely self-reliant, because in the end no one cared about them but them. For all the talk about customer relationships, the customer wouldn't notice if they dropped dead. As personal philosophies go, Gitomer's is a mad jumble. One minute he's telling us that sales is all about friendliness, the next that it's all flannel and that no one cares for anyone but themselves and that we die alone. First he shows us photographs of his family, then tells us that work-life balance is simply a question of making enough money so that you can spend your time however you like. He does not fuss over how you achieve that balance along the way to making all that money. He sets up a very big tent, held up by his jokes and his insistence that he alone is telling us the truth. If only we could strip away the dishonest niceties of our work, he urged, sales would be so much more fun. If instead of calling a customer to ask if they had any more questions, we called and said, "I'm calling about the money. Is it ready?" If instead of being polite to our competitors as we meet them in a customer's lobby, we walked up to them and said, "Hey buddy, you want to see something you haven't seen in a long time? Here's a signed contract." If only we could behave like the animals we are and not like constrained social beings consumed by our anxiety over other people's opinions. Gitomer seemed like a man condemned to speak the unvarnished truth in a world of jargon and lies. His remarks were startling only for the backdrop against which he makes them, the stilted world of formal business practice. The inconsistencies of his message were a reflection of the inconsistencies of life. Trying to smooth it out leads only to falsehood.

When I first read Gitomer, his pitch reminded me of those infomercials promising that "in just five minutes a day, you can go from a flabby stomach to rock hard abs with our revolutionary new system." Dave Stein, a leading sales writer and consultant, told me that Gitomer was part of a profound problem in how sales is taught. "Only in sales do you see all this. You don't find accountants looking for 'Six Quick Ways to Beat GAAP and Fool Your Auditors.' But salespeople are always looking for the next trick, the next silver bullet. Every new book that comes out, whether it's *Snap Selling* or *Solution Selling*, or Gitomer's books, they are very destructive because they prevent attention being focused on the right place, which is solving the customer's problem. There are no shortcuts, tips, or tricks."

The airport books, he said, prevent rather than provide solutions. They offer the salesperson the hope that the cure to what ails them is just one book away, just as your *Baywatch* body is just one ThighMaster away. What salespeople really need, said Stein, is to understand how modern companies and individuals buy, how they think about procurement as a source of strategic advantage. And then they need to understand the discipline required to sell to people who think like that. "If a salesperson doesn't understand the changes to purchasing, procurement, buying, whatever you call it, they are going to be run over like a squirrel in the road." And Gitomer, he said, offers no help achieving this kind of understanding.

I took his point. Gitomer is shallow. He is trite and vulgar. But really, his purpose is not to solve all your problems. His silver bullet does not lead to better selling, but rather comfort and companionship in the process. He is there to reassure you that you are not alone fighting this often godawful battle. He shares your pain and is ready to do what you would never do because you have fears and commitments. You may quietly yearn to tell your boss he's a jackass and walk. Gitomer would do it. He is the salesman's alter ego, combining gallows humor with sunflower-bright optimism to get you through the day. It is a different kind of faith from that engineered by Apple and practiced by its most ardent customers. That faith is one of austere ritual and blind devotion to a quasi-religious leader who promises miracles and transformations. It's akin to what we see in direct-sales organizations, where peddlers of cosmetics and plastic kitchenware are brought together in revival meetings by their charismatic leaders to get ginned up to sell. Gitomer's faith is more like Leonsis's faith in the future: realistic, ironic, and fundamentally trusting. Since the fates can render all our efforts meaningless in a moment, why not be truthful and optimistic, rather than dishonest and glum? Like Carnegie, he believes that friendliness and good humor are contagious and will come back to us as prosperity.

For anyone who spends their life devising elaborate sales systems, Gitomer is the Antichrist. "I cannot believe that in this day and age, you would go through a sales process," Gitomer told us. "You spend your week learning some system and then by the time you get into the meeting, you've forgotten the whole damn thing." Throughout the room, heads were nodding and faces smiling. I'm not even a salesman, but I felt like standing and offering up a lusty "Amen!"

Chapter 5

LEVELING

If I believe in something, I sell it,
and I sell it hard.

ESTÉE LAUDER

To be born a black woman on a Mississippi Delta planta-
tion in the 1860s was a curse, and for her first thirty-seven
years, Sarah Breedlove battled the predictable horrors of
poverty, prejudice, and physical abuse. Orphaned at seven, married
at fourteen, widowed at twenty, she worked as a cotton picker, cook,
and washerwoman. It took her until she was thirty-seven years old,
and bending over a laundry bucket one day, to realize she made
so little money that she had no chance of ever being able to retire.
Something had to change.

For several years, she had been battling hair loss with an array
of tonics and potions. The one that impressed her was sold by a
black woman entrepreneur, Annie Malone. So Breedlove moved to
Denver to work as a sales agent for Malone. Remarried to a newspaper reporter named Charles James Walker, she quickly left Malone,
adopted the title "Madam," and struck out on her own, selling

Madam Walker's Wonderful Hair Grower, a scalp tonic, which she said had been revealed to her in a dream. Over the next few years, she went door-to-door to black households across the American South, pitching her product in any church or club that would host her. She refined her sales pitch through her encounters with customers. Since many of them, like her, had grown up on farms, she described the scalp as if it were soil. "Do you realize that it is as necessary to cultivate the scalp to grow hair as it is to cultivate the soil to grow a garden?" she would say. Scrape away the dandruff clogging up the scalp as you would aerate soil and hair will grow, she claimed. No scalp was beyond saving. "Every woman who wants hair can have it, no matter how short, how stubby, or what the condition of the scalp may be," she told her agents.

By 1912, Madam C. J. Walker had become a wealthy, promi-nent, and influential member of the black business community. She was also starting to make a name for herself as a fund-raiser and donor to black causes. As A'lelia Bundles describes it in *On Her Own Ground: The Life and Times of Madam C. J. Walker,* that summer, when Walker arrived in her chauffeur-driven car at the National Negro Business League convention in Chicago, she was expecting to be heard. The event was chaired by the NNBL's founder, Booker T. Washington, who believed in entrepreneurship as vital to the prog-ress of African Americans. As the convention wore on, Washington called on a succession of bank managers and business owners to talk. Walker and her friends had made it clear that she wished to speak. But Washington repeatedly overlooked her. On the third and final day of the convention, Walker decided she had had enough, rose from the floor, and interrupted Washington as he prepared to introduce another speaker. "Surely you are not going to shut the door in my face," she said to the audience in South Side Chicago's Institutional Church. "I feel that I am in a business that is a credit to the womanhood of our race. I went into a business that is despised, that is criticized and talked about by everybody—the business of growing hair. They did not believe such a thing could be done, but I have proven beyond the question of a doubt that I do grow hair!" She said that she had been frustrated in her efforts to get the attention of Washington and his peers. "I am a woman that came from the cotton fields of the South. I was promoted from there to the wash-tub. Then I was promoted to the cook kitchen, and from there I promoted myself into the business of manufacturing hair goods and preparations. I am not ashamed of my past. I am not ashamed of my humble beginning. Don't think because you have to go down in the wash-tub that you are any less a lady! Everybody told me I was making a mistake by going into this business, but I know how to grow hair as I well as I know how to grow cotton."

Her success supported her claims. By this time, she had started an institute in Pittsburgh, named Leila College, after her only daughter, to train a team of Madam Walker "hair culturists." She owned her own factory and salon in Indianapolis, and had expanded her business into the Caribbean and Central America. She employed more than one thousand sales agents, women like her seeking a way out of poverty and the harsh position society had assigned them. She would soon be spending $10,000 every year (close to $250,000 today) to educate young black men and women in southern colleges. But when she finished her speech at the convention, Washington carried on as if she were not there, quickly introducing a speech by Mr. W. W. Hadnott of the Prudential Savings Bank of Birmingham, Alabama.

Starting in 1917, Walker would gather her sales agents from all over the country at an annual convention. Since hair was the subject, hats were forbidden. But Walker talked not only about her products, but also about the opportunities for self-advancement and self-confidence offered by a life of entrepreneurship. She also used her position to campaign against the injustices done to African Americans, and was constantly lobbying politicians and newspaper editors to end the lynchings and mob violence against blacks that still bedeviled the country. Her success as a saleswoman eventually brought the ultimate trophy of her times, a mansion she called Villa Lewaro, twenty miles north of Manhattan along the Hudson River. She hired an Italian gardener to create gardens to rival those of her neighbors, the Rockefellers, Morgans, Vanderbilts, and Astors. When she died, in 1919, the *New York Post* wrote that her success in business was a rare but vital example: "Mrs. Walker demonstrated that [Negroes] may rise to the most distinctive heights of American achievement. Men who do nothing but sneer at what Coleridge-Tayler composed, Paul Laurence Dunbar wrote or Booker T. Washington built will be all respect when the Negroes have their full quota of millionaires." Once asked the secret of her success, Walker said it came down to nothing but hard work. "There is no royal, flower-strewn path to success," she said.

Estée Lauder had a similar view of her own success. She was born Josephine Mentzer in Corona, Queens, one of nine children of Hungarian Jewish immigrants. Her father ran a struggling hardware store. But as an adult she was Estée, the glamorous peddler of eternal youth, friend of the rich and royalty, a philanthropist and saleswoman extraordinaire. From the time she was building her business in the 1930s and 1940s to her death, at the age of 97, she would descend on the stores that sold her products to meet her customers and touch them, a dab of cream on the cheek, a spritz of perfume on the wrist, insisting on physical contact with the women who made her rich. These were lessons she taught all her sales staff. Don't just stand there. Touch the customer. Keep talking to them and never turn your back. It went back to her early days in business when she was told she didn't have enough money to fund a serious marketing campaign and she decided to "go viral," long before marketers seized on that term. "Telegraph, telephone, tell a woman," she would say, as she used word of mouth to build her brand. She pioneered handing out free samples or "gifts with purchase," as they came to be known, as they were more intimate, and much cheaper, than buying advertising. Like Madam C. J. Walker, she used her gift for selling to flatten every business and social obstacle in her way.

Mary Kay Inc., The cosmetics firm, founded by the late Mary Kay Ash, a self-made Texas businesswoman, hands out a diamond bumblebee pin to the saleswoman who best symbolizes a triumph over impossible odds. Given the size of its body compared with its wings, there is no way a bumblebee should be able to fly. But it does. In her autobiography, Ash wrote: "We're not only in the cosmetics business, we're in the people business. And, as a people-oriented company, our goal is to offer women opportunity. And these women, in turn, fulfill the needs of other women by teaching them good skin care. In other words, our whole reason for existence is to give people the opportunity to enrich their lives." Those who sell Mary Kay products are not just selling lipsticks and mascara. They have committed to a broader philosophy about how entrepreneurship can change lives and flatten social barriers.

Direct-selling companies have now taken this message around the world. Avon opened in Russia in the early 1990s and immediately attracted thousands of women trained in science and engineering who craved the chance to make some money independently of their husbands by running their own business. As one of Avon's sales directors put it at the time, "They come to us like mice and we turn them into firebirds." In Hindustan, India, Unilever's Project Shakti offered village women the chance to buy soaps and shampoos that they could sell on to customers. Like any direct-selling company, Unilever offered sales training and claimed it was creating "micro-entrepreneurs" where none had previously existed. In its promotional material, it boasted of how Shakti was erasing social stigmas. A single mother was quoted saying: "When my husband left me I had nothing. Today everyone knows me. I am someone."

What each of these individuals and companies has done is provide an alternative to the more hidebound, bureaucratic forms of capitalist organization. While most companies are tightly managed with strict rules and controls, direct-selling companies are distributed and loose, and rely on the promotion of a powerful shared culture to keep people in line. Where other companies pay you for your time, in direct selling you eat what you kill. Where other companies demand you put work over family and friends, direct-selling companies encourage you to make work and family inextricable. And the hiring standards are so low, anyone can have a go. Direct selling has proved to be a powerful antithesis to the norm, a very different means of balancing the routines of working life with our hunger to retain some sense of individuality. To sell Mary Kay cosmetics is to choose a distinct and well-defined alternative to traditional corporate life.

The prejudices we find against salespeople are characteristic of resistance to a challenge from below. For generations, the English aristocracy belittled anyone in "trade," out of the reasonable fear that given time these new moneyed classes would soon be buying them out of their stately homes and usurping their hold on public life. Salespeople are the "trade" class in business, disparaged and threatening in exactly the same way. Managers are dependent on them, but fear their power, which seems an uncontrollable, Dionysian force, overwhelming to those in the neater world of financial spreadsheets and strategic plans. Madam C. J. Walker and Estée Lauder succeeded because they could sell other women on the benefits of their products. This was not a talent that had to be acquired at an expensive school, or deployed according to certain professional rules when they reached a certain age. It was a sharp weapon to use as and when they wished, to carve through a society that granted women few opportunities to become independently rich and powerful. Avon and Mary Kay used the promise of advancement through selling to attract ever more saleswomen to their ranks. Their experience proves that the ability to sell, in the right hands, can be an extraordinary social leveler.

William James, the brother of the novelist Henry, and a psychology professor at Harvard, wrote a chapter in his book *The Principles of Psychology* titled "Habit." It was seized on by the sales industry. *Salesmanship* magazine called it the "greatest ginger [pep] talk ever written." James argued that the way to develop excellent habits was through constant repetition of thought and action. The moment you resolve to do something, you should do it. And these habits are best formed young, as after the age of thirty, your will and ability to change is grossly weakened. "The greatest thing in all education is to make our nervous system our ally instead of our enemy," he wrote, and the way to do this was to train it in the direction you wanted it to go, so that your life formed a fixed and unbending pattern, rigidly espaliered against the brick wall of self-discipline.

This idea and its derivations appear throughout the sales literature of the past one hundred years. It goes back to Aristotle, who said that we are what we repeatedly do, and thus "excellence, then, is not an act but a habit." John H. Patterson, the founder of the National Cash Register Company, which was the model for IBM, was a pioneer in developing a large, homogeneous sales force to address the new mass market of the United States. He believed, like James, in molding a salesman's habits, from his dress to his behavior to his competitive instincts. At one point, Patterson became obsessed with numerology and especially the power of the number five. He had letters drafted to salesmen listing the five things they should and should not do. In his 1913 book *Scientific Sales Management: A Practical Application of the Principles of Scientific Management to Selling*, Charles Wilson Hoyt wrote that the proper training of the salesman "even goes down to the individual motions and work of the salesman. It goes so far as to insist upon the substitution of exact methods of work by the individual salesman for scattered efforts." Everything a salesman said or did was now codified. The larger-than-life peddlers of the nineteenth century, who would barge into a rural home and fiddle, joke, and yarn their way to sales, were replaced by men in blue suits, clean-cut and orderly, capable, as Patterson's NCR put it, of letting "the light of reason into dark places."

This emphasis on habit and self-discipline, bordering on superstition, occurs in many fields. We see All-Star baseball players stepping into the batter's box, then stepping out again, fastening and unfastening their gloves, and tapping their helmet before readying themselves to swing, following the same quirky pattern before every pitch. Nelson Mandela makes his own bed each morning—even when he stays in hotels. It is an act of control and self-respect that he developed during his years in jail. Ritual and habit provide the smooth craft in which to navigate the turbulence of life, whether it's a hitter's poor hitting streak or the effort to build postapartheid South Africa. For the salesperson trying to build a business against difficult odds, economic, ethnic, or social, it is no less important.

It is four thirty in the morning and I'm running up a hill in Roland Park, one of the ritzier suburbs of Baltimore. Beside me, breathing lightly, bouncing on his toes so effortlessly it's as if he is being worked by a celestial yo-yo, is a man some call the Termite. Ten minutes earlier, he had rapped on my door to rouse me from bed. This is how every day begins for him, whether in frigid winter or humid summer, forty-five minutes up and down the streets of his neighborhood, clearing his mind and preparing himself for the day ahead. "It is important to get my energy right," he says. As we run, he has a story to tell about every house and street. That's where the quarterback for the Baltimore Ravens used to live. Over there is a partner at Morgan Stanley. That brick mansion burned down a couple of years ago, killing two teenagers. This street is full of young families and artists. The hardest part of the run is the first five minutes, grinding steeply upward past the brick walls of the Baltimore Country Club. Seeing me wince, the Termite told me: "You do this first thing in the morning and the rest of the day is easy."

For Guillermo Ramirez—or Memo, as he is known to his family, friends, and many customers—energy is everything. He hews to William James's advice to make his nervous system his friend instead of his foe, and his habits have served him well, helping him to flatten a world tilted against him. He arrived in America at the age of nineteen with nothing and now owns twelve properties around Baltimore and runs a general contracting business with fifty employees with sales of $8 million a year, even in the darkest days of 2008–9. Each time I mentioned to his friends or customers that I was studying his sales skills, they laughed or rolled their eyes, as if to say, "You've got a live one." He earned his nickname the Termite because once he gets inside a house, he is all but impossible to displace, burrowing through the walls until everything is repaired or upgraded. His energy, recharged on these early-morning runs, propels him through his long days and keeps him alert to the fantasies and weaknesses of everyone he meets. It is the source of his self-efficacy, his belief in his own mastery of life. He believes he controls his own fate.

Motivation has been described as a desire to maximize one's rewards by attaining a "cognitive mastery of the causal structure of your environment." You want to know how the world around you works and to control it to your own advantage. It is the kind of desire rarely sought for in tests of ability. But the strength of that desire, that motivation, is what feeds persistence, resilience, and optimism, the coping mechanisms to help you through life's inevitable defeats. Memo has made a routine of his early-morning run, a superstition even, because he worries that the slightest lapse in control could lead to disaster. His motivation is doubtless more robust than he fears, but by worrying for its fragility, he makes nurturing it the center of his life.

Once we get back home, he pours out two glasses of carrot juice. We down them and he instructs me to be ready to leave in twenty minutes. It is still dark when we climb into the front seats of his gray Lincoln Navigator and his phone begins to ring. All across

Baltimore and its outlying suburbs, his men are stirring: Mexicans, Ecuadorians, Hondurans, Guatemalans, Chinese, even a couple of native-born Americans. As we drive to the nearest Starbucks, Memo begins a paean to his car. It is indestructible, comfortable, capacious, American, unlike the Prius he had for a couple of years, a nod to fuel efficiency that ended on the side of the road with two bags of concrete, three Mexican laborers, and a blown battery. "A reliable car is key. If I lose a day because of a car, it's a big deal."

All day long, the phone rang and Memo talked, an uncontainable flow of thoughts and emphatic declarations studded with an explosive laugh, like a flock of tropical birds hurtling skyward. At Starbucks, he bought the largest size possible of straight, black coffee and a multigrain bagel. The coffee is nothing like the good stuff he drank back home in Oaxaca, but serves its purpose. We drove on, pulling up at bus stops and building sites, loading and unloading workers dressed in paint-splashed jeans and T-shirts, sending them off with flurries of Spanish profanity.

More than two hundred years later and ninety miles south of Philadelphia, where Benjamin Franklin established the code of the American salesman, Memo, a first-generation Mexican immigrant, is keeping it alive. He has never read a sales book in his life, but if you spend a day with him, you see why he doesn't need to. He has energy, discipline, optimism, and resilience, and these have taken him a very long way.

I first met Memo in 2005, when he was painting a set of bookshelves in a terraced house in the Hampden section of Baltimore. Or, rather, he was arranging to have them painted. It has been a while since he did much handyman work himself, though none of it is beyond him. He was dating a friend of mine at the time, and now they live together and have a daughter. He made an indelible impression on me then, as he does on everyone he meets. He is of medium height, slim, with a ponytail of black hair hanging down between his shoulder blades. His dark face slopes up and back and his teeth flash a brilliant white. He carries himself with absolute confidence, shoulders back, his hands darting ceaselessly to touch an arm, a shoulder, to make contact with whomever he is talking to. The contrast is even more apparent when he has two or three workmen stand around him, slope-shouldered and snickering like teenagers, huddled behind the leader of their gang. He keeps himself fastidiously clean. Every day he wears the same uniform: Levi's 501s, leather boots from Nordstrom, shirt and V-neck sweater from Joseph A. Bank. And he is fanatical about control. He keeps only one telephone number in the contacts section of his phone: "Mama," his mother in Oaxaca. If anything was to happen to him, whoever found the phone would know whom to call. Every other number, for his scores of clients and workers, he keeps in his head. "This way, I can afford to lose my phone," he says. He keeps his hair long, he says, so he can cut his own hair without needing a barber. His entire personal and professional life in Baltimore is contained in twelve square miles, which means he is never more than fifteen minutes away from any situation. During meetings, he writes nothing down, however complex the discussion, because it forces him to deal with issues as they arise. William James advised us all to "seize the very first possible opportunity to act on every resolution you make," and Memo compels himself to do exactly this. Except for his accounts, which are meticulous, he never files anything for later. He has no "to do" list, because everything is taken care of the moment it crops up. For all that Memo has acquired in life, he still believes that all you can control is yourself, that nothing else is certain. This attitude propels him out onto the streets at 4:30 A.M., and onward through his day.

Memo was born in Oaxaca. His father ran a junkyard for cars and buses and his mother ran a restaurant. From his parents, Memo learned the two key elements of his eventual line of business: fixing things and sales. When a customer arrived half-tipsy at his mother's restaurant, she would tell the chef to add a little extra salt and spice into the customer's dish, to crank up the heat in his body so he would order more beer. His father would take broken-down machinery and bring it back to usable, profitable life. Memo also developed a view of business as problem solving for others. When he was seventeen, he was sitting in a bar around midnight when the bar ran out of beer. He had an idea. He would buy a tricycle and deliver beer to bars in central Oaxaca after midnight. The tricycle became motorbikes with coolers, and thus was born his first business. "I learned the basics, selling what people need and realizing they were ready to pay more for beer in the middle of the night than they were during normal delivery hours."

His girlfriend at the time was his English teacher, an American ten years his senior. She became pregnant and decided she wanted to return home to Maryland to have the baby. Memo chose to follow her. "I quickly found that Americans aren't as friendly when you move to the U.S. as they are when you're just visiting." After two days living at his girlfriend's parents' house near Baltimore, he began looking for a job. He read the help wanted ads in the newspaper and found one for a car mechanic. His girlfriend and her father both offered to drive him to the interview, six miles away. He declined. "If I get the job," he told them, "I'm going to need to get there myself." This was classic self-efficacy. Memo believed then and now that he has the means to control his own destiny. Asserting that he could walk the six miles to work was both an expression of his self-belief and a means of strengthening it.

So he woke up early the next day and walked. He found the garage, an untidy, unloved operation, and its owners, a father and son who had long since stopped communicating. Memo held up a copy of the newspaper ad and said: "I want to work." "I told them in my bad English, I can clean, I know the measurements of the tools, I can take things apart and put them back together. I was young and I could see the father looking at me and thinking 'He can be my little bitch.' He asked me when I could start, and I said right now, and I just began tidying up the garage, figuring out these American pneumatic tools. Over time, the owner began to trust me and I began to fix brakes and shocks and deal with customers. After several months, the son was basically working for me, because I could deal with his father. Then I went to this party and met a contractor who was talking about plastering and how you can make a lot of money doing that: $80 an hour."

Memo told him that he could work Saturdays and Sundays, at least to start with, and recruited the son of the garage owner to drive him around in his truck. Within a few weeks, Memo had left the garage and was working for the contractor full-time, soaking up every piece of advice and information he could. When the contractor's wife began an affair with another man, Memo found himself picking up ever more pieces of the business from his distracted boss. "I became the front man and began to understand what it was the customer needed. The customers began to give me the checks for his company and they began to see me as the business."

We pulled up at the home of Memo's ex-wife to pick up his teenage daughter. He does this every morning, to spend twenty minutes driving her to her $25,000-a-year private school, which he pays for. The American woman he came to America for is no longer his wife, but remains his business manager. He rolled his eyes at the complication of it all. Our next stop was the first customer of the day, a couple in their late thirties, both bankers. Memo explained that the husband was always traveling and the wife was left at home with her own high-powered job and an adopted child. They had over-spent on their house, but could not stop spending on making it just so. The wife, in particular, was fussing over every detail and then fussing over the bill. "When people can't afford what they want, they become rude," said Memo. When we arrived, the wife was dressed for work and the nanny had not arrived yet. The wife took us straight up to the bathroom. There was a tiny splash of paint in the sink she wanted scrubbed off. She wanted the electrician to rewire the lights so that the shower light would come on separately from the lights above the vanity. There was something not quite right about the way the drawers were sliding, but at least she was happy about the new door handles. "Don't worry, don't worry," said Memo at every turn. "Let me take care of it." He listened with his head slightly bowed, his ears cocked toward her, his face serious.

We stepped outside. There was an issue with the back porch light. It pointed outward when it should have pointed down. Memo looked up and explained in detail the various issues around lighting the back porch, showing where the wire ran, where it would have to run to have the light on the other side, offering up various colors and options for the light, moving from place to place and extending his arms in a broad arc to show the area a new light would illuminate. Finally he turned to the woman and asked what she would like. She hesitated, clearly baffled by the number of choices, her fingers held to her lips. Memo broke the moment with his own suggestion, a dark fixture to match the trim, motion-sensitive, so it wouldn't blaze into the house all night long, pointing at an angle down the steps. The wife tilted her head and agreed. Memo turned to the electrician who was standing in the garden and nodded. "We'll take care of it today," he said, and then we were off.

"It's always one more thing, one more thing," he said once we were back in the car. "It's hard to be effective selling to people who don't know what they're looking for, who keep coming up with all these small things." The phone kept ringing. Wally was installing an air-conditioning unit on the third floor of one house. Arturo was painting the exterior of another. It was payday the next day, so he had to make sure any outstanding accounts were settled. Memo's momentum was unrelenting. He was always moving, calling, selling.

The next house we visited belonged to an older, retired couple who were rehabbing a garage into an art studio and redecorating the top floor of their house for their children. The wife went upstairs with Memo and looked despairingly at the piles of boxes on the floor. "Would you like me to clear all this out? Put it in the basement?" he asked. "Yes, please!" she replied. The husband was trying to figure out how to get more light into his new art studio. Memo suggested cutting panels out of the existing door and replacing them with glass. The more expensive option would be to put in a new glass door. The husband went for the latter.

"It's why I go to all my sites every day," said Memo as we left. "The sale doesn't stop when you get the order. It keeps on going all the way through the job. I never send someone else to check on the work. I go myself and then once I'm inside the house, there's always something else. That's why they call me the Termite. Once I'm inside, I'm hard to get out."

"In and out, in and out" is how Memo describes his day, constantly seeing people, always thinking about the next meeting, maintaining a busy schedule. Sometimes the projects are large, such as buying a house and remodeling it, but when the economy is down,

LEVELING

it could be just fixing a leaky faucet or caulking a window. But staying busy is vital. "It's good for my health to stay busy. I feel like I'm doing something good for myself, my family, my customers. Even if I'm broke, as long as I'm busy, I know something eventually will come."

Memo has a clear idea of the house he will one day build for himself in Oaxaca with the fortune he has made in America. He has imagined it fully in his own mind. It will be in the center of the old town, around a courtyard. The floors will be of thick stone, the walls plaster, ideally suited to the weather. He will close the shutters in high summer to stay cool and light fires on the dampest days of winter. There will be no air-conditioning or central heating. He will do the roof so no one has to think about it for at least a century. The wiring and plumbing will be simple and accessible, no fancy dimmer switches or built-in stereos. He will eat fresh food bought each day from the market, so no need for a vast refrigerator. It will be the opposite of the fussy, fragile houses he spends his time fixing in Baltimore. His will require almost no maintenance.

We found ourselves on the top floor of a brick mansion with a trim blonde in her sixties who was wearing workout clothes and talking to Memo with her hands on her hips, as if she were about to teach a gym class. Until a couple of weeks ago, the top floor of her home was a warren of former servants' rooms, tucked into eaves and dormers just beneath the slate roof. The woman's two sons liked it up there, so she had called in Memo to fix up one of the bathrooms. "It started with a toilet," she said. Now the entire floor had been opened up and was being remodeled and repainted. Today's issue was lighting. The electrician had proposed a few ideas that the client

157

hadn't liked. So Memo picked up a pencil and began to draw circles on the ceiling where he envisioned installing spotlights. "We could have one here, and here," he said. The woman looked up and nodded. "And then perhaps another one here and here," he went on. "I think this would brighten that side of the room." Then he passed the woman the pencil to make her own marks, pointing to the spot in the center of the ceiling where he thought she needed another light. She reached up and marked a cross.

"I was making the point that she was the boss," he said back in the car. "She's alone in a big house and her family is not there very often. This is one area where she has control. Her husband doesn't question the bills for this work. If I just solved every problem for her, it wouldn't be so satisfying for her." So he gave her the pencil.

We made a quick stop at a small ranch house where a young man greeted us at the door in his pajamas. There was something the matter with his sump pump. The house was built over a spring and the basement often flooded. The man explained that he had been online and reckoned he needed a new pump. Memo rolled up the sleeves of his shirt and sweater, took a hammer, and gave the pump a thwack. Nothing. "I'll have someone come to replace it," he said. Before he left, he spotted a dartboard, picked up a dart, and threw a 17. "Pretty good," said the man.

If that were your own sump pump, what would you have done? I asked once we had left. "I'd have spent half an hour unscrewing it, cleaning it out, and putting it back." Why didn't you do that back there? "That's not what he wanted. He wanted a new pump. When you add up the plumber's time to install rather than repair, and the cost of the new pump, it's not a big difference. But this guy had looked online, tried to figure out the problem, and he wanted peace of mind. So that's what he's getting. It's a big show, man. Keeping everything going, everyone busy, everyone happy. A big show."

It was 10:40 A.M., and Memo did a quick tally of his sales so far. A door, seven lights, and a sump pump: $2,000. The cost of the materials would be $1,000, then there would be taxes, permits, and labor. Memo himself would make around $300. It's nothing like what he was making a couple of years ago when the real estate market was still booming and he was able to make several hundred thousand dollars on every house he flipped, but it's work, and he'll take it. "People who want to work can find it even in a recession. You just have to get your prices right and adjust your expectations. But you have to keep working, to keep the energy levels around you, to attract more work."

He picked up a water bottle cap and rested it in the palm of his hand. "I live in constant fear that someone is going to come and snatch it all away. You think you have it, and then"—with his other hand, he took the bottle cap—"suddenly you don't. That's why I keep doing everything face-to-face, to make sure I still have the customers and work I think I do. For me the sale is not selling one thing. It's selling the second and third thing. When you make your first sale, it isn't complete until you've made your second, and so on and so on. The best salesman is the one who gets the same customer over and over. Then you get their friends, brothers, grandmothers, and finally you're buying their sister's house. Once you have word of mouth, it's a multiplier. It's everything."

For a man so self-possessed, I wonder how he can look so deferential in the presence of his customers. "I am their servant," he says. "I am the punching bag. To be a good salesman, you have to be good at taking the blows, dealing with other people's problems.

Customers don't like big egos." But they do like energy. Meeting an older man, a retired businessman, Memo played the hardworking immigrant. The man pulled me aside at one point to say that compared with all the American contractors he has used, Memo and his team work twice as hard for less money. With a younger wife fixing up her first family home, Memo was more flirtatious, the super-competent handyman who is going to make everything right with his smile and his jokes, brightening up the midmorning blues and creating a different kind of bond. "You have to be very careful about what you give of yourself in different situations, but in every one, when you're selling, it's about attraction." Whenever he does have time to read or watch movies, his favorite subject is love, the history of love, how it changes across time, place, and people. "Countries fall apart for lack of love. We need it in everything we do."

As the day rolled on, Memo's energy did not flag. At a large Victorian house, a woman was fussing over three new bathrooms even while the rest of her house could have used work, from the peeling paint and worn carpets to the roof. According to Memo, the woman's husband had decided to try renovating the bathrooms himself. But after weeks stretched into months, and tile and grout lay in the hallway and toilets backed up, the wife, who earned more than her husband, had decided to punish him by spending $70,000 on three new professionally installed bathrooms. "She is trying to make her husband feel guilty," said Memo. "She makes the money, so even though the rest of the house needs help, she is using the bathroom project to tell her husband how useless he is. He doesn't make much money and he can't even do a simple renovation. As long as the handyman husband exists, we are in business."

We arrived at another house to look at a wiring problem in the bathroom. The wife told me the wonderful thing about Memo was that he didn't give her very many choices. He made it easy for her to decide what to do. During our visit, the husband emerged and asked Memo to look at a fence several hundred feet away on the road. Memo scampered over the rocky garden to look. He then offered to fix a rotting beam next to the garage. After we left, he told me, "My purpose in going over to the fence was to make the husband feel powerful. If he asks me to look at his fence, I go do it. Did you see how he told his wife to go inside?" At one point during our conversation, the wife had come out only to be told by her husband that what we were discussing would be of no interest to her. We were discussing the state of the U.S. economy. "He likes to be in control, so I encourage that feeling. I try to hear what the customer is saying and then I interpret it back to them in my words and my behavior."

After we had been at the house for twenty minutes, I noticed Memo was conspicuously looking at his watch. "When I create the feeling that I'm leaving and ask 'Anything else?' the problems start pouring out. I'll be coming back to fix that beam and the fence, and there's a problem with the swimming pool heater. It's all to get the next sale, and the next one. A salesman is like a fish, always swimming, moving, never resting in case you get gobbled up. I am like a fit fish."

Memo has never studied selling formally, but is bubbling over with ideas about what it takes. It takes preparation and good health, the contagious power of a sunny disposition, and great mental alertness. It takes an early-morning run and carrot juice to keep the mind and body fresh and resilient against all the slings and

confusion the day will inevitably bring. It takes organizational discipline and serious acting chops. It requires charm and quick thinking, the ability to apply pressure in the moment and yet keep in
mind the larger picture. It also requires a dose of cynicism. Throughout our day, Memo kept returning to the subject of Bernie Madoff.
Every day, Memo feels he sees people ignoring reality, striving to
create an environment for themselves as if it will somehow eradicate
all the other problems in their life. Sometimes a leaky toilet is just a
leaky toilet. But other times, a bathroom renovation is revenge or a
substitute for affection. The salesman's job is not to solve these issues
but to feed them, to let these fantasies flourish, to allow the psychological need to be satisfied, however briefly. "Madoff gave everyone
a reality check, but when you think about it, it's amazing that it
took so long for reality to catch up with him. For decades, people
were ready to buy what he was selling because they so wanted it to
be true. He woke the country up to what was going on everywhere,
people avoiding reality and buying fantasies."

As a boy in Oaxaca, Memo used to accompany his mother to
the local market. One day, she was shopping for tomatoes. She saw
what she wanted at one stall, but the vendor had to move several
boxes to get to them, which he did. She then asked the price. It was
too high, she thought. So she kept going around the market. None
of the other tomatoes were as good, so she returned to the first stall.
But the vendor was cross and refused to sell her the tomatoes, saying
she had been rude to walk away after he had gone to so much effort
to get them for her. She stared at him and said, "I came back. Isn't
that enough?"

To be a decent salesman, he is saying, nothing can be personal.
If someone wishes to buy, that's enough. The insults, the efforts, the
suppression of self, it all becomes nothing. "I used to take things

personally," says Memo. "If someone bullied me, I'd spend time worrying why these guys were messing with me. Until I learned to stand up to them." The simple act of taking action freed his mind. It gave him control.

That's not to say managing his ego doesn't still take work. At one point, a former customer called to see if Memo could come to repair the shoddy work done by a cheaper rival. The customer suggested that Memo come around the next Tuesday. Memo offered Thursday. After he hung up, he told me that he could easily have done it Tuesday. But for his own sense of self, he had to show the customer who was boss. If he can do this sometimes, it helps him keep his pride in check during the periods when he is nodding, bowing, and serving.

The longer I spent with Memo the greater my regard grew for his skills. He has a knack for dropping ideas into conversations with clients and leaving them bouncing, as he put it, like a basketball dropped from a great height, bounce, bounce, bounce, long after he leaves their house. He would come in to fix a door and mention in passing that the kitchen might need a fresh coat of paint. A week later, the customer would call: Do you have time to paint the kitchen? He approaches selling like a tennis player would a match. "You never want to get figured out. You never want to be off-balance, but you want everyone else to be." And yet everything is done with an easy charm, a sense that he and his customer are playing one of those elaborate games that make life worth living, to-ing and fro-ing around a commercial transaction much as you would in a romantic or intellectual one. It is a game with lures and snares, but to play it well is part of living fully. To be able to sell well for Memo is also a great source of personal strength. "What a recession does is create confusion. But once you have built something from scratch, you know you can do it anywhere, anytime again."

The most venerated of all Oaxacans, he told me, was Mexico's nineteenth-century president Benito Juarez. His parents were peasants and he was orphaned at the age of four. He did not attend school until he moved to Oaxaca at the age of twelve. He worked as a domestic servant, but his employer was so impressed by his intelligence that he paid for him to attend a seminary and later study law. During his career, Juarez confronted the Church, the great European powers of the time, and powerful business interests. He was the first Mexican president without a military background and the first full-blooded indigenous Mexican to hold the highest political office. But to Memo, his most remarkable attribute was his willingness to act, not to wallow in his past and his traditions, but to try to do something for himself and for others, to pursue a romantic ideal of Mexican nationalism by the most pragmatic means. To level out an unfair system so that he and others could flourish. Had Juarez and Benjamin Franklin, both daring optimists and vigorous men of action, been alive today, they would have understood Memo, the ponytailed figure running hard through the Baltimore night, along a path that, as Madam C. J. Walker observed, is never strewn with flowers.

Chapter 6

ART AND COMMERCE

Making money is art and working is art
and good business is the best art.

ANDY WARHOL

Capitalism may seem an intellectual abstraction, but selling engages all of us every day, demanding we match our wits and practicality to our hopes. The novelists Salman Rushdie and Peter Carey began their careers writing advertising copy—even poets must eat. Film directors frequently cut their teeth making commercials before moving to Hollywood. Then to win an Oscar, they need a producer willing to lay siege to the hearts and minds of the Academy. Mozart and Michelangelo were artists for hire, creating their greatest work at the behest of wealthy patrons. No great artist can thrive without also being a great salesperson—or at least having one on their side. Art and commerce do not sit at separate ends of a spectrum of values, one ethereal and noble, the other a necessary evil. At the heart of any rich artistic and cultural life are the people who sell art.

Three men dominated the twentieth-century art trade in New

York City, very different in personality, yet consistent in their ability to spin extraordinary value out of work of no practical worth. The first was an Englishman, Joseph Duveen, who came to America in the late nineteenth century armed with the simple observation that "Europe has a great deal of art and America has a great deal of money." During the decades that followed, he transformed the family antiques business he had inherited into the preeminent art dealership in New York, Duveen Brothers. He provided the template for every great art dealer who has followed. He occupied lavish premises, built a peerless network of contacts, and controlled the supply of key works of art while using his personality—charming, clownish, knowledgeable, and endlessly diverting—to attract and retain his clients. Andrew Mellon, the famously solemn steel baron and secretary of the treasury, once told him: "The pictures always look better when you are here."

S. N. Behrman's *Duveen*, which first appeared as a series in the *New Yorker*, describes in detail how Duveen would stoke the desire in rich men and women to acquire the works in his gallery. One day, a favorite client of Duveen's, Lady Lavery, asked if she could bring a California industrialist to see his galleries. Duveen agreed as a favor to his friend, though he considered the man an unlikely prospect. When the Californian arrived, Duveen ignored Lady Lavery's protests and told the usher to keep him waiting for half an hour. When he finally deigned to meet him and escort him around his galleries, he showed him a Rembrandt. When the man asked its price, Duveen told him it was $100,000. The industrialist said he'd take it. Duveen then asked what other pictures he owned. When he discovered the man had a meager collection, Duveen refused to sell it on the grounds that "I can't possibly sell a Rembrandt to a man who owns no other pictures." He encouraged the man to buy a few lesser works, which he duly did. Only several years later did he permit him to buy the Rembrandt. Not only did Duveen enhance the scarcity value of his works, he also made customers yearn to be worthy of owning them. It was quite a trick when you consider these were men used to acquiring whatever they wanted with no more than the flourish of a check.

The wife of the press titan William Randolph Hearst complained to Behrman of a similar experience. "You couldn't buy anything from Duveen. Everything was either in reserve for somebody else or he had promised it to his wife or for some reason he wasn't ready to sell it yet. Rockefeller, for example. He used to collect colored tiles and things in a modest way, and then he heard Duveen had something better and he went in to his place one day to buy. But he couldn't buy. Duveen wouldn't sell him anything. That was true of my husband and all his friends. . . . Duveen didn't want to sell his stuff, but they always badgered the poor feller till he gave in."

Time and again, Duveen would guide his clients through what Behrman described as the "silken portieres of his salesmanship." One of his favorite tricks was to set up a painting in a velvet-hung room in his gallery on Fifth Avenue. The painting would sit there alone on an easel, beautifully lit, awaiting the visit of a potential buyer. The client would be left to contemplate the work in reverential silence. If, after all this ritual, the client declined to buy, Duveen would consider it a grossly philistine act, however outlandish his asking price. "The ladies felt that he and they were fellow-epicures at the groaning banquet table of culture," wrote Behrman.

Like Majid El Fenni, Duveen focused as much on buying as on selling. He was not just seeking items he could sell for more than he paid. He was trying to control the market for his art, to develop and exploit the scarcity of the works he sold. The more he paid for paintings at auction, the more they came to be worth in the minds of his clients. He paid the highest prices for paintings, even during the Depression. In July 1930, when the rest of the art world was struggling, Duveen paid four and a half million dollars for a single collection of works. He teamed up with the art historian Bernard Berenson to form a cartel controlling the flow of Renaissance art across the Atlantic. Berenson provided the academic seal of authenticity, while Duveen did the selling. Not all of Berenson's attributions have stood the test of time, but Duveen was rarely challenged successfully during his lifetime on the provenance of his paintings. "Why should they like me?" he once asked of his clients. "I am an outsider. Why do they trade with me? Because they've got to. Because I've got what they can't get anywhere else." Every salesperson should be so lucky.

Duveen's clients tended to have made their fortunes in brutish industrial businesses. Duveen not only sold them paintings, but helped them build the homes in which they would hang them. He organized steamship tickets and tours of Europe, even weddings, ushering his clients into the gilded world where their hard work and risk taking had won them a place. Ultimately, as Duveen saw, he allowed these men to buy the immortality their business careers never would.

Henry Clay Frick made his fortune turning coal into coke and selling it to Andrew Carnegie's steel factories in the late nineteenth and early twentieth centuries. His rough treatment of striking workers caused him to be widely loathed. Duveen not only sold him paintings, but also helped him build and design the mansion in Manhattan that now houses his eponymous collection. As Behrman notes, of the twenty-three lines devoted to Frick in the *Encyclopaedia Britannica*, ten describe his life in industry while thirteen describe his work as an art collector. "In these thirteen lines, he mingles freely with Titian and Vermeer, with El Greco and Goya, with

Gainsborough and Velázquez. Steel strikes and Pinkerton guards vanish, and he basks in another, more felicitous aura. The old boys take him cozily under their wings; they carry him along. For the pleasure of their company on the golden shore, Duveen made Frick pay heavily."

Duveen possessed what Behrman called the "unusual spirit of friendliness." "He wore friendliness like a nimbus, and let it shine upon an enormous miscellany of people connected—sometimes directly, sometimes very indirectly—with art: critics, museum directors, restorers, architects, decorators, and servants of all grades, including deck stewards on ships." When it came time for his clients to hang their pictures, Duveen made sure their staffs were paid handsomely and received large tips. This ensured him not only excellent service but also an unusually broad network of informants. Butlers would tell him if their bosses were hard up, or heading for divorce, and might have to sell a painting. All those people who passed invisibly in the lives of the very rich, catering to their needs, were Duveen's eyes and ears.

His promiscuous amiability paid off most spectacularly in his pursuit of Andrew Mellon. Duveen had studied Mellon closely, going so far as to rehearse possible conversations with his butler Morgan, who impersonated Mellon. He was convinced he could turn him into a fine client. All he needed was to meet him.

In 1921, Mellon was visiting London and had taken a suite on the third floor of Claridge's hotel. Duveen kept a suite on the fourth floor and happened to be there at the same time. Duveen's valet and Mellon's valet were, inevitably, friends, and so one afternoon, Duveen received word that at that very moment, Mellon's valet was helping Mellon on with his coat before he left the hotel. Duveen scampered out and caught Mellon in the elevator, feigning complete surprise to be meeting him in London. He told Mellon, "I am on my way to the National Gallery to look at some pictures. My great refreshment is to look at pictures." Mellon joined him and by the time the afternoon was over, was so intoxicated by art he was determined to buy from Duveen's own collection.

Duveen's greatest deal with Mellon, however, occurred fifteen years later, once Mellon had decided to bequeath his collection to the new National Gallery of Art in Washington, D.C. For Duveen, the idea of a National Gallery was the perfect solution to the problem of limited wall space in the homes of his wealthy clients. With the American National Gallery, these clients could now buy from Duveen on behalf of the gallery and take their place in the pantheon of national benefactors. Mellon, at the time, was living in an apartment in Washington close to Dupont Circle. Duveen rented an apartment on the floor below, filled it with the works he wished Mellon to buy to seed the National Gallery's collection, and installed a caretaker. He explained to Mellon that it was easier to do it this way than for Duveen to travel back and forth from New York with individual items. He gave Mellon the key to the treasure-filled apartment.

Duveen's caretaker reported back that Mellon often came down in his dressing gown and slippers to spend time in Duveen's apartment. Occasionally, he would entertain people there rather than in his own place. Finally, he told Duveen he wanted to buy everything in the apartment. It was the largest sale ever recorded in the art world: $21 million for forty-two items.

In October 1975, an article appeared in the *New York Times* titled "Making the Buyer Beg—And Other Tricks of the Art Trade." It was a cynical depiction of New York's art dealers, especially their then reigning prince, Leo Castelli. It accused him of manipulating the prices of his artists' works, bidding up prices at auction to stoke the lucrative private markets. Castelli wrote to the paper a robust self-defense: "As a dealer in contemporary works of art, it is my right and privilege to sell them at any prices I determine and to make different prices to different prospective purchasers as I may determine in my own interest or in the interest of the artist. Various factors influence my determination—the distinction of the purchaser and his collection, the frequency with which the purchaser makes purchases from me, my personal relations and friendship with the purchaser, etc. Anybody who does not understand this attitude by a dealer is indeed naive." His friend the psychologist Bernard Brodsky wrote praising Castelli for his role in funding, supporting and creating markets for new American artists. "Rather than be characterized as a notorious money-maker, Leo Castelli should be honored as an American who has no minuscule share in bringing to the fore what is great in America."

The dustup between Castelli and the *New York Times* encapsulated a challenge for art dealers. Unlike Duveen, Castelli made his name dealing in the works of living artists. Without the likes of him, most artists would languish in unpaid obscurity. They require these carnival barkers and market makers to go out and bring attention to their work, to gather up collectors and museum curators and hustle them into showings and clouds of mesmerizing pixie dust that result in the setting of prices, and thus a livelihood for the artists. It is cultural sausage making, a process no one particularly wants to see but which must happen. In a 1963 speech in honor of Robert Frost, John F. Kennedy said, "I see little of more importance to the future of our country and of civilization than full recognition of the place of the artist. If art is to nourish the roots of our culture, society must set the artist free to follow his vision wherever it takes him." Such political high-mindedness is fine, but few things are more likely to liberate an artist than a large check from his dealer.

Castelli, like Duveen, was a genius at what he did. And remarkably, he did not become serious about it until he was forty-nine years old. Castelli was born Leo Krauss in 1907 in Trieste, a cosmopolitan town tucked into the corner of northeastern Italy. At the time of Krauss's birth, Trieste was part of the Austro-Hungarian Empire, but in 1919, it became part of Italy. Krauss became Castelli when his father, a Hungarian by birth, married into the Castelli family and took their name. Castelli grew up like many others in Trieste gliding effortlessly through four or five European languages and cultures. He trained as a lawyer and spent his early years as an insurance salesman. While working for an insurance firm in Bucharest, he met and married Ileana Schapira, the daughter of one of Romania's wealthiest men. The couple moved to Paris in 1935, where they immersed themselves in the art world. Castelli opened his first gallery in 1939, but closed it shortly afterward when World War II erupted. In 1941, Castelli and his wife fled to New York.

After the war, the Castellis engaged with the art world of their new adopted city, though Leo was still more a dilettante than a serious salesman. He began to deal a little in Parisian abstract painters, but he had little interest in dealing with either dead artists, as Duveen had, or artists who had already been discovered. He wanted to uncover the new. He later told an interviewer: "The secret was, in part, knowledge about art of the past. I studied art history and figured out that one movement followed another and that there were changes that occurred periodically. . . . [Abstract Expressionism had] dominated the scene for a while, so I felt that something else had to happen. I tried deliberately to detect that other thing." Castelli saw his role as someone who could make culture happen, who could spot the new and bring it to broader notice.

That "other thing" turned out to be two young southern artists who had recently come to New York to make their names. The story goes that Castelli had seen Robert Rauschenberg's work in a minor exhibition and was invited one Sunday afternoon to visit his studio in lower Manhattan. Rauschenberg offered Castelli and his wife a drink, "with or without ice." Castelli asked for ice and Rauschenberg said he had to pop over to his neighbor, who kept the fridge which they shared. Castelli followed him and was staggered by what he saw: "paintings of flags, red, white and blue, plain, and a big all-white one; targets with plaster casts above them; alphabets, numbers; and all in a material I hardly knew—encaustic." Castelli invited the creator of the works to join his gallery, and the twenty-seven-year-old Jasper Johns said yes.

On February 3, 1957, Castelli opened his New York gallery in his apartment at 4 East 77th Street, in a town house owned by his father-in-law. He stored his furniture in the basement, rearranged his living room and his daughter's bedroom, hung paintings on the walls, and invited people in. Johns's work proved a sensation. It appeared on the cover of *Art News*, an unprecedented tribute to a new artist, and the then director of the Museum of Modern Art, Alfred Barr, decided to buy four of Johns's paintings on the spot. As one biographer wrote: "Sixteen years of taxiing on the runway around New York—noting trends, contributing sporadically, waiting and waiting—had allowed Castelli to assemble a range of acquaintances throughout the art world that no one plunging in precipitously could have anticipated."

Unlike the stereotypical fast-moving salesman, Castelli was extraordinarily patient. Steve Jobs once observed that one only connects the dots of one's life in retrospect. The life Castelli had lived up until 1957 may have seemed disorderly and without purpose, but from the moment his gallery opened, every decision and seeming happenstance took on meaning. The languages he spoke, his charm, his private wealth, his taste and knowledge equipped him for his work in a way that no amount of career planning could. All of a sudden, he was the best-prepared art salesman in town.

Over the next thirty years, Castelli demonstrated a remarkable eye for new artists and a knack for dispatching them triumphantly into the critical and commercial markets. Roy Lichtenstein, Ellsworth Kelly, Dan Flavin, Richard Serra, Donald Judd, and Julian Schnabel were among those Castelli sold. His gallery, which moved in the 1970s down to SoHo, was famously approachable. Castelli worked in a glass-walled office visible to all, and he was happy to talk to anyone who came in, client or not. As one profile noted, "If there was the possibility of an agreeable encounter at his gallery, Mr. Castelli seized it, whether or not any business would result. He behaved as if business were a subdepartment of sociability."

He won the devotion of many of his artists by putting them on stipends early in their careers, paying them monthly checks while waiting for their work to sell, thereby freeing them from the financial distractions that might have stifled their creative efforts. He offered them enthusiasm and encouragement of the kind every experimenter needs to keep going. He described the thrill of discovering and promoting a new artist: "When I first saw the work of Johns and Stella, I was bowled over. I just felt sheer, pure enthusiasm. And then you get feedback from a mysterious consensus out there that you are right. Then, of course, you intensify your push and drive. Anyone can discover an artist, but to make him what he is, give him importance, that's really discovery." It is also really salesmanship, though Castelli never considered himself a hustler. Late in his life, he said that he got into art because of the possibility of being involved in work of "groundbreaking importance. As far as the selling of that art is concerned, the devil can take the hindmost."

Whether his diffidence about commerce was candor or European artifice, it is hard to know. What is known is that Castelli frequently ran into financial difficulties, from owing money to not collecting debts, giving to museums works he could have sold for millions and keeping artists on stipend even while their works weren't selling.

As a salesman, Castelli was unique. His ability to sell was the product of his experiences over time. No one else had his background, his private money, or his eye, or certainly not the same blend. But he did have attributes consistent with those we find in great salesmen. He adored his product and was more than capable of making others feel the same way. He conjured up a seductive world around himself and his artists and invited others in. And like Duveen, he had an extraordinary gift for making friends.

He was also a resilient optimist. The dealer Mary Boone, whose career he helped start, recalled sitting on the terrace of a restaurant with him at the annual art fair Art Basel. "There were two lovers down below in the river. All I could think was, 'That water is so dirty and cold, what could those people be doing, bathing in that water?' Leo looked down, raised his glass of champagne and said in Italian, *La vita inizia domani!*—'Life begins tomorrow'—to toast the couple. That was Leo's attitude towards life: he always looked to the positive side of everything."

. . .

Castelli's heir as New York's dominant contemporary dealer has no reputation for warmth. Whatever criticism Castelli faced for mixing art and commerce pales compared with the judgments leveled against Larry Gagosian. "He's not a salesman," said one New York art critic. "You don't see him working the floor. He's like a visitor from another planet, an extraterrestrial trying to communicate with our species." Though he's an opportunist, says another, "his opportunism is transparent, it's not underhand: it's all overhand. He is not complicated. He's like a shark or a cat or some other perfectly designed biological mechanism." Even if he is a dealmaker, he is one with rare panache, according to the artist Jeff Koons, one of Gagosian's longtime clients. "Larry enjoys these different types of transactions, that type of energy. It's kind of like a sexual energy." Yet if the definition of an entrepreneur is someone who finds a way to commercialize an innovation, then Gagosian is one of the greats. He has Duveen's flair for showmanship and for understanding the inner passions of his customers, and Castelli's desire to bring new artists to the market. He is also magnificently and unapologetically in business for himself. Whether he is passionate or not about the work, he revels in the life it has brought him, the homes around the world, the luxurious cars, the New Year's parties in St. Barts.

A prominent buyer of contemporary art told me that he once received a call from Gagosian offering him a particular work. Gagosian told him he had chosen this collector among many as he considered him worthy of owning the work. The price was not to be discussed. The implication, however, was that if the collector did not buy the work, he would never again be welcome in Gagosian's top tier of buyers. Duveen would have recognized the trick: bump up your prices by creating a sense of scarcity and erecting a velvet rope around your product.

I met Gagosian some years ago around the time he was establishing his first gallery in London. Though he has often been written about and has a prominent role in a very public business, he rarely gives interviews. Unlike Castelli, he is not the kind to step out of his office to chat with a dentist and his wife who chance upon his gallery, which happens to be one of the most remarkable spaces in Manhattan, large white room after large white room, like a mental asylum, atop an art deco building on Madison Avenue. When I arrived to meet Gagosian, I found nobody in the gallery. I shouted "Hello" into the empty space. Nothing. I walked through a couple of large rooms before finding a receptionist sitting behind a counter. She pointed me to a chair. A couple of minutes later, Gagosian's secretary walked me down a long corridor of art books, arranged as neatly and densely as if they were an art installation themselves. Suddenly she stopped and there to my left, amid the shelves, was a tall thin door, with no ornament, no plaque, and no handle. I pushed it open, at her invitation, and standing in the doorway staring down at me was Gagosian, a big man with a tightly cropped helmet of silver hair. He looked like a recently minted Russian billionaire, an ex-KGB man suddenly given a lucrative oil concession for services rendered, wearing a houndstooth jacket, baggy beige slacks, and a turtleneck sweater. His hands were folded over his groin, like a soccer player defending against a penalty kick.

I had been warned in advance that Gagosian refuses to talk specifically about clients and prices. Fortunately, I wanted to know something quite different: how a boy from the San Fernando Valley, the epicenter of American mall culture, had found his way to such a preeminent position in the art world, gliding past all the history of art Ph.D.s who gazed enviously at him from their squirrelly cubes across Manhattan.

His office, like the rest of the gallery, was a soothing white. Though it was noon, a single opaque window in one corner let in a late-afternoonish light that fell gently on paintings and sculptures lined up neatly on ledges around the walls. It had the austere calm of a private papal chamber. Gagosian's voice was soupy and languid, like warm ocean water, monotonous, low, confidential and self-effacing, evidently an effective tool for slackening an art buyer's wallet. His family, he says, had no interest in art. "I didn't even know there was such a profession as an art dealer growing up. I didn't know it existed. That you could make money selling paintings, representing artists, or working in a museum, it was something I'd never even heard of." But after leaving college, where he majored in English, Gagosian began selling posters on the streets of the Valley and on the beach in Malibu. "It was sort of an interesting fluke. These weren't even art quality posters. They were kind of kitschy, schlock posters. But through poster selling, I became exposed indirectly to art. I'd get little catalogues for these kind of crummy posters and there'd be maybe something a little more expensive, a little finer, and I'd say, maybe I'll try to sell that. It was through selling posters literally on the sidewalk that I got interested in art."

It was a "collage of things" that stimulated his interest. "It wasn't reading one book or whatever. It was maybe a magazine, *Artforum*, *Art in America*, or going to a studio and talking to artists—more that way. It was more kind of an accretion or exposure to information and then finally going to a museum. It's kind of embarrassing, but my family wasn't the kind that went to museums. And living in Los Angeles, living in the San Fernando Valley, you know, museums were the furthest thing from my mind." He came to New York in his early twenties to visit his aunt and uncle. "I'll never forget it, when I got out of the cab to walk to their apartment, just the look of the city, the feel of it just hit me. Immediately. I'd never seen anything like it. And it just made everything else look pale by comparison. Mind you, I'd never been to Europe at this point or really traveled that much, so I was a pretty blank slate in terms of travel experience. But it was a palpable thing. The people on the street, the way they looked, the buildings, the energy, something about it. It was beautiful, just beautiful."

He determined one day to return, and it was Castelli who made it possible.

They met by accident. Gagosian had seen a photograph by Ralph Gibson; he called up the photographer and was invited to his studio. Gibson's dealer at the time was Castelli's then wife, Toiny Castelli. When Gagosian finally made the move to New York, he rented a loft in SoHo, across the street from Castelli's gallery at 420 West Broadway. As Gagosian told Castelli's biographer, "I had a reputation, for no particular reason—[what with] my family background, my lifestyle, the fact that I sold posters—but Leo legitimized me. He would call me to go have a margarita with him at Tre Merli after work and would tell me all the bad things people said about me—it made me laugh! If I ever had a lot of success, I owe it to Leo. He was a gold mine for me."

When Gagosian started out, rival dealers disdained his West Coast glitz and hustle. He streaked like Day-Glo across their world. "I didn't know any better," he told me. "I really couldn't be something I wasn't. I couldn't pretend to be some hyperbred European. I did the best I could, really. Which was just a matter of being practical. I wanted to have a career in art, I wanted to have a gallery. I had a lot, and still have a lot, of ambition. But I didn't have the background or the social or professional structure to kind of plug myself into. I've never apprenticed at a gallery or an auction house, so if it looked brash, it wasn't like I was trying to be brash or draw attention to myself. I just didn't know any other way to go about it."

Living in SoHo, Gagosian not only had Castelli across the street, but he was surrounded by the group who would dominate New York's art scene in the 1980s: Francesco Clemente, Julian Schnabel, Cindy Sherman, Eric Fischl, and others. "They all lived in downtown Manhattan without exception. There was this great kind of community in the restaurants, the bars, the studios, and I was extremely excited to be in some way at least on the periphery kind of involved with that, exposed to that." He had embedded himself in exactly the right social network to enable him to succeed.

Gagosian's lifestyle tracked the great economic boom of New York's last three decades. Besides his home in New York, he also has a large house in the Hamptons, designed by Charles Gwathmey, and a penchant for expensive cars. Art is an extension of this pattern of consumption. "Art is very compelling," he said. "Being able to own art, things that you enjoy looking at, that you enjoy thinking about. What are you going to do with money? Hopefully give enough of it away to help other people. But in terms of consumption, art engages so many things, your emotions, your eye, your intellect, your financial acumen. I think that's one of the reasons that people who are quite wealthy, who can afford to, buy art. It's not just buying a car. It's subtle. It's a different kind of value system. It's certainly a different level of appreciation and beauty. I happen to like beautiful cars, but paintings, a work of art is, you know, can be very profound. When it's good, it can be profound." There is the pitch. Just as Duveen captivated the industrial titans of the early twentieth century, so Gagosian grasps the ambitions of the financial moguls of the early twenty-first. He sells much of his work to money managers. He understands the importance of value and status to buyers who see art as a way to flex their newly acquired financial muscle and who want their Hirst or Warhol, Twombly or Koons not in a year or two, but now. He also grasps that they want profundity as well as decoration. Gagosian is as competitive as they are and understands that assembling a collection can be as much a fast-moving arms race as an act of scholarly accretion.

Like Castelli, he also has the good manners to express mild disdain at the commodification of art that has served him so well. "I think there's too much focus on money in art," he said. "Coming from me, you might find that disingenuous, but I think it's kind of a contaminating thing, and if you focus on money, on making artists rich and making yourself rich, you lose it, you become something else. Artists who think about making money, that's what they end up making. They don't make art. I think Picasso liked making money, but that's an extreme case. Artists, I think, want money, but there's a difference between that and wanting to become rich by being an artist. I mean, you don't go into art to become rich." No, but you don't want your creativity to lead to poverty either. The reason why Gagosian can sell, and perhaps the reason why other dealers find him so maddening, is that he is not infatuated with art as an academic or ethereal pursuit apart from our elemental needs. Van Gogh's suicide or Mozart's dismal, lonely, premature death are not romantic tales, but tragedies of highly creative people failing to cope with the exigencies of real life. A Gagosian or Castelli might very well have made their lives more tolerable and thus even more productive. No art history Ph.D. ever made an artist's life more livable. The art salesmen do that.

It was New York that Gagosian wanted as much as a role in the art world. He wanted his piece of the city's life. Coming from outside, he sold his way in and up to the top. He used his talents as a salesman to level the playing field of an otherwise forbidding industry. He made himself the equal of people who thought themselves superior. And for that he may never be forgiven.

The fact that art has little or no utility makes the salesperson all the more important. And the harder the viewer must work to understand the art, the harder the sell. To sell the bright lights, stomping dancers, and toe-tapping tunes of a Broadway show requires a mastery of marketing. You can sell a guaranteed good time. To sell the squiggles and graffiti of Cy Twombly takes a different kind of genius, an ability to place complex work in its intellectual, aesthetic, and cultural setting and persuade a skeptical world that it is an achievement worthy of admiration and millions of dollars. The same applies to any nonessential product. A book that tells you how to build a kitchen table has a distinct value. A book that promises a unique literary journey takes some selling—the persuasion of trusted critics, the social proof of broad distribution and an appearance on bestseller lists, the stoking of word of mouth, and the creation of more tangible experiences such as book club meetings.

For scientists it is similar. If you come up with a slightly better animal feed pellet, companies will shower you with money. Create a chemical no one yet understands, and you have to sell the world on your belief until the proofs come in. As a society, we claim to venerate the innovators and buccaneers, the people who "think different." Yet we force them to sell their ideas and creations hard before we dare reward them.

In order to sell the art that now fills our museums and enriches our national life, Duveen, Castelli, and Gagosian had to hustle, by which we mean they had to shuttle ceaselessly between the economic, structural, and psychological aspects of selling. Without the dealers' efforts to create and sustain the market for their artists' goods, there would be no museums to curate them. Without the sales forces of publishing companies going chain to chain and store to store offering variety and quantity, books would still be a rich man's hobby and authors their dependents. Without the great producers of Hollywood boasting that their film is better than all the others and berating anyone who thinks otherwise, we would have no Oscar winners.

The management writer Peter Drucker once said that "the aim of marketing is to make selling superfluous. The aim of marketing is to know and understand the customer so well that the product or service fits him and sells itself." It is a recurring managerial fantasy that one day we will be able to eliminate salespeople entirely and replace them with the scientific tools of marketing. Certain industries lend themselves better to this aspiration than others. When you are selling a familiar product again and again with slight adjustments, you can depend on marketing. But when you have a new, unproven product of dubious economic value, you still have to sell. No database could have replaced the network of domestic servants who supplied Duveen with information. No survey could have induced Castelli's gasp when he first saw Jasper Johns's encaustic flags. No marketing manager could ring up a billionaire the way Gagosian does, and tell him he has to buy this work or risk never buying from him again.

Selling is not merely an adjunct to art or music or whatever cultural pursuit one might prefer existed uncontaminated by commerce. It is essential to how and why we create, and to the satisfaction that comes when others agree that our creations are worthwhile. Cultural institutions tend to be full of people who are flummoxed by selling. Understanding selling's social purpose, as the great dealers do, and enjoying its possibilities, are crucial steps to becoming any good at it.

Chapter 7

THE ZEN OF SALES

A sk a hundred salespeople the secret of their work, and ninety-five will say "listening." They may even touch their ears as they say it. Listening is selling's golden rule. It's about what the customer wants, not what you have. Once you've made your pitch, shut up. Don't talk yourself out of a close. Have your customer's interests at heart and you can sell him anything. All these aphorisms are derivations of the basic advice to listen more than you talk. But contained in that advice is one of the biggest challenges in sales. More than how to prospect, seduce, or close, it is: How can you realistically claim to be serving a customer's best interests when at least half your brain is calculating how to extract the most money possible for what you are providing?

The simplest response is just to say you have the product that serves the customer's best interests. Your product, your price, and their need are all a perfect match. But this is rarely the case. Few salesmen can honestly say that what they sell is an upgrade to their customer's life, rather than a means to the salesman's own enrichment. This is not to criticize every act of superfluous selling and spending. No one needs a $50,000 car or even a Snuggie, but if you want one and can afford one, why not buy it? Economic growth and human advancement emerge from the churn of nonessential commercial activity. But how about the subprime mortgage sold to an illiterate immigrant? It is partly the immigrant's responsibility to know better, but it's also up to the mortgage broker to choose whether or not to sell a product he knows may well harm the buyer, for the sake of a quick fee. Politicians make election promises they know they cannot keep, but which serve the purpose of making them appear to be servants to the public's will. Once we have lived through a few election cycles, we come to tolerate their hypocrisy as part of the political sales process. To sell and to serve seem to be contradictory activities, the one dominant, the other submissive. And yet, we are told, to succeed in the former, one must excel at the latter.

Augie Turak has been grappling with this question for most of his adult life. I learned about Turak while talking to a man in his fifties who worked in financial services in New York. I had asked my usual question: Who's the best salesperson you know? Everyone, I found, had an immediate answer. It was a cousin, a parent, an old school friend, the person who had sold them their car or house or pension plan. These encomiums were usually followed by the claim that this person "could sell anything." The type of salesperson they had in mind tended to be the gregarious, back-slapping sales type, the wicked but irresistible uncle who could make you laugh while picking your pocket and trying to sleep with his best friend's wife; the person at the center of the backyard barbecue, in whose company stress evaporates and life seems brighter. Augie Turak, I was told, had once been this man. But he had since become something quite different.

We spoke first on the telephone, and our conversation ran to an hour and a half. A few weeks later, we met in person in Manhattan. Turak looked like a lost, elderly tourist, in a battered baseball cap and ratty old raincoat, smoking on the sidewalk—a twenty-first-century Loman. He had flown up from his home in North Carolina to advise a start-up company on sales and business ethics. I had been told in advance that he could be intense. He is tall, burly, and ruddy, his gray hair swept back from a wide, lived-in face. His front teeth are yellow from smoking. He is a compulsive, unstoppable talker. It is intimidating at first until you let the surges and undertows of his monologue pull you along for the ride.

Turak grew up in Pittsburgh, one of eight children. His grandfather was a steelworker and his father worked for the Pennsylvania railways and later as a labor negotiator. He went on a scholarship to Hotchkiss, the elite prep school in northwestern Connecticut, where he flourished intellectually, and then to the University of Pittsburgh, where he began searching for something outside the lines of his formal education. One night at the Theosophical Society of Pittsburgh, he heard a talk given by Richard Rose, a Zen practitioner and "hell-raising West Virginia hillbilly" who lived sixty miles west of Pittsburgh. "Even though I had a great career path mapped out, this stuff blew me away," Turak told me. Rose harked back to Chinese Zen, insisting that spirituality was not about finding inner peace, but about approaching truth, however brutal it might be.

That fall, Turak did not return to college. For the next five years, he studied under Rose, working on his farm, talking to and teaching anyone who might listen. To support himself he learned to install carpets. "Rose didn't believe in any of this communal living-off-the-land crap. He taught me determination, to be on time, to never quit. I was fired four times as a carpet installer before I learned how to do it."

Turak moved to Cleveland to start a group to teach Rose's philosophy. "I knew I was either going to make it or collapse and go home. But I wanted to please Rose. I wanted to be like him. When I arrived in town, I knocked on the door of the Catholic Church and asked the priest for a place to live. He pointed me to a house in Little Italy. I got my first carpet installation job there, and was fired. That was the low point. But I went back to my room, got the phone and the Yellow Pages and started to call every carpet company within a hundred miles of Cleveland. Every single one of two hundred said no. Making those calls took me a week. The next week, I went back to the beginning and started through the list again. When I got to K, Kilgore Carpets, I got Mr. Kilgore himself on the phone. He was a big blustery guy. I said it was Augie Turak and asked if he had a job. He said, 'Didn't I tell you last week we didn't have a job?' 'Yes,' I told him, 'but a lot can change in a week.' He said, 'Boy, I've got to meet you.'" Turak took the job and learned all he needed to know about carpet installation. After a few months, the time came to move on and Kilgore asked him to stay. "Before I left, he said to me, 'Never be too goddamned proud to come back to us.'"

Turak remembers this as the moment of complete conversion to Rose's worldview. He had put himself in an abject position and emerged triumphant. He had a great education, a promising path ahead of him, and yet had chosen to put himself through this entirely avoidable ordeal. It was no dilettantish, résumé-padding adventure to lend color to his life, like the modern fashion for climbing Mount Kilimanjaro or spending a couple of weeks working for Habitat for Humanity. It wasn't even like a Mormon mission, a rite of passage required by his religion. It was an entirely self-directed journey into the forbidding seas of rejection. I asked him why he bothered to do it, and his answer explained much of his later success in sales: "Luke Skywalker doesn't need to be a Jedi. But we pay $16 to sit on the edge of our seats to watch him become one." All of us, he believes, crave the classic hero's journey, the transformation of being, that comes only through doing the very hardest thing we can. One of his favorite films is *The Devil Wears Prada*, because Anne Hathaway's character "puts her life in play. She goes against everyone's advice and sticks with this job, and when she realizes the Devil wants her to quit, she says 'I'll never, never, never quit.' She refuses the temptation to give up and emerges a swan. We all want this in our own lives, but many of us are just satisfied voyeurs."

Rose, he said, would tell people that the first step on a spiritual path was to walk around the block every evening. Then walk twice around the block. Then three times. Then at the same time every night. "People thought it was some kind of metaphor, but it wasn't. People just don't do it. They don't start by just saying, 'Tomorrow I'm going to be on time for my meetings, and the next day after that.'" Everywhere Turak has lived since he met Rose, he has stuck on the refrigerator a saying from a Chinese Zen master: "You must study hard and never slacken in your efforts, because if you do, you will be nothing but an ordinary being." The process of becoming a better person, and a better salesman, is not hard to understand. There is no magic to it. But doing it, day after day, with unremitting effort, distinguishes the extraordinary from the ordinary.

Such effort requires sustained attention and discipline, the foundations of the Buddhist notion of mindfulness. Instead of letting our minds skitter back and forth, tortured by regret or anxiety, we must focus instead on the present. In Turak's view, personal transformation and sales success do not depend on changing our behavior, as James Patterson of the National Cash Register Company believed, or our thinking, by adopting a more positive attributional style. Rather it relies on our accepting and inhabiting this moment. As the Serenity Prayer popularized by Alcoholics Anonymous puts it, we must possess the "serenity to accept the things we cannot change; courage to change the things we can; and wisdom to know the difference." Simply by walking around the block every night, then twice, then three times, we learn to attend to and accept the present. Acceptance leads to contentment and reduces the stress that can so easily undermine a salesperson's ability and ruin their life.

After five years with Rose, Turak returned to college and graduated. Under pressure from his father, he applied to and was accepted at law school. But he never enrolled. "This was the Devil trying to divert me from my path," he says. Instead he became a salesman. "Sales," he said, "turns out to be the greatest laboratory in the world for studying human nature. Because there's money on the line, you get more honest feedback. Sales flushes people out. You see who they really are. As they say, sales talks, shit walks." Turak found sales to be an ideal profession for understanding himself and his fellow human beings. Yes, you can lie, cheat, and fake, but over the long haul, you must confront the truth and its consequences. For a man who had no patience for the consolations of deceit, selling was the perfect gig. "Rose created desperation in me by saying that if I didn't do the work, I'd end up like all the other slobs. They might be good people, but they're ordinary." That, of course, was precisely Willy Loman's worst fear: "I am not a dime a dozen. I am Willy Loman!" Turak's urgent need to be extraordinary found its outlet in selling.

His first sales job was selling photocopiers for 3M in Boston. By the fourth month, he was the top salesman in the Northeast region, and on the final day of the month, he went out to celebrate. The next day, he arrived in the office to see his name on the board with a "big fat 0 next to it." Every month, he had to start afresh to retain his title. He found each sale a puzzle he needed to solve. "I realized that if I do this and this and this and this, then the guy will buy. As a salesman, you're managing the process, setting up the dominos like a kid, and then when you let them go, you can say 'I did that.' I found that of everything you can do in business, sales is the cleanest. It's hand-to-hand combat. He's saying no, he's saying yes, your job is to figure out what's going on. If you're bringing in the money, the internal power is an incredible rush. I loved the power that sales gave me."

When one of the other salesmen at 3M asked him the secret of his success, "I told him the more calls you make, the more appointments you get, the more sales you make. It was what they taught us in sales class. But they didn't want to believe it. Then another salesman told me, 'It's those blue eyes of yours,' and I turned around and told him, 'That's fucking bullshit. I work my ass off. That's my secret.' The secret is always the same thing. Work your ass off." He told me he once got a reference from an employer who said "Augie Turak could learn Chinese in a weekend if he had to." When his father announced he was going on a diet, Turak bet him money he could lose more weight. His father declined, saying, "Hell, you'll just stop eating to win this." "Anything I said I was going to do, I just did it. You can learn determination."

In 1978, Turak met Lou Mobley, a retired IBM executive who had worked closely with Thomas Watson Jr., the longtime president of IBM, and founded the IBM executive school. Since retiring, Mobley had thought about how corporate life might be improved, how people could be given more space to be themselves. He evolved his own theory of results-based management, whereby people were judged by their output rather than their ability to work in a bureaucracy. He settled on a farm in Clarksville, Maryland, and soon attracted a ragtag group of intellectuals, hippies, and, according to his wife, Dorothy, "lost souls who didn't read and wanted the one-on-one learning." They would arrive at the weekend to talk with Mobley about the inadequacies of corporate life, capitalism, and organizations and to dream of better, more humane systems. Turak arrived one night in 1978 and was still up talking the following morning. Mobley offered Turak a room in his home and an education in both business and philosophy if he could boost sales at his struggling consulting firm. Turak doubled the sales of Mobley and Associates in each of the next two years. At IBM, Mobley had worked in the most regimented sales organization in American business history, a place where the salesman's behavior, attitude, and pitch were prescribed down to the minutest detail. It was commercially successful, but the methods left Mobley with questions. In an interview with *Selling* magazine in 1993, Turak explained Mobley's thinking. "Most people want formulas, very, very simple formulas. A pitch. That's what they want from their churches too. They want the preacher to give them a pitch they can live their whole life by. That will work in all situations. That will always get the order. Which means getting to heaven. Lou used to say that the first eighteen years of your life, you're learning to be like everybody else. But from the age of eighteen on, he said, what we should be learning is differentiation, uniqueness. And what it usually takes for uniqueness to happen is a mind-blowing type of experience. What an executive has, and what a good executive salesman has, is a taste for the different. I guess the old saying would be, don't prequalify too much. Don't always assume this guy is going to buy and that guy is going to buy. Keep your mind open."

In the 1980s, Turak moved on from Mobley to sell MTV and Nickelodeon to cable networks. These were the rough-and-tumble days of cable. MTV in particular was a swashbuckling young place to work, and Turak said he was the kind of boss who bounced his secretary on his lap, wore sharp suits, and spent his night on the town. "It was my time in the wilderness after ten years on this spiritual path. I was twenty-eight years old, with an expense account, a lot of nightclubs and girls. I was off to the races for a few years. This was the most fun time in my life. But deep inside I was dying."

As a salesman he kept getting better and was soon promoted to a new role as a sales manager. "Most people don't understand what brings about peak motivation. But I can create passion. I can do it right now. I can lean across the table and put my hands around your throat. You will become passionate." He compared his approach to the Marine Corps. "Look at what soldiers will do for a bronze star or football players for a sticker on their helmet. In the Marine Corps, you do things for others you would never do for yourself. It's about the esprit de corps, the few, the proud, the Marines. In sales, you don't manage individuals, you manage the room, the energy. You go in first and demonstrate how to do it yourself and then you create the conditions for other people to want to do it. It's a relentless job. Change, change, change. You're onstage all the time but you have to keep these guys on fire. When I managed teams of salespeople, I wanted them elbow to elbow. I wanted noise. I wanted everyone to be sitting between two people who were selling. People have to believe that what they're doing is bigger than they are. That's transformative."

One of Turak's favorite tricks was a game called Top Gun. He would come onto the sales floor and throw down a cowboy hat. Whoever picked it up was Top Gun for the week. They then had to go around the room and challenge everyone to a sales contest. If you agreed to the contest and the Top Gun outsold you, you paid him $1,000. If you outsold the Top Gun, he paid you $1,000. Turak remembered a member of his sales force, a man called Scott, who had been quiet and sold poorly, until one week, he grabbed the cowboy hat, seized the challenge, and won. Afterward, he told Turak: "Augie, once you've tasted it, you never want to go back." Another salesman, he recalled, made 150 calls a day for three months and didn't make a sale. His roommates came and told Turak they were concerned about their friend's dark moods. But a year later, he had salesman of the month awards piling up on his desk. "He substituted for complete lack of talent an unbelievable work ethic," said Turak. He had shown that crucial capacity for rebounding from rejection. "Failure is very, very powerful. If I was having a bad sales slump, I'd take a breath and say to myself, 'This is a numbers game. This is all good. Two hundred rejections mean I'm due a hot streak. I'm burning up my bad luck.'" It's one thing to say this on rejection number 7. Quite another to say it on rejection 177.

Turak believes that salesmen need "goat rodeos," a term he picked up from a manager at Microsoft in the 1990s. At Microsoft, you'd be sitting at your desk at 5 P.M. on a Friday and the phone would ring. It would be Bill Gates telling you he'd be presenting your product in Tokyo on Monday morning. You had better have it ready. For the next seventy-two hours, you would work nonstop to achieve the impossible. Three successful goat rodeos and you would have made your bones at Microsoft. They were the means of transforming your sense of what you could do. Turak saw the intensity of a sales floor as a similar means of taking people beyond their ordinary expectations and giving them the chance to do more than they ever thought they could.

. . .

Turak eventually moved from MTV and Nickelodeon to A&E and then to Adelphia Communications, a cable company, before starting his own company in North Carolina selling database software. It was much harder than selling to cable networks, but he persisted and sales grew. Then in 1998, he went skydiving and broke his ankle. The weeks of recovery triggered a profound depression.

"It was the start of a classic midlife crisis," he said. "You realize you're on a treadmill going nowhere at the same time you realize you're running out of gas as you get older. It's the old feeling that you've climbed up the ladder but the ladder was up against the wrong building. It happens to lots of salesmen. You think 'I have the Mercedes. I've been laid. And this is as good as it gets? Now what?' You've been thinking the hole in the soul can be fixed by worldly success. And now you realize nothing will save you and you turn to drugs, alcohol, antidepressants."

The worst thing about his depression, he said, was that he couldn't imagine anything that would make him feel better. He had all the money he could ever need, and yet there was nothing he wanted to do with it.

In desperation, he went on a retreat to a Trappist monastery in South Carolina. He stayed for several weeks. He had spent the previous twenty years chasing the fleeting rewards of the salesman's life, but it took the company of the monks to help him realize what he had been missing. The monks served God and their community with utter selflessness. They worked on their farm from well before dawn until well after dark. They prayed incessantly. There was no contradiction between who they were and how they behaved. They had decided on the purpose of their lives and acted on it.

Turak's time with the Trappists taught him that for all his professional experience and his time with Rose and Mobley, he had never fully grasped the idea of sales as service. The monks did their work, providing the highest level of service, without the slightest need for recognition. Unlike the salespeople he had worked with, they did not complain about commissions, or scrap and claw for that trip to Hawaii. Their service sold itself. It was not a means to an end. It was the end itself. It was a message Turak was eager to take out into the world. "Every time I did, I got people saying, Fine, but how does this service and selflessness shit apply to real business problems? What's in it for me?"

Intellectually, it is easy enough to see that the best salespeople turn themselves into the means by which customers achieve their purpose. Focus on serving customers and the financial rewards will follow. But to act on that idea requires an unusual abandonment of ego. "It takes years to learn to behave this way," said Turak. "It's why sales managers have to say repeatedly: 'Shut up and ask questions. Shut up and ask questions.'" Turak's epiphany with the monks took him back to Rose's version of Zen. Before enlightenment, you must chop wood and carry water. Walk around the block once, then a second time and a third time. Listen to the customer and keep listening. Don't let your mind wander to what's in it for you. Inhabit the moment. Be mindful. If you do this right, the rest will just happen. Even when the bills are piling up, the quota has to be met, the sales manager is shouting, just keep doing it. That is the Zen of sales.

Never before had I shopped as much as I did in the months before my wedding. There was the ring, the suit, the honeymoon, not to mention the fuss around feeding the hungry hordes who would be arriving in the name of family and friendship. Two buying experiences defined this pre-wedding splurge. The first was the engagement ring. I went into the process in a rather typical state of bachelor panic, fearful of both the expense and the risk of buying something that would undermine all the hard work I had already put into convincing my girlfriend that I was worthy of being promoted to spouse. The first store I visited was Van Cleef & Arpels on the ground floor of the Bergdorf Goodman building on Fifth Avenue. I felt uncomfortable the moment I entered. There were no visible prices, just glass cases full of glittering gems and predatory-looking salespeople. I felt like a mark, the kind they must have seen a thousand times: single dumb male in search of ring.

A woman behind the counter caught my eye and asked how she might help. Engagement ring, I told her. Burmese ruby, if possible. It was what my mother and grandmother had, and I wanted the same. I mentioned my budget and I could feel her shrink away. It was money that I had stashed for just this moment, and it was a lot to me. But the saleswoman gave me the distinct impression that I was a disappointment. She sighed and unlocked her tchotchke case to produce a display cushion set with rings in my price range. They were slender gold bands topped with colored stones set as petals around a minuscule central diamond. They looked like dime-store trinkets. Definitely not the classy declaration of intent I was looking for.

"Really, that's all I can get?" I asked. The woman shrugged. This was it. This was where my finances put me in her world. In the kitsch category. She didn't have any alternatives, a payment plan option, even a suggestion of another place to go. I had found my step on the economic ladder and it was well beneath her contempt.

My next stop was 47th Street, New York's diamond district, a jewelry bazaar. The problem here was not lack of choice, but over-abundance. Every store had everything at every price, to the point where I ceased to trust anything. Without a guide through this world, I felt like I could spend my hard-saved thousands on a chunk of cut glass set in tin and then return for a refund only to find the salesperson, even the store, gone.

My eventual solution was to buy at auction. A friend of my future wife worked in the jewelry department at an auction house. She found a Burmese ruby ring in an upcoming auction, vouched for its authenticity, and suggested I bid on it. I left a fixed bid, waited and soon had exactly what I wanted, a Burmese ruby ring, handed to me in a ziplock bag. I tucked it in my jacket pocket and then left in search of a suitable box in which to present it. I walked up Madison Avenue, passing store after intimidating jewelry store, until I reached Fred Leighton, a vintage jeweler on the corner of 67th Street. I pressed a buzzer on the door and was let in. A large woman wearing heavy makeup was helping someone who looked like her identical twin, except topped with a bird's nest of red hair. Their fingers, ears, and necks were laden with gems.

"Can I help you?" the saleswoman asked. I held up my ring in its bag.

"I just bought this ring at auction and I need a box for it."

"We don't have boxes," she announced flatly. I could see boxes all over the store. Surely there must be one they could spare.

"I'm happy to pay for it," I said, assuming for a moment that she thought I wanted the box for free.

"We don't do that here," she said, and turned back to her client. Fine, I thought, as I walked back out onto the street. Screw you, Fred Leighton. Screw you, Fred Leighton, because even if I make more money than anyone in history, I will never, ever spend it in your store. And I will tell all my jewelry-loving friends never to spend money in your store. I may even use that imaginary fortune to buy pages in the very magazines you advertise in and publish pictures of your schlocky goods being worn on farmyard animals. That's how I feel about you right now. I came to you in a mood of rare delirium, a man about to propose to a woman, high on life and love—and you treated me like a bum. That's what your salesperson just did. They poisoned your name for me. Forever.

Contrast this with my experience at Paul Stuart, a clothing store in midtown Manhattan. I went there looking for an outfit to wear on my wedding day. Nothing elaborate, just a nice dark suit. Paul Stuart, I had heard, was just the place. As you pass through its large glass doors, you step out of the hubbub around Grand Central Station into a 1960s version of Manhattan. Everything is infused with amber light, from the tan carpet to the dark wooden walls. The salesmen wear pressed suits and polished shoes with flashes of individual exuberance—pocket squares and vibrant colored socks. You feel as though at any moment, someone might hover into view sipping a martini, talking about tennis. It was a pleasure to go into Paul Stuart. I asked someone for the suit department and was directed upstairs, where a man in his fifties wearing horn-rimmed spectacles took me to a rack that ran the length of the room.

"What are you looking for?" he asked.

"A suit to be married in."

"Well, congratulations."

"Thank you." He looked me up and down.

"Dark gray or navy," he said. "Two or three button?"

"Three, I guess."

"Of course. You're English." He riffled through a rack of suits, and glanced back again to gauge my size. "These are our standard light wool suits," he said, pulling out a couple. "You can spend a lot more on cashmere, but I think this is what you want." In a few moments, he had diagnosed me correctly. I don't wear suits often. I'm not very interested in clothes. All I wanted from this suit was that it be appropriate and well-made, evidence that I had made an effort for this day of days. Beyond that, I couldn't care less whether it had three buttons or two, single vent, double vent, or no vent at all, three or four buttons on the cuff. I just wanted to play the percentage shot. This salesman saw that and helped. He didn't do what everyone else I met in the course of preparing for marriage did—try to upsell me on the grounds that it was my wedding day, and how do you put a price on that? He alone did not try to exploit the commercial opportunities of my wedding.

After I had chosen my suit, the salesman took me to a fitting room where an Italian tailor measured my pants and advised me that I should have them cuffed. Once again, I took his advice. I trusted him. And I've trusted Paul Stuart ever since, returning whenever I needed clothes for a significant event, a shirt for a christening, a tie for a wedding. Time and again, Paul Stuart's salespeople have repaid my trust.

Even the simplest of retail sales transactions comes larded with complexity and the potential for customer loyalty or hatred. I told all this to Martin Shanker, a sales trainer in New York who has worked for companies ranging from JCPenney to Ralph Lauren and Cartier, training their sales staff. He is a slight man with a pompadour of red hair who resembles the actor Danny Kaye. He is an expert on the nuances of sales and service.

"The best salespeople like people," he told me. But the problem, he said, is that most salespeople are like the women I encountered at Van Cleef & Arpels and Fred Leighton. They have no interest in people unless they can see the value attached to them. They don't let the sale emerge from their willingness to serve. They decide whether or not they like the customer only once they have seen the size of his or her wallet. "The really good salesperson starts out in love with every customer," said Shanker. "You can't profile. The customers who come dressed to shop aren't always the biggest shoppers. Today especially, those shoppers don't want to stand out." He told me that the Broadway star Mary Martin would peek through the stage curtain before every performance and whisper to as many of the audience as she could see, "I love you, I love you." By the time the curtain went up, she loved them so much she wanted to give her best possible performance.

If only a salesperson could do the same thing. To every customer, repeat in her mind "I love you, I love you" and then bathe them in affection. You would not need a sales manager looking over every shoulder to be sure every interaction was superlative. You would, to use Steve Wynn's phrase, have "split the atom." You would have achieved the Zen of sales.

Unfortunately, says Shanker, many salespeople who do the job for money resent their subservient role. Given the choice between talking to a stranger and finding out what product at what price would best meet their needs, they would rather hide in a back room or manipulate the customer for their own financial advantage. They see no personal reward in providing excellent service as a platform for a long-term relationship. After all, the benefits of that relationship are more likely to accrue to their employer rather than to them.

Shanker learned his trade at Macy's, where he rose to be a vice president, and later at companies selling wholesale to department stores. It wasn't a natural move to start helping companies improve their sales staff, but he realized that few knew what they were doing. Sales trainers, he found, were preaching the same decades-old self-help routines and closing tricks. Meanwhile, highly trained businesspeople with MBAs and financial qualifications went limp if they ever had to deal with "soft" subjects like communication and basic sales. Basics, such as never asking yes-or-no questions early in the sales process, were simply never taught. Salespeople skipped the dialog, the questioning, the eliciting of information, the staging of a sale, in their rush to close. For many, their laziness was a matter of habit. "People sell by habit," Shanker told me. "We all do what we like to do and we do what we think we're good at," regardless of how much better we might be.

Shanker realizes he cannot turn everyone into a crack salesperson, but he believes he can reduce the gap between a customer's expectations of a salesperson and reality. In department stores, he just tries to get staff to smile and ask open-ended questions. He tells them never to go up to customers and ask, "Can I help you?"—precisely the kind of question to elicit a yes-or-no answer right off the bat. The deadliest phrase a salesperson can hear is "just looking." To explain his point about restraint, he raised his palm and asked me to put mine against it. We were sitting in the lobby of a Manhattan hotel surrounded by middle-aged bankers having job interviews. Hesitantly, I complied. "What are you doing?" he asked. I didn't think I was doing anything. "You're pushing," he said. Indeed I was. "It's quite normal. Everyone does it. But when you're working in a store, you have to refrain and pull back. If you walk into a store and someone immediately says hello and walks toward you, it's quite aggressive. It's counterintuitive to refrain and hold back, to watch a customer's behavior before reacting."

The manipulative aspects of sales, Shanker insists, can easily be learned. Closing techniques can be taught in fifteen minutes. The hard part is building a relationship with a customer. When I bought my wedding suit, the salesman never had to ask "Shall I ring this up?" After ascertaining what I wanted, he asked me what I liked about each suit I tried. When the list of "likes" for a particular suit ran on, without any countervailing dislikes, there was nothing left to say. I had found the one. He allowed me to prove the purchase to myself. What enabled the entire transaction was the trust he created at the outset, not any slick moves in the close.

When companies hire Shanker, the first thing he asks is not what they want done with their salespeople, but rather what they want to do with their company. He needs to know what is required of the salespeople at a corporate level. Are they expected to shift volume? Or nurture a luxurious brand? Are they supposed to build long-term relationships? Or to facilitate low-cost, impersonal transactions? What is the point of the sales force? As he puts it, "I get paid to change sales behaviors in line with higher goals." A department store chain with thousands of salespeople on meager salaries is a very different challenge from a jewelry chain with four stores and twenty highly paid employees. In both cases, however, Shanker regards salespeople as "interactive ads." A slovenly salesperson on $30,000 a year who mistreats customers, who then share their bad experiences online or through word of mouth, can easily undo the effects of a multimillion-dollar advertising campaign. So Shanker tries to match the service to the level of customer expectation. A visitor to Wal-Mart expects low prices rather than great service, so even a smile exceeds expectations. At JCPenney or Gap one expects middling service, clothes neatly folded, and a clean changing room. But at Cartier, Louis Vuitton, or a Ritz-Carlton hotel, the customer really wants to be spoiled. Surprise and delight, the buzzwords of customer service, are the result of your experience exceeding your expectation, which varies depending on where you are. The market, the product, and the customer will dictate the competencies you need in salespeople. The peppy, flirtatious, gossiping type might thrive at Neiman Marcus, but flop at an ecclesiastical wholesaler. Different settings need different types, and there is only so much you can do to train them.

The manager of a large private equity firm once told me that sales forces were one of the greatest challenges he and his partners faced. They could acquire a firm and reengineer its balance sheet while standing on one finger in a hailstorm. Changing manufacturing and supply chains was harder. But sales. Boy. Often he went through two or three sales managers before finding one whose actions matched the owners' intentions, who did not simply come in and try exactly what he had done elsewhere before with the same kinds of salespeople. "Sales managers tend to hire people like themselves," he said. "They might be good for one kind of selling but not another. But by the time you realize that, you've lost months and then it takes more time to fire and rehire again." He conceded that while he felt comfortable in most areas of business, understanding sales and the culture of salespeople remained an enormous challenge.

Shanker draws lessons from couples therapy and applies them to selling. He is a devotee of the late American psychologist Carl Rogers, who advocated "active listening" during arguments. Often, he says, when a couple fights, what is heard are the strong words themselves, rather than their underlying meaning. He cites the example of a woman he trained at a furrier. She said that her boyfriend had become upset with her and confronted her using strong language. In the past, she told Shanker, she would have taken each point and argued it out with him. But now she just let him vent and when he was done, looked at him and said, "I guess you want the relationship to be over." He sat down and said that was not what he meant at all, and started again in more measured tones. What had begun for this woman as a sales lesson in reading and understanding a customer's true wants had become useful to her in her personal life.

I wanted to believe that the best salespeople care deeply for their customers, that success in sales follows the abandonment of self, rather than the greedy exploitation of others. Turak, Shanker, Memo, the man who sold me my wedding suit, and the loose-robed approach of the Kasbah all argued for the truth of this ideal. Indeed, many of the techniques and trappings of sales seemed unwittingly to move the salesman's focus away from the self. The insurance men like Oka and the infomercial masters like Sully who memorized their pitches, the IBMers with their military precision and identical suits, the storytelling service people at Steve Wynn's resorts, the self-effacing, glad-handing graduates of Dale Carnegie's course—all of them were adopting one or another strategy to dissociate their work from their egos. They were aspiring to a model of sales both nobler and more economically efficient than the Machiavellian models typified by the Hull-Dobbs system and pharmaceutical disease mongering. These were not the salesmen of David Mamet's *Glengarry Glen Ross*, victimized, duplicitous, and desperate, Marx's capitalist nightmare made real. All were trying to sell by silencing the clanging gongs of ego, by accepting success and failure with equanimity. This does not mean they shed every quirk of character, to become robots programmed and deployed only to sell. Rather it means that in the process of selling and the moment of the close, they seek to transcend the mistrust and gamesmanship of their profession, to apprehend the truth of what they did. This readiness to confront this truth, and remain Zen in the face of it, is a mark of the greatest salespeople. Fortunately, technology is enabling more of it.

Chapter 8

HYBRID VIGOR

I would rather teach engineers than
anything. . . . They're so bad to start with it's a
great joy to see them learn how to open their
mouths without chewing their tongues up.

DALE CARNEGIE

oward Anderson's wet-suit class was the only sales course I
took in two years studying for my MBA at Harvard Business School. And it was scarcely a course, just an optional
couple of hours one afternoon in a sparsely filled lecture room.
Anderson is an imposing man, tall with windshield-size spectacles,
a slight limp from years of hard physical exercise, and a Borscht-belt
sense of humor. In his determination to force the realities of sales
down the throats of reluctant MBA students steeped in theories and
spreadsheets, he lights up a classroom like few teachers I've ever seen.

The wet-suit class goes like this. You are working for a wet-suit
maker, Divers' Delight, and you have to sell your firm's product to a
chain of diving-wear stores. Your suit is made of space age material
and can keep those who wear it five degrees warmer than rival suits.
But it's also much more expensive, $400 versus $250 for an ordinary

suit. You'll be pitching to a customer base that has seen numerous start-ups come and go, failing to deliver what they promise. But your customers are also determined to stay on the cutting edge. The major discount chains are now selling wet suits too, and they need to be different to survive. Your challenge is to get them to buy twelve wet suits, two in each of three sizes for men and women.

As the class learns over the course of two hours or so, in order to sell those suits, you have to discover what really scares your customers, which is being drawn into a price war against the discount chains, and what they really want, which is to run a sustainable business selling to serious divers. The buyers can assess the technical advantages of the wet suit themselves. Your job is to convince them that you can provide a steady supply; that they will make a good margin; and that customers will elbow each other out of the way to buy the suits at their stores. What you're selling to the diving store chain isn't a more expensive wet suit that keeps buyers warmer. It's the possibility of increasing and sustaining profits by remaining on the technological edge of their industry.

Since retiring from his business career, Anderson has devoted much of his time to teaching. One fine spring morning I returned to Cambridge to attend one of the sales classes he teaches at MIT's Sloan School of Management. Sunlight poured through the windows as students trickled in, many in sweatpants, clutching cups of coffee. A few minutes after the scheduled start of class, Anderson shut the doors and set up the case. "I am the chairman of Sand Hill and we've got a nice piece of business here if we can do it." He picked out a student, a Chinese woman, and told her to come to the front of the class. "This is where you're going to be in two years after all," he said, meaning that managing sales will soon be an essential part of her job.

The purpose of the day's case was to demonstrate that selling is as much about mustering resources and support within your own company as it is about gathering those things from your customer. The customer is offering to pay $75 million for your product, but in order to get to that price, you have to secure concessions from different branches of the company, the finance division, production. "It's easy to think about salespeople as individual giants on the earth. But this is a team sport," said Anderson. "As a CEO, I'm going to be rip-shit if we don't get this $75 million." The case forced students to think about how the various compensation systems (salary, hourly wage, commission, etc.) in effect throughout their firms might encourage conflict or collaboration among different groups of employees.

Being a sales manager, Anderson told the class, is like being a primary-school teacher. You are managing groups of unruly individuals who need to be told again and again how to behave. It's also one of the most transparent roles in business. You either make the numbers or you don't. Throughout the class, he presented a series of classic sales manager problems. Two salespeople want credit for a single sale. One salesperson worked the sale, but the contract was ultimately signed at an office in another salesperson's territory. Who gets the commission? A saleswoman flies out to a meeting a day early. The flight is considerably cheaper than if she flew out the following day, so she bills the firm for an extra night in a hotel. She thinks everyone wins. She gets an extra day in California on the weekend and the firm saves money overall. But it's a breach of company policy. What if everyone did this? In another case, a medical products firm is having trouble getting its sales force to sell a new product. How do you persuade them to sell it? The class ran at a hectic pace, as if Anderson barely had time to say all he needed to. "You have no idea how real-world this is," he told his students.

As we walked back to his office, past a door leading to the MIT economics faculty (a cluster of Nobel laureates), he told me that at the beginning of each course, "I ask, How many of you have carried a quota? It's always none. Sales is the one area you can actually measure. That scares B-school students no end." Getting an MBA without studying sales, he told me later, is like getting an MBA without studying accounting, a class required by all business schools. You're just not credible.

Anderson grew up in Atlantic City, New Jersey, where his father, a wholesale grocer, was constantly haggling, buying and selling for his business. It was relentless, fickle work. His parents lived through the Depression and wanted security above all for their son. His mother urged him to become a teacher, because teachers continued to be paid even in the worst days of the 1930s. His father advised him to become a lawyer. At eighteen, Anderson took a job as a debt collector. It was tough work that involved bullying, threatening, and cajoling people into paying up, and it was a uniquely challenging form of sales, because the collector had to convince the debtor to part with money he'd already shown himself unwilling or unable to pay. It taught Anderson a crucial lesson: sales is based on collection, not billing. "No one at the Harvard Business School taught me this," he says. Like Majid El Fenni and Tony Sullivan, he grew up in a family where buying and selling were part of life. Like Sullivan, he cut his teeth collecting money. His environment honed a temperament already well suited to selling.

Anderson attended the University of Pennsylvania and then went straight on to Harvard to study for his MBA. As he prepared to graduate from Harvard in 1968, he spoke to the dominant recruiters at the time, large industrial firms and banks, but could not get excited. So he prepared to start his own consulting firm, and within eighteen months of receiving his MBA, he founded the Yankee Group. He was twenty-four years old. He chose the name because it resonated well in Boston, where he settled, with its connotations of thrift and hard work. Anderson focused on technology and communications.

After working in debt collecting, selling industry research to CEOs was a cinch. "When I was a young salesman setting up the Yankee Group, I'd cold-call companies. I'd call the switchboard operator and ask for the name of the CEO's secretary. Gertrude. Then I'd call back a few minutes later and say, 'Hi Gertrude, is Ray in?'" The Yankee Group quickly grew, adding seminars and ever more research products. As he built his team, Anderson liked to hire a particular kind of salesman. "Ex-athletes from first-rate schools who were the first generation in their family to go to college. They loved the chase and were very coin-operated," meaning they responded well to financial incentives and commission-based pay. "If you put a group of salesmen together and ask them to rank each other in terms of competence, if you don't have a fistfight, you have a problem."

As a big, funny, profane, and highly competitive man himself, Anderson had no trouble managing in this environment. He put his own office between the sales and research divisions so he could maintain the balance between the two very different cultures. "I liked strong sales but not too strong. A salesman left to run amok would do anything to get a contract." He balanced the risk-taking of an aggressive sales culture with extremely conservative financial management. The combination worked, and success enabled Anderson to start Battery Ventures, a venture capital firm within the Yankee Group, which drew on its knowledge and contacts. Battery

Ventures invested $3 billion in two hundred companies and Anderson became a rich man.

Over the course of his career, Anderson saw the practice of selling transformed. The smart jocks he hired were joined by technical specialists. The arrival of the Internet, which allowed people to find almost any piece of information they wanted, and software to do prospecting, transformed the salesperson's role from bully to persuader. The most useful film a modern salesperson can watch, Anderson says, is *Lawrence of Arabia*, a constant back-and-forth of persuasion and resistance under the most arduous circumstances imaginable.

Lawrence, played by Peter O'Toole, is a British soldier stationed in Egypt during World War I who believes he can unite the feuding tribes in the Arab peninsula into a single force to fight the Turks and drive them out of Damascus. It seems a preposterous ambition. Lawrence's first achievement is to convince the British generals to send him on a three-month expedition to "appreciate the situation." As the film unfolds, we see Lawrence build credibility with the suspicious tribesmen by forgoing the comforts of a British officer and copying their harsh way of desert life. He drinks only when they drink. He eats their food, though it makes him gag. He wears their clothes, speaks their language, and can even identify their numerous tribes. When eventually he does meet up with the ragtag tribal forces, he finds them demoralized after taking on the Turkish guns with just horses and swords. What they need, the leader, King Faisal, tells Lawrence, is "a miracle."

At this point, we witness one of the most extraordinary moments in cinema: Lawrence thinks. How many movies show a man simply lost in thought, pacing around searching for the answer to a problem? It brought to mind something Ashok Vemuri, head of

American operations for Infosys, the Indian services company, told me, that he will often ask his salesmen how much of each day they spend thinking. If they reply "not much," he assumes they are not doing a good job. Even Tony Sullivan, presented with a new gizmo and asked to pitch it on the spot, says no. First he must think. Presented with Faisal's request for a miracle, Lawrence doesn't come up with some glib, first-pass answer. He wanders around the desert and thinks.

The solution, he finally tells the Arabs, is to cross hundreds of miles of forbidding desert and take the Turkish stronghold of Aqaba from the rear. The Turkish guns there are fixed, pointing out to the sea. An attack from the desert will surprise them. The Arab leaders tell him it is impossible, but Lawrence cajoles and persuades, playing to the vanity and ambitions of each so adeptly that one of them, having succumbed, sneers admiringly at his trickery: "Thy mother mated with a scorpion." When they cross the desert, Lawrence seals his credibility by going back into the blazing heat to find one of his men, who has fallen from his camel. The Arabs urge him not to; he will surely die. It is written, they tell him. "Nothing is written," says Lawrence. As with every great salesman, he refuses to hear the word no.

For Anderson, this is the most important film any aspiring salesperson can watch because it describes the sales process not as one of desperation, rejection, and deceit in the pursuit of financial reward, but as one of subtlety, craft, and imagination in pursuit of a larger, collaborative goal. "Sales has dramatically changed over ten years. It used to be you were a gunslinger"—in a shootout against the customer and your rival salesmen. Nowadays, Anderson prefers to think of it like this: "A great tennis player can play tennis against his customer, but it's lose-lose. You win, your customer hates you. You lose, your customer thinks you're lousy. Far better to play doubles with your customer against another team." That other team is the customer's rivals. One way to think of his course, he says, is not as a course for salespeople, but rather as a lesson in the perspective of buyers.

All this is good news for the engineering students at MIT. If Anderson's sole purpose was to turn each of them into old-school salesmen, the kind of hard-ass ex-athletes who populated his firm in its early days, it would be a futile mission. Every so often, the raw talent might wander into his class, but trying to teach this kind of selling would be pointless. He believes his students will flourish because of "hybrid vigor," a biological term used to describe the superior function that occurs when you mix two genetic breeds. Left to pollinate alone, for example, maize becomes gradually weaker over time. When two separate lines are forcibly pollinated, however, the maize becomes more vigorous and produces much higher, more predictable yields. So with engineers and salesmen, when an engineer learns how to sell. The engineer-salesman is a higher-performing creature than an engineer plus a salesman together. "That's not to say that just by giving an engineer a briefcase, you make him a salesman," says Anderson. Something deeper must occur for the hybrid vigor to take effect, some rare combination of intellect, curiosity, and will, of the kind that occurred in the career of Seddik Belyamani, the $30 Billion Man.

Seddik Belyamani could feel at home anywhere. A French-speaking, Moroccan-born American citizen, he can flit across borders as if they did not exist, sliding in and out of cultures as if they were well-worn shirts. The frictions that inhibit so many businesspeople as they ply their trade internationally never affected him. For two decades, he skipped around the globe as the head of commercial airline sales for Boeing, selling to American bean counters and oil-rich sheikhs, to ego-swollen African dictators and French government bureaucrats. He sold $30 billion dollars' worth of Boeing's planes, keeping tens of thousands of Americans in their jobs.

He is a short, well-built man with a rolling gait, neat gray hair, and soft features. He could be anything from a well-to-do contractor or plumber to a retired cabinet minister. He was quiet, polite, and modestly dressed, with not a gold Rolex in sight when we met in a hotel lobby in Boston. He grew up in Casablanca, one of six children. His father was a teacher and politician, who despite his modest income insisted all six of his children attend college. "It was a matter of honor to him," said Belyamani. It made for a tough, demanding, stressful household. "My father was a politician, but he was an honest one, which meant he died poor." As a boy, Seddik was fascinated by electronics, from hi-fi systems to telephones, and desperately wanted to attend the École Nationale Supérieure des Télécommunications in France. But despite his excellent performance in the high school baccalaureate, he was not accepted, and was offered a place instead at the École Nationale Supérieure de l'Aéronautique et de l'Espace in Toulouse, where many of the faculty were involved in establishing the European airline maker Airbus. The plane he took on his first trip to France, he recalls with a smile, was a Boeing Constellation.

In Toulouse, he received a thorough grounding in aeronautical engineering, even working with his professors on the wing structure of the Airbus A300, one of the company's first, great planes. "What we didn't learn, though, was how to market an airplane or what makes one airplane better than another. What airplane do you design for what customer? The answer is not in the back of a book." He realized that "Airbus were dreamers. There was no connection between what they were building and what might sell. Boeing had much better insight into the market."

In order to rectify the gap in his learning, Belyamani applied for and won a place at MIT to study management and economics, with a focus in accounting. It was the kind of academic work not available in the French system. He studied integer problems in mathematics and the challenge of maximum utilization of aircraft. "It's the difference between math and Sudoku. Sudoku involves numbers, but it's a logic problem, not a math one. How does an airline schedule its crews, its routes, and its planes to ensure it is yielding the maximum profit?" After MIT, he was hired by Eastern Airlines as a programmer to help solve the yield management issues he had studied, but then moved in 1974 to Boeing to work as a financial analyst. "I did cash flow analyses on aircraft purchases, which allowed me to understand how airlines think and how they are evaluated by the market." It also prepared him for his next move, into sales. "The path to creating a good salesman is not by parachuting him into the job. You make him an analyst, make him talk to his counterparts at the airlines, make him crunch the numbers. Because then it's much more likely he'll find the hook. And every sales campaign needs a hook. What makes this plane work for this airline?" This is hybrid vigor at its best, the antithesis of a narrow specialization in sales as a unique business function.

Belyamani's first sales assignment was in Africa, because he spoke French. After a couple of years, though, he feared he would spend the rest of his career at Boeing specializing in Africa and the Middle East. So during a reorganization of the sales division, he went to the head of sales and complained that he was being punished for speaking three languages. If he just spoke English, he would be working in the huge North American accounts. His boss took his point and rewarded him with an assignment in the Asia-Pacific region. It wasn't the plum North American assignment he was hoping for, but the area was growing fast.

Despite the complexity of his product, Belyamani's sales approach never deviated from the classic three-stage process. First you build trust. Then you qualify the product. Then you close the sale. One of his favorite clients was Omar Fontana, a swashbuckling Brazilian entrepreneur who founded Transbrasil airlines. He and only he made the decisions for his airline. "I spent many nights downing scotch with him. We both played the piano and we'd do that in his mansion in Brasília. He bought only Boeings. He was the only decision maker. After a night of scotch and piano, he'd buy." With another executive, he climbed Mount Rainier in Washington State. "I don't like mountain climbing, but it was important to him and we discovered a great bond. Later I went with him to Salzburg, fly-fishing, skiing."

Throughout his career, Belyamani tried to read the minds and hearts of his clients. "You should always be trying to find a common interest. I once knew the head of a major airline and I'd been struggling to find out what made him tick. Then at a business dinner, a customer on the other side started talking about scuba diving and the CEO opened right up. Bingo. I figured this guy out."

Another way he found to build trust was to back away from the easy sale and offer advice in the customer's interest. He once advised the owner of an Indian start-up airline not to buy Boeing planes, but to lease instead. "He couldn't believe it. He said to me, 'Your job is selling airplanes, and you're telling me to go elsewhere?'

But he started leasing, and after three years, he calls and says, 'I'm ready to buy now.' He ended up buying Airbuses, but that was only after I left." Also vital is to build relationships as deep inside your target company as possible. "If you piss off someone in the back room who feels ignored by the Boeing salesman, that person could end up at the top." Everyone from the doorman to the CEO needs to be handled with respect. Just as Anderson knew how to talk to the CEO's secretary, and Duveen greased the palms of butlers and chauffeurs, so Belyamani took a very broad view of his network of contacts. You never know who is going to matter and when.

Building trust in so many different countries required a high level of adaptability and sensitivity. "You have to be much more attuned to watching and learning. In the Middle East, we don't conduct business in Arabic, it goes immediately to English. But I use some Arabic words at the beginning and it creates empathy, an affinity. Sometimes, I talk in French. I have very good relations with Air France. It helps you create and build credibility. I can tell jokes in French. Being able to laugh and have something interesting to say, a joke, a riddle. You can't just go into a meeting and sit back. I remember meeting the French with an executive from Boeing who started the meeting by leaning across the table and saying, 'What can I do for you?' It was very bad. You have to be able to engage in a conversation before you start talking business."

The next stage, qualifying the product, he says, is a question of detective work, analysis, and intuition, which leads to understanding your target's decision-making process. It begins in the parking lot, seeing whose car is parked where, as you try to establish the hierarchies both formal and informal within the firm you are trying to sell to. It continues in the waiting rooms and hotel lobbies where you run into the engine makers and parts suppliers who form part of the airplane ecosystem and are waiting on line like everyone else to sell. When Belyamani started at Boeing, the choices between planes were more obvious. Some planes just traveled farther than others, or covered the distance faster. He once sold a plane to Air Mauritius simply because Boeing's plane was the only one that could fly non-stop from London to Mauritius. End of pitch.

The longer he sold, however, the more the competing product lines converged. It became harder to differentiate between one company's plane and another. "Then it really does become about relationships and trust," he says. "You have to have something more than just the hook. You need an advocate within an airline who will accept your hook rather than a rival's and then champion it within his own firm. When your person within the airline needs arguments and data and you're able to provide them, that's the best situation. That way, you not only can explain the benefits of your solution, but also translate them in a way that he understands them. Say your plane has a range of 5,000 miles. Show them some routes on their schedule that cover 5,000 miles."

At this point, the salesman needs to be like Janus, the two-faced Roman god, one face looking at the customer, the other at his own company. Toward his own colleagues, he becomes the orchestra conductor, coaxing more vibrato from the analysts, less from the noisy brass of marketing, more subtlety from the timpani of engineering, all in an effort to keep the restive audience, the client, engaged. "When you have a complex airline organization, where there's a sales committee involving finance and operations, you have to develop good relations across the board so they'll tell you where you stand. They'll help you figure out what you need to do to make the deal. You have to do the rounds. You talk to the finance team, who tell you they have a credit crunch and will need to delay payments. You take care of them. Then the operations guys say we need more pilots, so you're going to have to buy us a simulator to train them. You take care of them. As a salesman, your job is to figure out how to make everything fit."

During his entire career, Belyamani took a single, one-day course in negotiation. He has never read a book telling him how to sell. And yet he is a remarkable example of Anderson's theory of hybrid vigor. He is a mathematician, an engineer, a man of many cultures and languages, who when deployed to sell became more than the sum of his parts. He could piece together everything it took to sell a plane. He would keep an eye on national industrial strategies and political shifts. He tracked airline deregulations and changes in environmental strategies. In tight contests, he would arrange for advertisements to run in local media lauding Boeing's planes, so airline executives would see them over the breakfast table. "You never know for sure why you win or lose. You have to work everything to try to win, to try to overcome all these objections. You can't pinpoint any one thing which leads to the close."

The close, the final step in Belyamani's process, is an art in itself. One time, Belyamani found himself sitting at a potential customer's house at 1 A.M. The customer was surrounded by his senior team, and they were haggling. Each man had a list of requests and Belyamani was exhausted and confused. "By this time, I had no idea what they were talking about. It was too late to call headquarters in Seattle to find out if these were $1 million or $50 million issues. I just sensed we were getting down into the nitty-gritty. I had made the sale, but the customer was trying to gobble up as many crumbs as he could in these final moments."

Belyamani turned to the CEO and said, "I have no idea what these guys are talking about. But how about I give you $50,000 per aircraft and we make this whole list disappear.'" The CEO was silent, so Belyamani suggested they call Alan Mulally (then head of Boeing) and tell him they'd struck a deal. The CEO didn't believe Belymani could call the head of one of America's largest corporations in the middle of the night. "So I called Alan and said, 'It's Seddik.' Alan put the phone down. So I called again. 'Alan. It's really Seddik. I have the CEO of the airline here and he wants to tell you personally that we have a deal.' Then I put the receiver to the CEO's ear. He couldn't refuse. Sometimes you have to figure out a trick just to make it happen. It's all on-the-job training. You can't teach this stuff."

Belyamani has found his life as a salesman to be deeply fulfilling. It satisfied the various sides of his personality—the engineer, the mathematician, the strategist, and the charmer. The money was good, but the learning and opportunity to excel at such a complex task mattered too. His hybrid talents allowed him to flourish. Though he says he loved to make deals, he didn't get off on simply changing people's minds. He did not thrive on his skills as a persuader. He could have built airplanes or programmed routes or even run an airline. But he found selling to be a job that matched perhaps the rarest aspect of his personality: the Mary Martin aspect. "I like people. I like to please people. I like to solve their problems. I give people the benefit of the doubt. It has served me well. My general rule is to be gullible. I'm not constantly calculating, looking for the dark side. I am always looking for the bright side. Even if someone's bullshitting me, I give them the benefit of the doubt. I trust people and move on. Sometimes you'll be wrong. But people who do it the other way are missing the good part of life."

Howard Anderson and Seddik Belyamani enjoyed long, successful careers thanks to their ability to sell. They paired their genetic inheritances to a range of experiences to develop their skills. Anderson was not just smart and determined, he also worked as a debt collector and was later bold enough to set up his own business soon after getting his MBA. Belyamani's ethnicity might have inhibited his career progression thirty years earlier, but coupled with his education, it made him a unique ambassador for Boeing as its international markets grew. Both emphasize the importance of serving your customer, getting on their side and helping them solve their problems. It is certainly seductive, and seems far more wholesome than aggressive, manipulative modes of selling. But if your purpose is profitability, it may not always be the way to go.

In the academic sales literature, there are two dueling views of the most effective form of sales: customer-oriented versus performance-oriented selling. Imagine two companies. The first sells industrial equipment to a few hundred customers all over the world. It is highly profitable and has few rivals. Its sales force is well educated and well paid. They don't come up with products and try to bully them onto their customers. Instead, they are engaged in a long-term conversation, finding out what their customers need and then developing products to match their requirements. They never have to cold-call. The salespeople receive constant coaching in products and selling approaches. Each step of the process is measured, so every sale, successful or not, can be examined for improvement. Each failure is considered an opportunity to learn. The salespeople are never forced to choose between the company's ethics and meeting the quota.

The salespeople at this first company live close to each other in an affluent suburb, and the company organizes trips for them and their wives and is always inviting in speakers and arranging events where they can learn to be better at their work. They are also encouraged to involve their customers in their events, to create a "win-win" climate that spills over into their commercial relationships. Their base salary pays their bills, but they also have the chance to make an additional 25 percent each year on commission. Naturally, their friends at other firms are always pestering them to tell them about any openings. During the annual strategic review, the head of sales is always consulted. Are the revenue goals achievable? Will they disrupt the salespeople's hard-won relationships? Might there be conflicting incentives that inhibit the salespeople from achieving these new profit goals? No strategic goal is set without the sign-off of sales.

The second company is in a very different position. It is selling software solutions to small businesses: cheap accounting, payroll, and tax systems. Prices are low and margins slim, especially once the cost of selling is taken into account. The business has been bootstrapped by its founders, who are used to running it on fumes. Salespeople are hired through advertisements on free online message boards. They are paid solely on commission, and must be willing to work nights and weekends, without benefits. They must sit in cubicles under glaring fluorescent light and their calls are closely monitored. They must make at least eight calls an hour and are expected to close one in thirty pitches. Each successful close earns them $50. The top earner at the company works eighty hours a week and makes $6,000 a month before tax. Employees here are given a three-hour orientation when they join, and a stack of sales scripts from which they are not permitted to deviate. These scripts contain the pitch, and deal with every objection a customer might throw at them. Salespeople are expected to use them to maneuver customers into a position where they cannot say no. If their coercion does not appear to be working after six minutes, they must end the call and move on. The managers listen in on calls, but see no value in trying to improve the selling process of a poor salesperson. A failure to make sales is regarded as a failure to follow the established process and is grounds for dismissal. A good salesperson in their eyes is simply one hungry and disciplined enough to recite the scripts. Hiring and firing involves almost no cost to the company, so the high turnover rate is, from a financial perspective, trivial. Employees find the work stressful and dehumanizing, but they have few choices in life. They dislike trying to coerce people into buying, but their managers consider ethical squeamishness an unaffordable luxury.

The question is whether either company could sustain the other's sales culture and survive. If the industrial products company started treating its customers as quick hits, without considering the long-term consequences, it would quickly run out of them. If the boiler room began spending money on retreats and customer orientation sessions, it might quickly see its business model collapse around its ears.

Fans of customer orientation say it creates a virtuous cycle. Buyers and sellers no longer have to fight each other. They can be partners. Salespeople are less stressed and thus more capable of selling. They don't suffer the psychological wounds of having to coerce customers every minute of every day. A culture of learning replaces the culture of selling at all costs, which leads to long-term growth and the development of trust. Fans of the selling orientation say that salespeople are fundamentally coin-operated, and that the more pressure you apply, financially and personally, the more likely they are to sell.

From a managerial perspective, both approaches can work. What matters is the context. The boiler room may be unappealing for its treatment of people, but for certain products and services sold as one-off transactions, it is enormously effective. It allows a business to play the odds, through dozens of calls to make each sale, and avoid overinvestment in any one employee or customer. The learning-oriented environment works when you do need sales-people to build trust, to act in your company's long-term interests, to persevere in the face of difficulty and establish real relationships with customers. Applied in the wrong setting, though, it can lead to a lazy, excuse-filled culture where sales are being constantly delayed and long-term profits are never realized.

Riding sidecar to the customer versus performance debate is another one about the comparative benefits of working hard versus working smart. People who respond to setbacks by working harder tend to be those driven by the need to perform in the next week or month. They don't change their routines. They just make more calls and try to close more deals. They are focused on their performance, not on their learning, like a piano player banging out the same tune with the same mistakes ever more furiously, hoping to get better but without bothering to pause and practice his scales. Those who work smart are the ones who take the time to learn from every step in every sale and who adapt and improve, laying the groundwork for a more profitable future. Evidently the hard worker would pre-fer a performance culture, while the smart worker would prefer a customer-oriented one.

But these arguments lead us nowhere. Certainly nowhere very optimistic. Sales cultures, under this view, are determined by the business, not the other way around. The people who sell are victims of the market's hidden hand. If you happen to be in a great busi-ness with fat margins, you can afford a humane sales culture. If not, you must endure men like Frank Pacetta. Pacetta was a legendary sales manager described in *The Force*, an account of a year in the life of the Xerox Corporation's Cleveland sales team, published in

1994. He was in many ways a clown, like Michael Scott, the office manager played by Steve Carell in *The Office*. As the author David Dorsey wrote, Pacetta created a "culture of ironic phoniness" that permitted people "to do outrageous things," which in turn exposed them to manipulation. The farther you venture from your real self, the more vulnerable you become. He liked to quote Vince Lombardi and frequently compared sales to sports, a field of human activity where there are clear winners and losers, where risk can reap reward and where grit and talent must be blended to yield success.

Pacetta would throw violent temper tantrums and churn through staff who failed to meet his standards. Patience, he once said, is "for someone without a budget." Like many of the least appealing salesmen, he boasted of being able to sell "snow to an Eskimo." He would hold contests among his district managers every month. The winner would get to park their car in the garage, rather than in the open lot, while the loser received an ugly doll on a rope which they had to hang in their office. According to a profile in the *Wall Street Journal*, Pacetta insisted his reps keep themselves clean shaven, that fat reps lose weight, and that men's shirt collars be starched so "you can skate on them." At office parties, he banned slow songs in case they prompted office romances, and danced alone in order to protect his status as manager and boss. He asked job prospects to sell him his own desk, and to tell him whether or not they'd paid their own way through college. He preferred those who did, the "grinders" as he called them. He lavished customers with expensive golf outings and recognized his staff with endless parties, plaques, and praise. "When you're in sales," he explained, "it's lonely and it's a war, and you want to hear your name." His methods sharply increased sales and made him a legend within Xerox.

The success of men like Pacetta poses a difficult problem. His methods were vulgar and in some cases downright unpleasant. He exploited people's vulnerabilities for the unimpressive purpose of selling photocopiers. And he bragged about it. But from Xerox's perspective, he closed sales. We might wish for a more benign climate for salespeople, in which they are motivated to learn and improve, to feel a strong sense of inner purpose and develop meaningful and long-term customer relationships. But when your business is failing, it's Frank Pacetta you call.

Or at least that was always the view. But I sense that this notion of sales as football by other means, a world where, to quote Lombardi again, "if you can accept losing, you can't win," need not prevail forever. In fact, it may even be in retreat.

Martin Nowak, a professor of mathematical biology at Harvard, believes that humans are more cooperative than we think. Charles Darwin may have taught us that only the fittest survive, but he also revered the complex and mutually dependent relationships between living things. Darwin used this analogy to help us understand what he meant: "It is interesting to contemplate an entangled bank, clothed in many plants of many kinds, with birds singing on the bushes, with various insects flitting about, and with worms crawling through the damp earth, and to reflect that these elaborately constructed forms, so different from each other, and dependent on each other in so complex a manner, have been produced by laws acting around us."

As both a mathematician and a biologist, Nowak has sought to understand the logic behind our behavior, to answer a question posed at least since Plato: How should we behave toward each other in order to maximize both our individual advantage and that of society as a whole? It is a near-impossible question to answer, as the variables seem infinite. We might like to think that someone who deceives us for a short-term gain may suffer in the long term. But it doesn't always happen. The true altruist may find herself endlessly taken advantage of. Religion offers us the consolation of notions like karma, and the Golden Rule, to treat others as you would have them treat you. But worldly success has always seemed to adhere to a knottier system. Thieves, hypocrites, and abusers of the common good can thrive while honesty, decency, and diligence are ignored. By analyzing broad biological patterns, however, Nowak believes that over time, cooperation wins out over ruthless competition. It may not always happen in a single individual's lifetime, but over the life of large groups, cooperation triumphs. It explains why cells collaborate within our bodies to help each other survive, and why friends help each other with no immediate promise of reward. It is not just conflict that moves us forward, but mutual assistance.

Nowak defines five basic mechanisms of cooperation: direct reciprocity, you scratch my back and I'll scratch yours; indirect reciprocity, in which decent acts enhance your reputation and benefit you in the future; spatial games, the idea that it pays to be good to those who live near you; group selection, the power of the tribe; and kin selection, or the old idea that blood is thicker than water. For all these reasons, we are often better off cooperating than we are competing. Sadly, there will always be moments of opportunity for anyone willing to exploit a highly cooperative society. The moment of maximum trust and cooperation is when the virus of dishonesty takes hold. It is why con men prey on church congregations. History, according to Nowak, can be read as a tale of cooperation leading to great empires and achievements, which are inevitably undone by exploiters of that cooperation. After a period of conflict and mistrust, the cooperative spirit returns even stronger than before, and humans march onward.

Selling offers the opportunity to be cooperative or competitive in various ways. Salespeople can be pitted against each other within a company. They can decide to serve their customers or to rip them off. They can build trust with customers over the course of a career or engage in lots of highly profitable one-off transactions in which they never see the same customer twice. Companies can choose to develop a culture of cooperation and learning to keep their employees fulfilled and their clients well served, or they can run a boiler room, churning and burning toward profitability. But if we believe, as Nowak does, that cooperation is always best, we must find a way to let it flourish, to create an environment where reciprocity makes sense and the ties of proximity, group membership, and kinship can thicken. Religious missions have succeeded in persuading people to give up the very things they enjoy most, from drink to sex, in part because they created communities of believers who then felt ashamed to let each other down.

Technology offers us a less controversial means of encouraging cooperation. By applying new technology to old-fashioned sales problems and not forgetting that this remains a human activity, we can discover hybrid vigor of a very different kind: a new sales culture, neither hard nor soft, neither bullying nor sappy but one that relies on transparent information and enhanced cooperation.

The offices of Salesforce.com occupy a large warehouse space overlooking one of the loveliest urban spots in America, the Embarcadero, where ferries come and go across San Francisco Bay. The staff is young and the atmosphere buzzing. If you ever felt anxious about the state of American economic life, a visit here would quickly restore your faith in its energy and potential. Outside the offices of the firm's founder and chief executive, Marc Benioff, is a small stand of potted trees soaring some ten or twelve feet surrounding a couple of sofas and a coffee table. Lurking amid the trees is a three-foot statue of Yoda, the cryptic sage of the *Star Wars* films, green, long-eared, and wise. "Marc likes to go in there and consult him for advice," said one of Benioff's assistants, flitting past.

Benioff is a colossal man, six feet five, broad-chested, with a mane of brown hair. He dresses casually, in slacks and a sport shirt, and when we met he was wearing a white electronic device around his neck, the size of a box of matches. It was monitoring how much he moves during the day, as part of his latest effort to lose weight. His office was full of stuffed toys and more *Star Wars* paraphernalia, much of it sent to him by Alan Hassenfeld, the chief executive of the toy maker Hasbro and a board member of Salesforce.com. Benioff lopes around, an iceberg of calm in the volatile waters of the technology industry. He is often accompanied by his equally mellow golden retriever, Koa, named for the Hawaiian word meaning "spiritual warrior." Koa is known, in that Silicon Valley way, as the firm's "chief love officer." Benioff adores all things Hawaiian. He believes in infusing his company with *mahalo*, the Hawaiian spirit of gratitude. The conference rooms at Salesforce are named after Hawaiian islands and volcanoes.

Benioff is the kind of West Coast capitalist it would be easy to loathe. He is worth hundreds of millions of dollars and yet professes his devotion to the antimaterialist Buddhist philosophy of the Dalai Lama. He runs a hard-driving, cold-calling sales firm and has published a book called *Compassionate Capitalism*. He is a showboater, a bomb thrower, and a marketing guerrilla, and yet to meet him in person, he's the loosey-goosey, everything's cool Jimmy Buffett of tech.

What makes a good salesperson? I asked him. "We are not static people. We are the product of our experiences over time," he told me, leaning back against a table in his office. Along one shelf stretching the length of his office were dozens of books about selling. He said he has glanced at a few of them, but most are worthless. "There are so many kinds of selling that it is not a generic art. The guy who sells a car is different from a vice president at Salesforce.com. Some are learned skills, some are innate. It's your genetics and physical mold plus a lifetime of successes and failures that condition who you become. In that sense, sure, salespeople are made. The skill set can be learned." His answers suggested he had just been communing with Yoda. We are who we are as a result of our genetics and the lives we lead. We are the salespeople we are because of those same forces. Now, go forth, young Jedi. His company, however, reflects just this belief, that there is not one kind of sales process, nor one kind of buying process, nor one kind of successful salesperson, but many, which must be accommodated and allowed to thrive.

Benioff founded Salesforce.com in the spring of 1999, and the company is now striding toward adolescence with revenues of over $1 billion a year from providing Internet-based sales software. Its products give salespeople an easy way of scheduling, maintaining contacts, and organizing their materials, contracts, and targets online. They also help managers keep tabs on their salespeople, where they are in a sales cycle, who they're talking to and when. This is not something all salespeople care for.

Ken Auletta, writing in the *New Yorker*, captured the gulf in attitude between the technology firms of Silicon Valley and traditional forms of selling. In 2003, Mel Karmazin, the defiantly old-school chief operating officer of Viacom, which owns CBS television, MTV, Paramount Pictures, and numerous other cable, radio, and publishing businesses, went to see the top brass at Google. Whereas Viacom still depended on fleets of salespeople to sell advertising on its various media, to advertise on Google, you didn't need to talk to anybody. Anyone could sign up, set a budget and targets, and receive monthly bills. You also received metrics to help you judge how effective your advertising had been. As the CEO of Google explained to Karmazin, "Our business is highly measurable. We know that if you spend x dollars on ads, you'll get y dollars in revenues per industry, per customer." Karmazin was horrified. "You buy a commercial on the Super Bowl, you're going to pay two and a half million dollars for the spot. I have no idea if it's going to work. You pay your money, you take your chances." He loathed the idea of automating advertising sales. He felt it neutered the process. "I want a salesperson in the process, taking that buyer out for drinks, getting an order he shouldn't have gotten. You don't want to have people know what works. When you know what works or not, you tend to charge less money than when you have this aura and you're selling this mystique." Viacom at this point was selling $25 billion worth of advertising a year. To demystify it, he half-joked to Google, constituted "fucking with the magic."

The same might be said of Salesforce.com. In one sense, selling is the most measurable activity in business. Either you sell or you don't. Much harder to measure is all that goes into a sale, all the meetings, casual conversations, relationship building, and closing that result in the check being signed. For managers this is a nightmare. It demands enormous levels of possibly unjustified trust. They would much rather know on a daily basis who is doing what so that they can coach salespeople, adjust tactics, or manage expectations before the quarter ends and their target is either met or not. Many good salespeople, however, like to see themselves as great athletes, who can take their skills and succeed anywhere. They would rather not share their secrets and relationships, even with their own employer. Look at the results, they will say, don't fuss over the process. It's a classic problem. Employees want to be individuals, and businesses would rather they weren't.

When Benioff started Salesforce.com, he was still working as a senior vice president at Oracle, the enterprise software firm. He rented a one-bedroom apartment in the building next to his house on Montgomery Street in San Francisco and hired three programmers to develop a way to provide enterprise software as a service.

At the time, enterprise software was a product you bought on CD-ROMs or paid to have installed over months for millions of dollars. Benioff, who had been one of Oracle's top salesmen, envisioned a subscription product that could be delivered, updated, improved, and maintained over the Internet. He saw business application software being sold as a utility, for which you paid each month the way you would for electricity. He set up his programmers with folding chairs, computers on card tables, and two posters from Apple Computer's latest marketing campaign, which showed the Dalai Lama and Albert Einstein with the words THINK DIFFERENT. The founding team all wore Hawaiian shirts to instill an "aloha spirit" in the firm.

Benioff had powerful backers, not least Larry Ellison, the multibillionaire founder of Oracle, who acted as mentor and investor. A legendary salesman himself, he was ready to lend his flame to Benioff's. Benioff later wrote that Ellison "taught me that accomplishments are fueled by faith. When Oracle entered its darkest days, every employee, customer, analyst, and even the people closest to him doubted the company would rebound. Even in that difficult climate, Larry's resolve never faltered." His salesman's optimism kept the dream alive. More specifically, Benioff learned the "Larry Ellison playbook." Always have a vision; be passionate; act confident even when you're not; think of it as you want it, not as it is; don't let others sway you from your point of view; see things in the present, even if they are in the future; don't give others your power.

Salesforce.com quickly took off. Within a few weeks, the office had spilled into Benioff's home. Ethernet cables were draped from the office window and through the branches of redwood trees into his bedroom. A few weeks later, the company moved into proper offices where, as Benioff describes, "it was an archetypal California start-up scene with a dog in the office and a mass of young and energetic people wearing Hawaiian shirts, working hard, and subsisting on pretzels, Red Vines licorice, and beef jerky." Benioff proved himself as adept at performing marketing stunts as he had once been pitching multimillion-dollar software systems to corporations. In 1999, one of the then giants of business software, Siebel, was hosting a conference for its users in downtown San Francisco. Benioff paid actors to picket the conference holding signs saying NO SOFTWARE. He hired other actors to come along pretending to be journalists covering the demonstration. Siebel's executives then called the police, who lined up to protect the phony protesters. A crowd gathered to watch, local television came, and every person attending the Siebel conference was given an invitation to a Salesforce.com party that night. The publicity led to hundreds of new clients signing up for the service.

At the official company launch, Benioff rented out the Regency Theater in San Francisco and decorated the three levels as hell, purgatory, and heaven. Hell symbolized existing enterprise software, which cost millions and often went stale by the time it was implemented. It was filled with actors in cages playing enterprise salespeople. "Help, get me out," they screamed. "Sign this million-dollar license agreement. I need to make my quota." Heaven was Salesforce, where harps played and light poured in. The B-52s received $250,000 to perform, and Benioff told his audience: "We are going to be a $100 million company three years from now" and "the last dot-com." A few weeks later the dot-com bubble, along with the NASDAQ, deflated. Nonetheless, Salesforce.com kept growing. To every journalist who visited, Benioff spun the line that they were seeing "the end of software" as they knew it and that Salesforce.com was the pioneer of an entirely new industry. Soon it became conventional wisdom.

In addition to the splashy marketing stunts, however, Benioff also instituted a rigorous sales process tailored to his product. Unlike other enterprise software, which required long sales cycles, laborious installation, and expensive contracts, Salesforce.com's product could be bought online with a credit card and set up in just a few minutes. Benioff's idea was to "seed-and-grow" by offering customers free trials before using the software. His sales tactics were simple but effective. The Salesforce.com website was set up to capture potential customer information. Media coverage drove traffic to the website, which in turn drove free trials and subsequent sales. Customers were then offered user seminars, upgrades, and support to keep them engaged with the company. During the dot-com fever, Benioff would go to several parties a night in San Francisco and collect business cards. The next morning he would turn them over to his sales team. "They hated it," he says. "They tried to hide as they saw me walk down the hallway, but luckily the office was a big open space, and there was nowhere for them to go. I also encouraged the team to call everyone they knew and to routinely ask friends of friends for referrals." It was no different from the traditional methods of selling life insurance, but it worked.

Benioff also used telesales and cold-calling, other old techniques looked down on by most tech firms, which preferred either no-touch online sales or high-touch teams spending weeks at clients' offices. Benioff found that he could hire energetic college graduates, train them for a few weeks, and in relatively short order have them pounding the phones for business the way companies sell cable service. As much as he could, he streamlined the process of selling, stripping away aspects that would allow a salesperson's individuality to affect the process. For instance, he insisted that the product be priced low and there be no discounts, so that salespeople couldn't slash prices to generate volume. The pricing never changed, whether you were selling one subscription license or a thousand. You closed now at this price, or you did not close at all. The more salespeople Benioff hired, the faster his company grew.

The dot-com crash changed Salesforce.com in two crucial ways. It went from billing customers month-to-month to billing them for annual subscriptions, the same way you might pay for a magazine. This gave the company cash up front so it could cover expenses rather than wait a month or two to collect. It also washed away many of the firm's smaller customers and forced it to attack larger businesses. It was time to grow up. So Benioff went out and hired grown-up salespeople. Like Jim Steele.

After I'd spent a few hours at Salesforce.com, with the Yoda statue outside Benioff's office, the bowls of candy, and the chief love officer, Benioff's dog, Jim Steele, the "chief customer officer and president, worldwide sales," came as a welcome dose of sobriety. He wore pressed jeans, a sport coat, and a collared shirt. He had a firm handshake, a rich deep voice, and a TV weatherman's hair—thick, boot black, and carefully groomed. He didn't pull the hippie capitalist routine you find around the technology business, the Steve Jobs vegan-bully, materialist-spiritualist schizophrenia that permeates the culture. Steele was born and raised in New Jersey and Pennsylvania. He studied engineering in college and then spent a year and a half on the IBM sales training program, which he recalls was like a military boot camp. "They told us, one in three will survive and make it through to sell for the company, but that this was where you learned the business. That if you could sell yourself, you could sell your product. They made us feel so proud to be IBM salesmen. We were taught to dress like the CEOs of the companies we visited, and told that if we had the will to win and the will to listen, we could learn the rest." He spent the next twenty-three years at IBM. Straight up and down corporate America, an engineer with a sales pitch.

IBM moved him west and eventually he left during the tech boom to join the software firm Ariba. In 2000, with Ariba plummeting from its bubble heights, Benioff called Steele. Weeks of interviews ensued at the office, over dinner, at sports games. Benioff even had Steele meet a psychiatrist. "Marc told me to come and see what it was like. He said, 'What's the worst that can happen? You come to Salesforce.com, you try some new things, and if they don't work, we just flip back.' He told me to be different. At first, I was passive and resistant to change. But as Marc says, if it ain't broke, break it." Steele was sold.

"During my interviews with Marc, he started showing me the Salesforce system. I hadn't done a product demonstration since 1979 when I'd gone to a firm on Wall Street to demo an IBM check-processing sorter and the demo went so badly, I vowed never to do another one again." That changed once he arrived at Salesforce. "We're salespeople selling to salespeople, so we're selling what we're using. I often tell prospective clients, 'Let me show you what's going on in my business' and show them how I use the software as a salesperson and manager, and within five minutes, they're drooling. All sales managers want the same thing, accurate visibility into their pipelines and the activities of their sales force. If you're passionate and can translate what you're doing to what they're doing, you're going to win every time."

Steele insisted that there is no magic to sales, just two absolute requirements: work hard and be a good listener. Even in a company deeply rooted in technology, the basics of sales remain the same as they are in the Tangier souk. "What motivates salespeople is the thrill, the rush, the living on the edge, the idea that they're going to close the big one. It's a hero mentality," he told me. As a manager, Steele has to keep that hero mentality alive for his people. "If they feel too confident that they can do the job, or they start to not like where they're working, they'll disengage. The best salesmen in the world are like five-year-old kids chasing a soccer ball. They're all running to exactly the same place. They'll always choose the hot company, so your job is to remain that company."

For the good salespeople, he says, there are always other jobs, other firms, other opportunities. Theirs is the most portable talent in business. So for Steele, staying hot and keeping salespeople engaged is at the heart of his job. It applies to himself as much as his team. Steele is fifty-three and says that in order to keep coming to work he needs to be inspired each day. He must always feel that he is choosing to work at Salesforce, not that he must. He cannot just drag himself through the week. At IBM, he went through one of the hardest periods of his career when he ran the Southern California region. Over a few months, he had to fire two thousand people. To turn the region around, he had little but his own will. "I didn't have the experience, the products, the market leadership, or the positive press I have here." It was depressing to sell in that environment, so he appreciates being at a place where people are enthusiastic, where personal loyalty has been engendered over months and years, and where the goal is an "environment where you can have fun and make money."

I asked him if he took selling personally, wondering in my own mind how any ego could take the volatility of such high-volume selling. I imagined that in order to cope, he would view the process objectively, as a game to be won or lost. Coolness amid such heat, I imagined, would be the only way to succeed. Did he have loose robes? His answer surprised me. "I take it all personally. I once spent a week in Korea selling a $50 million deal. The client then chose another vendor. So I stayed back to persuade him. I begged him for a chance to prove we had the best solution. I genuinely believed we did and eventually we won back the deal. I never believe it when a customer says it's not you and they blame other people. You have to get them to lay out what it will take to win, and if I've done that and I still haven't won, you bet I'll take it personally. It's how you will things to happen after you've gone through all the steps and presented all the substance. You can either talk yourself into conceding or convince yourself into winning. It's a refuse-to-lose mentality. It's either David against Goliath, or you're just a small dinghy adrift in the ocean." This is a sentiment Mel Karmazin might well endorse for its suggestion that the salesman's "magic" still matters.

Even though Benioff insists "we're not just P. T. Barnum out there with a hat and cane saying roll up," the P. T. Barnum element still counts, an astonishing fact when you consider the array of systems Salesforce has in place to facilitate sales and minimize the variance that occurs when individual talents are left to themselves. Every salesperson at Salesforce is supported by sales development staff, who provide them with leads, so they can focus on developing and closing deals rather than filling their pipeline. Every aspect of sales is measured. Salespeople must make a certain number of calls per week, have a certain number of meetings, and keep their monthly pipeline filled to a predetermined value. They are measured on visibility, the extent to which their forecasts differ from their achieved quota; effectiveness, the number of deals they close; productivity, the time it takes to close each deal; and lead management—the volume, response time, and conversion time of leads. They are monitored to ensure that they follow up with customers within twenty-fourhours of any inquiry. Salespeople are constantly reminded that being measured matters. Every minute they spend in the bathroom or on a coffee break haunts them.

Were George Orwell to visit Salesforce, he might find all this monitoring to be confirmation of his vision of 1984, a world where everything you do is watched and weighed. Martin Nowak, however, might see this as a system designed to minimize obfuscation and mistrust and enhance cooperation. Salesforce uses technology to reduce the classic tensions that arise within sales organizations. Its technology generates so much data about customers on the basis of their industry, geography, and buying habits, that if salespeople complain that their territory is weak, their sales managers can counter the point using reams of facts. It uses its own software to support salespeople with plans, customer testimony, and war stories from other salespeople in different parts of the world. Salespeople are encouraged to share their success stories in a public forum for other salespeople to read, a virtual form of Steve Wynn's storytelling, or standing at the bar after work telling your colleagues about how you crushed it. The firm has a quota club system, whereby people who meet quota are congratulated in person and immediately, and an e-mail is sent recognizing the fact to senior management. Precise compensation levels are not published, but somehow the big success stories always leak out to encourage others. Humans remain utterly human in this setting, but they are given tools to minimize evasion and suspicion and allow each person to prove their worth in cold, indisputable, meritocratic numbers. Technology provides the transparency that leads to trust. Humans still provide the magic.

And then in the Hawaiian spirit of *mahalo*, gratitude, Salesforce is always seeking new ways to motivate its employees. It prints up life-size posters of high performers and plasters them all over the office. It rewards any salespeople who hit 100 percent of their quota with a three-day trip for two to Maui. That perk ends up going to around 65 percent of the sales force each year. For the very top sales people, there is the Breakfast at Tiffany's special. During your trip to Hawaii, you are chauffeured to a Tiffany's store before its ordinary opening time, where an Audrey Hepburn lookalike greets you with champagne and takes you round to help you spend.

It is something no technology can yet do.

THE LEMONADE
STAND

We sell—or else.

DAVID OGILVY, *CONFESSIONS OF AN ADVERTISING MAN*

At the end of the summer of 2010, my two sons, aged seven and five, underwent a peculiarly American rite of passage. They set up a lemonade stand. To prepare, they spent hours in our garage hammering together a sign and a low table. While the sign was fine, colorfully decorated and correctly spelled, the table wobbled dangerously and had to be replaced at the last minute by a card table. The boys mixed lemonade and limeade in two separate pitchers, filled a bowl with Oreo cookies, took up position at the end of our driveway, and were in business. The first forty minutes were slow. People drove past and waved but didn't stop. But slowly, one after another, our neighbors kindly stopped by and bought the fifty-cent cups of lemonade for a dollar and told the boys to "keep the change." Our tribe was cooperating, Martin Nowak might have observed, for the promise of direct and indirect rewards, immediate thanks, and the enhancement of each individual's reputation. Over three hours, my sons collected $43. I suppose I could have ventured into the sticky area of cost of goods sold and profit margins, but I didn't. The gross sales went into their piggy banks, a few more steps on the slow march to the go-kart they both covet.

When I was talking to Martin Shanker he asked me a question I never expected to hear from a sales trainer: What do you most want for your children? There were lots of things, I said. Health, happiness, longevity, intelligence, friendships. He put it another way. If I were to die tomorrow, what skill would I most want them to have? He didn't mean an unplayable top-spin forehand or a knack for picking undervalued stocks. The answer, he told me after I fumbled to find my own, was this: the ability to meet their own needs. It is what all our parenting efforts boil down to. We want our children not merely to be self-sufficient, but to be able to meet the needs any human has in order to live a fulfilling life. What we fear most is that if we were to die, they would be as helpless as they were when they were first born.

Selling, in Shanker's view, is a crucial part of meeting one's own needs. We sell not just for the sake of it, but as a means to achieving what we want out of life. For some that will be money and the comforts and status it brings. For others, selling is an act of commercializing a particular talent. A painter sells his work so he can continue to paint without going broke or hungry, so he can paint and not lead the frustrated life of a moving man, short-order cook, or accountant, his true passion relegated to evenings and weekends in the basement. The pleasure a parent feels in watching his children run a lemonade stand is not that of the CEO watching his salesmen close deals. I have no great ambition for my children to sell soft drinks. Rather, it is the pleasure of knowing that they are figuring out how the world works, and that the only means to getting what they want is by managing their own thoughts and actions. Learning to sell, then, is as much a part of growing up as learning to read and write.

The Arts and Crafts movement, which came to the United States from Britain in the late nineteenth century, argued that selling should be an integral part of any child's education. Their reasoning was that children should not be taught to live upon the labor of others. They should not be educated to become members of a rent-taking elite. Rather they should learn by practice how to cultivate the land, develop their own food supply, and make whatever they needed to house, clothe, and equip themselves for life. "Let a child work until he craves the help of books, instead of studying until he forgets the need of work," said an early edition of *The Craftsman* magazine. The perfect school, then, should be a working garden or small farm, with buildings attached for carpentry, metalwork, sewing, printing, binding, painting, cooking, and so on. But at the front entrance should be a shop, where children should learn how to approach customers, how to interest them, how to explain the quality of their work and why it is priced the way it is. If children were not making something, members of the Arts and Crafts movement believed, then at least they should be out filling orders and drafting contracts to make the activity of their school self-supporting. Selling, according to this philosophy, was anything but Willy Loman's subjection to the capitalist grind. It was a means to escape the jaws of industrialized commerce. It was how you could live in a modern, capitalist society, while doing exactly what you wanted to do.

The Harvard psychologist Robert Coles wrote in his book *The Moral Life of Children* that morality is developed in the young by experience. He found extraordinary levels of moral sophistication among barely schooled children who had been caught up in the

South's school integration battles of the 1960s. Experience had given them empathy and a grasp of life's complexity. They were farther along the path of understanding morality's shades than their peers who had experienced no such adversity. This is not to say bitter experience is necessary to develop a moral sense, but some experience beyond the deceptive, sunshiny rhetoric often dumped in children's minds helps. Sales, with its many contradictions, hypocrisies, and moral challenges would be a fine place to start. Selling allows for the kind of moral confrontations which lead to personal examination and the banishment of fear. What Coles found time and again was that the most active idealists as adults tended to be those who started early considering the tensions they would face in life between their idealism and their need to satisfy the "practical" ambitions forced on them by their family, institutions, and peers. It was those who never considered these tensions who ended up disillusioned. I cannot think of a better practical education than selling for forcing anyone to think about who one is and how one might balance one's highest self with one's most practical, human needs.

When Shanker asked me why I was so interested in the subject of sales, I told him that my interest arose from my ambivalence. My feelings were divided between the two visions of sales I laid out at the start of this book: the positive view of selling as a means to human progress, and the negative view embodied by *Death of a Salesman*. He told me that we all know we have to sell to live but that almost everyone erects obstacles in their own mind to selling. We tell ourselves we are too shy, or that potential customers don't want to be bothered. We say we are too decent to dissimulate or manipulate. We blame our bosses or the market, or the latest fad selling system, which is too complicated to figure out. We blame the product even when history tells us that people will buy the most preposterous products: $500 sunglasses, most financial advisory services, steak knives. And yet every one of us has something we want that we can get only by selling. We want to feed ourselves and our families. We want financial security. We want to live fully, pursuing our passions, without going broke in the process. If the urgency of achieving those goals is felt strongly enough, then all the obstacles that inhibit us from selling melt away.

Shortly before Christmas I reconnected with Shanker, to take him up on his offer to walk me around a department store and observe the salespeople. We met on 59th Street and Third Avenue in Manhattan, at the entrance to Bloomingdale's, in an area that the father of a friend of mine used to refer to as the gates of hell. Whatever the weather, it always seems gray and grimy. The traffic is bunched up, half of it trying to get over to the Queensboro Bridge. Cops stand in the middle of the street yelling, steam billows up from the subway, and the sidewalks seem designed to trip up shoppers laden with bags. Inside Bloomingdales, it's not much better. The heat is cranked up, the air is thick with cloying, clashing perfumes wafting out from the cosmetics department, and the salespeople look defeated.

"We want to look like ordinary shoppers," said Shanker. "Let's see what kind of service we get." We began in menswear at the Dunhill counter. Shanker walked over to the shirts and ties and began riffling through them, purposefully. "I'm trying to look like I'm looking for something specific," he whispered. A saleswoman who had been standing at the cash register wandered off without acknowledging us. A man took her place. After a couple of minutes he came over, stood around ten feet away, leaned in, said, "Just to tell you, all the shirts on that shelf are 40 percent off," and then moved away again.

"He assumed we were sale shoppers," said Shanker as we left. "He didn't bother finding out anything about us. He had just been trained to say this one thing." We walked into men's fragrances. A middle-aged salesman was standing behind the Ralph Lauren counter arguing with an older woman about a refund. He had clearly lost patience with her and she was fumbling with a handful of receipts. When she finally walked away, he asked if he could help me while watching the woman disappear out of sight. There were four men's eaux de toilette in a battered-looking rack, called the "Big Pony" collection. One was described as "fresh and sporty," another "spicy and seductive," a third "energizing," a fourth "adventurous." I asked for a spritz of the fresh and sporty one on the back of my hand. The salesman complied, though his attention remained elsewhere. "So what's in all these?" I asked. "This one has lime and grapefruit, this is all about dark chocolate; we have mandarin to energize here, and fresh mint in our classic," he intoned as if reading his lease. "And how much are they?" "Sixty-five dollars for the large size and you get a free tube of shower gel." "I'll think about it," I said, and he turned immediately to rearranging his display.

"He clearly had good product knowledge," said Shanker. "But again, he didn't try to find out anything about you. When you asked to try that one scent, he could have initiated a conversation, but he didn't." As we drifted into a conversation about women's cosmetics, a passing saleswoman interrupted us. "Are you interested in trying some women's fragrances?" Even as I shrugged, she said, "Follow me." She led us to a counter where she was selling Guilty by Gucci. "This is one of our bestsellers," she said, spraying a sample onto a piece of card. "Very floral, very pretty. We sell a lot of this." She handed over the card for me to smell. "Also, if you buy the large size, you get a free cream and a jewelry box." "People like this?" I asked. "It's one of our bestsellers," she reiterated. She was confidently assuming that all I wanted to buy was what everyone else was buying.

We had been in Bloomingdale's for about half an hour by now and no one had yet bothered to ask me a single question about why I was there. I had been told about discounts, about the composition of fragrances, and about what other people were buying. For all I had learned about the importance of salespeople listening to customers, not one salesperson here seemed the least bit interested in me or what had brought me off the frigid winter streets into their store. Shanker assured me the level of selling would improve as we progressed up the store, as the items got more expensive. "Remember, companies tolerate a level of selling that fits with their business model," he said. "If there's no commercial advantage to having good salespeople, they will put up with what they can get."

Arriving in the women's wear section, I looked for an item I could credibly discuss. I spied a gray woolen shawl by AllSaints Spitalfields, a British company. There was one assistant in the AllSaints area and she was busy folding clothes and rearranging an accessories display. I peered ostentatiously at the shawl, rubbing it between my fingers and staring in her direction with a look of male helplessness. She ignored me and kept folding. Finally, I asked her, "What kind of wool is this?" "Huh?" she said, finally looking up. "What kind of wool?" "What kind?" "Yes." She came over and fumbled for the label. "It's a wool blend, with mohair and alpaca." "So you dry-clean it?" "Uh-huh. No, hold on." She peered again at the label. "Yeah, uh-huh, dry-clean." She then walked back to her accessories problem.

Except for the uninterested sales assistant, the AllSaints Spit-alfields area was great. The clothes looked terrific, the name of the label was picked out in lightbulbs, there was a dark wooden floor and service counter. It felt like a fashionable urban clothing store dropped into the middle of Bloomingdale's. So why was the service so poor? Was I so obviously not a customer? Shouldn't any sales-person know that you should never assume who is and who isn't a customer based on first impressions? The schlub in baggy pants and a sweatshirt might be a billionaire eager to spend. The elegantly dressed couple could be up to their necks in debt.

We kept going upstairs. The Armani section was beautifully laid out, spare and cream-colored, the clothes, worth hundreds of dol-lars each, were hanging from the racks like museum pieces. But there was no assistant in sight. Across the floor was an area devoted to L.K.Bennett, a label I'd never heard of. I walked over to what looked like a woman's trench coat, something I knew my wife had been looking for. It turned out to be a woolen overcoat. "Do you have any trench coats?" I asked the saleswoman. "No, we don't, I'm afraid," she said. "You can try Burberry, which is also on this floor, or the coat department upstairs." She seemed friendly and eager to help, so I continued the conversation. "Tell me about L.K.Ben-nett." It is a British line, she told me, aimed at younger, professional women, offering business and casual wear. Their strategy is to own their own stores across America, but they had made an exception by taking an area in Bloomingdale's. I thanked her and reported in, favorably, to Shanker.

"But she didn't sell you anything," he said. "She didn't even show you something else. She could have said, you know, maybe your wife has something else on her Christmas list, a belt, or a jacket." I told him that might have felt pushy. "But if she'd already established a rapport, it's her job to try to get you to buy something." He's absolutely right, of course. It's not the salesperson's job to be my best friend. It was her job to be liked enough that she could trigger a sale. I'd have certainly listened to her pitch, had she bothered to make it, because she had already earned my trust and attention. But she didn't. She let me walk away.

Shanker's point returns us to this psychological battle inside the salesperson's head: the need to sell and the need to be liked. Shanker told me that the good salesperson is the one who finds a customer's psychological need and satisfies it. Thus, what I considered "pushy" should be interpreted as an effort to find out what I need. The reluctance to sell me, therefore, should not be considered an act of politeness but a failure to meet my needs. The saleswoman who lets me go with the consolation that she remains likable should in fact be regretting her failure to scratch whatever psychological itch had brought me to her corner of Bloomingdale's. Had she engaged me in further conversation, she might have discovered that I was writing a book about sales and then sold to me on the basis that if I was to fully understand the sales process, I needed to buy something.

Of course this assumes that buying is a reasonable means of satisfying psychological needs. If you take the position that trying to get people to buy their way to happiness is fundamentally wicked, then you'll never reconcile yourself to most forms of sales. But if you take a more moderate position, that buying and selling are part of who we are, then selling in Bloomingdale's, engaging in conversations with shoppers and seeking a way to persuade them that what you have is what they need, should carry no fear. If you are rejected, at least you tried to do the shopper a favor. This is a much better means of coping with the psychological challenge of selling than the trite demand that in order to sell well, you must be passionate about what you are selling. The idea that every salesperson can be passionate about the product is pure fantasy. Most people sell what they hope can make them a living, whether it is missile systems or socks. To feel passion is a rare privilege. What changes in a sales transaction is not just ownership of a product, a trivial matter, but more important, the emotional state of the buyer. If you are looking for reasons to sell, satisfying other people's psychological needs seems more interesting work than pushing product.

Augie Turak told me a story of meeting a German woman at a swimming pool in Israel. When he told her he was a salesman, she said, "Don't you get tired pushing things on people all the time?" As they paddled around the pool, he suppressed his resentment of her question and drew her into a Socratic dialogue about the value of adding an elevator to a building. He asked, what's the economic value of adding the elevator? Eliminating the need to climb the stairs, she said. Sure, Turak replied. But think about it this way. How does an elevator change the way you price the different floors on a building? In a building without an elevator, the ground floor would be the most valuable, as it would be the easiest to reach. The top floor would be the cheapest. Add an elevator and what happens? Now you can call the top floor the penthouse and charge in rent many times what you charge for the ground floor. So what's the product you're selling here? Is it the elevator? No, it's the view. What an elevator does is uncover the value of an asset contained in every tall building, the view. You can extract the value of the view via the penthouse via the elevator. The building owner doesn't care if his tenants get tired going up and down stairs. He cares about the value of his property. Before the salesman came in, no one had thought to charge for the view. The salesman thinks of all this, not the elevator maker or the building owner who is already collecting his rents. The salesman envisions and creates value where previously there was none. Because he is by nature an optimist, he can make the best of everything.

Gerry O'Reilly, known to everyone in my hometown in Connecticut as Coach, is one such optimistic salesman. He is in his mid-eighties now, but remains tall and dapper, rosy-cheeked and bright-eyed with a word and a joke for everyone. If you bump into him and compliment him on his Barbie-doll pink sweater, he will say "cashmere, mere cash," and smile. When he meets a woman in her nineties, it's "Hello, young lady." Barely a sentence escapes without a wisecrack. In his company, the world seems brighter and more orderly.

His greatest passions, beyond his sprawling family, are the Catholic Church and Notre Dame football. On the mornings of game days during the football season, he visits the local shrine of the Virgin Mary, lights a candle and says a prayer, then returns home and lays out his Notre Dame blanket and other school mementos in front of the television before settling in to watch. Anyone who knows him knows better than to call or stop by during those three or four hours. On other days, he can be found watching the local high school sports team, timing the latest stars of the track team, or cheering on the swimmers, the football or baseball players. For crucial games, the real coach has called in Coach to give the locker room pep talk. "Any sport in a storm," he says. "That's me." The encouragement he gives to the young players, he admits, comes as a succession of worn but true aphorisms: "If it is to be, it is up to me"; "Success comes in cans, not in cannots."

He began his working life as a cosmetics salesman and ended it in a senior management role at Procter & Gamble. But if you ask him to describe himself professionally, he will always say he's a salesman. He was a young man living in Brooklyn when he saw an ad in *Time* magazine for sales training at Vicks. He applied, was hired, and was immediately sent out to sell Vicks products door-to-door to pharmacies and drugstores in western Pennsylvania and West Virginia. "It was a lonely, miserable life," he says. "At 7 P.M. you'd be driving alone past a farmhouse and you'd see a family sitting down for dinner. But at the time I had no attachments, and once I got back to the hotel, I'd run into the star salesmen, like Frank Zito of Old Spice. And I'd try to befriend them. If I was going to West Virginia one week, I'd offer to take their order forms in." The earliest and most important lesson he learned was that "people are more important than things." What mattered was to know as much about a prospect's business as the prospect did and then find a way to make a personal connection. "I'd always pick up the local newspaper, so I could ask, 'Did your boy's school baseball team win in Erie West?'"

He recalls his early days on the road with startling clarity. His $275 a month salary, plus car and expenses; the small store in Butler, Pennsylvania, where he walked in one day with a big smile and the owner said, "I don't know what you've got, but I'm going to buy it"; even the names of trainees, often the ones with the gilt-edged educations, who couldn't handle the work, moaning to Coach that it was all "out of the car, into the hotel, into the car, out to the stores," day after day. "I'd have guys who I'd take out into the field and I'd know immediately they couldn't sell their mother to their father." Coach says that he got so good at his work, it became like "strafing a nursery." "I'd give them all the usual lines. You can't sell from an empty wagon. Stack 'em high and watch 'em fly." And then there would follow the triumphant return to corporate HQ. "You'd live to hear that 'Way to go Charlie.' The 'here comes the man of the year.'"

When I asked him to recall the high point of his sales career, he didn't hesitate. "Calling on a Kmart in Fort Wayne, Indiana. I'd never called on this guy before, but when I got there, I saw the Notre Dame sticker in the car. I went into the store and asked 'Who's the Notre Dame fan here?' The man behind the counter said 'Me.' Turned out he was the owner, a Cuban immigrant who had always wished he'd been able to go to Notre Dame. After we spoke, I went back to my hotel at the airport and totaled up my sale to him. It came to $950,000. So I called him back and said, 'I've never written a million-dollar order.' He said, 'Neither have I,' so we got it up to $1 million. I couldn't wait to call in to my office and say, 'Get a pencil!' There were these moments of great joy, when I knew I had had a great day, and I got back to the hotel, had a couple of shooters with dinner, and then watched the NFL game."

Coach firmly believes that Lou Holtz, the famed coach of the Notre Dame football team, had it right about selling and the rest of life. "Ability is what you're capable of. Motivation determines what you do. Attitude determines how well you do it." In sales as in sports, ability and motivation are givens. Attitude is what makes the difference. It is what helped Coach through the years after his wife died of a sudden aneurysm, leaving him with four young children. The easy wisecracks, so rote, so 1950s plaid, so capable of charming everyone from a testy grandchild to a centenarian neighbor, accompanied the sunny disposition required to endure periods of profound anxiety. His salesman's shtick is evidence of his resilience.

Attitude is not something often addressed in the Valhallas of business thought and education. It is banished to the lowly realms of self-help seminars and motivational speakers. But as I thought about selling, I could not shake this image of Coach's younger self, driving alone through the country roads of West Virginia, gazing in at the farmhouses, downing his shooters at day's end and swapping tales with the hotshot from Old Spice. It seemed a truer business story than most. It dealt with business as it is, not as glossy magazine covers and CEO speeches would have us believe it is. Coach's story is about surviving not just the peddler's life, but life in general.

My adventure in selling brought me into contact with a wide range of people who convinced me that there is no "type" who can sell, but rather certain traits that determine success. In Tangier, I met not only Majid but also a languid English antiques dealer, Christopher Gibbs, who had sold the last of his business and retired to a splendid house overlooking the Straits of Gibraltar. Gibbs was for many years London's preeminent antiques dealer, selling a particular high-bohemian look to collectors including Mick Jagger and Sir John Paul Getty. As a schoolboy he developed a fascination with art and objects, and his father would reprimand him, as Gibbs said, "for asking people about their things." His career as a dealer was highly eccentric. He opened his first shop at the age of twenty and stocked it with things he described as "wonderful but in a bit of a mess." He sold taxidermy alongside dining tables and fragments of royal garters. At a moment of financial insolvency, he struck up a business partnership with Simon Sainsbury, the finance director of his family's eponymous British supermarket chain. Sainsbury introduced him to ideas such as "shelf life," advising him to get rid of products he had owned for too long, and encouraged him to expand his list of clients. Knowing rich people was one thing, knowing rich people who would actually buy from him was quite another. Over tea and rosemary biscuits at his house, Gibbs told me, "the darling grocer [Sainsbury] would say go to America, make a list of what you have and go to provincial museums and see the ghastly trustees, which I used to do." Like Duveen, Gibbs could ensnare buyers with the lure of his rarefied tastes, and set prices according to nothing more than his own enthusiasm. "I can sell things I'm mad about," he said. "And I won't budge on price. In fact, I'll jack it up." Yet despite all his success, Gibbs reached a point where he could no longer stomach the selling. Just as Memo dreams of one day escaping the contractor business of Baltimore and living in a maintenance-free house in Oaxaca, Gibbs has sold almost everything antique he has ever owned. It was never the product that exhausted him. "Really," he said, "it's the people you have to deal with."

For a saleswoman like Carolyn Klemm, however, the people she deals with as a realtor keep her going. Klemm is the top real estate agent in Litchfield County, a dreamy corner of northwestern Connecticut full of colonial towns and gentlemen's farms owned by wealthy New Yorkers. Her client list has included George Soros, Henry Kravis, numerous Goldman Sachs partners, and Henry Kissinger. Since starting her business, in 1979, after a career as a department store buyer, she has sold nearly $2 billion worth of houses in this one small market. Every Labor Day, she holds an end of summer barbecue at her home, a whitewashed Georgian brick manor house just off the town green in Washington, Connecticut. She has tents put up in the garden and Japanese lanterns hung in the trees leading down to the swimming pool. Caterers prepare vast quantities of fried chicken and coleslaw, home cooking for what Klemm insists is a "casual affair." Then around two hundred guests arrive—former, present, and future clients, bankers, writers, movie stars, business-people. And through this whirl passes Klemm, in her late sixties, recently widowed, wearing a bright pink jacket, puffing on a Benson & Hedges cigarette, throwing her arm around shoulders far higher than her own, and talking nonstop.

When I visited her at her office, furnished with a checkered sofa, piles of papers, and a chocolate brown Labrador named Teddy, she barely paused for breath. A typical Carolyn Klemm story goes like this. It is delivered circuitously, breathlessly, and with the relentless dropping of names and the adjectival use of "darling." "So I received a call the other day from an Englishman in New York looking for a summer rental. 'Hellooo, I'm looking for a rental,'" she said in a mock English accent, as if holding a phone to her ear. They get to talking, because that is what you do on the phone with Carolyn Klemm. "Most people have no idea how to answer the phone," she said. "I'm able to form a very quick connection."

It turned out the man was the creative head at a major retail chain—more than enough for Klemm to begin her trick of shrinking the world for him. "Well do you know Richard Lambertson and John Truex?" she asked, mentioning two handbag designers who share a country house in Litchfield County. "Or Calhoun Sumrall [a senior executive at Ralph Lauren]?" The man said he didn't, but naturally knew all about them. "Well, listen," she told him. "Rent a house up here and I'll make sure you meet all these people." The Friday after this conversation, she went to a cocktail party a couple of towns over from Washington and met an old friend who worked for Brooks Brothers. She discovered one of his employees was the Englishman's partner. The circle was closed, and the following Monday, Klemm's Englishman signed up to rent in Litchfield County over the summer and she had plans to host a dinner party for him in early June. "Most people can't remember their broker long after a sale goes through," she said. "Hopefully no one forgets me." Christopher Gibbs ended up exhausted by his clients. Klemm is energized by the effect she can have on them. Both reached the top of their respective areas of selling.

So too did Ashok Vemuri, head of the Indian business process outsourcer Infosys's operations in America. He came to the United States in 1999, leaving a comfortable and successful career as an investment banker in India. He had the salesperson's drive to test himself, to see if he could thrive in a Western economy. A few months after he arrived in New York, he and twenty other young Indian men arrived by bus in Portland, Maine, to make a pitch to Hannaford Bros., a regional supermarket chain. Vemuri recalled stepping out into the freezing cold in his thin overcoat. He had never seen snow before. The residents of Portland gathered in their doorways to watch this unusual-looking rabble walk down the street. The Infosys pitch was about offering cheaper, better technology and management systems. But at the outset, it was also about India itself. Customers would routinely ask if Indians could speak English. "We had to sell India as a place where educated people lived and worked," Vemuri told me, "as more than a land of snake charmers and elephants on the streets."

As Infosys's American business grew and Vemuri had to hire and train more salespeople, he said he was appalled by the caliber of people and how they were taught. "It seemed everyone had to be either Dirty Harry or the girl on the beach in her bikini teasing people." What he sought was intelligence, curiosity, and an agile mind, not the chest-beating alpha male of sales myth. He wanted low-ego characters who regarded client service as the highest goal.

When he hired, he tried to see candidates in as many settings as possible. He met them in the office, or at a restaurant for lunch. He met them with their spouse, even asked them to invite him somewhere. He was looking for salespeople who could make others comfortable, be articulate and convincing, and deal with the unexpected.

During the interview process, Vemuri asked candidates to pick a subject of personal interest and to make a short presentation. The six out of ten who picked a financial or technology services product were rarely hired. He preferred it if they talked about a more believable passion—a sport, a favorite movie, or a place they had visited. "It has to be interesting enough to them so they can tell a good story about it. I'm not looking for a business lecture, I'm looking to see that they can look at a subject in depth and from multiple perspectives and talk about it so people listen." He wanted salespeople who could talk the way Tony Sullivan talked about his holidays, brimming with enthusiasm and recommendations. He did not want chameleons or people who have imbibed every body language trick. "We want people who are well read, well informed, who are comfortable being themselves." He wanted authenticity. "I've had salespeople with terrible accents, who don't adhere to an acceptable Westernized dress code, who misspeak words, but they are terrific storytellers. They relate their story to your problem and can combine experiences across functions and geographies. They cannot hold a great conversation with the CEO about wine, but they can talk specifically about technology."

It is so different from what Norm Levine and the old-school insurance salesmen suggest, that to succeed you must cut your personality to a certain respectable cloth and skulk around for snippets of information so you can connect with your clients. Instead, Vemuri and Infosys recommended, as Dale Carnegie, Jeffrey Gitomer, and

Mrs. Shibata had, that you be yourself and trust the world to appreciate your intelligence, wit, and open-mindedness, whatever wrapping it comes in. It is a much more attractive vision of selling, because it claims that very different kinds of salespeople can succeed. You don't have to be clean-shaven, wearing a blue suit, and telling anyone who asks that all is "fine and dandy." You don't neeed to blend in with "the force" and willfully ignore the reality of the work. You can be exactly who you are, provided that you have the kind of attributes anyone should aspire to: open-mindedness, curiosity, acceptance of others, warmth, and resolve. All these are to a great degree learnable. If you can approach selling this way, you will be more than capable of dealing with the emotional challenges embedded in the work.

When the Dalai Lama first engaged with the West after fleeing Tibet in 1959, he seemed a remote, baffling figure, a young monk who spoke in long, philosophical ramblings, meandering along the most arcane pathways of Buddhist scholarship and thought. Few in the West could understand him, let alone sympathize. If he wanted the world to pay attention to Tibet's plight, he could not keep talking as he would to his fellow monks. So he learned a different way of speaking and presenting himself. As one biographer put it, he educated himself "in the language of the world, not changing his fundamental positions but constantly finding new ways to make them approachable." Sometimes he is charming, the smiling monk onstage at Radio City Music Hall spreading a philosophy of happiness. But when he finds it wins friends but not real help for the cause of Tibet, he will show flashes of anger about the world's abandonment of Tibet to Chinese brutality. It is a kind of adaptive selling, tailoring a message to an audience to achieve a specific purpose, sifting rapidly through the categories of customers to figure out which pitch will work best.

Nelson Mandela operated in a similar way. In *Playing the Enemy*, an account of how Mandela engineered a peaceful regime change in his country by winning over white South Africans, John Carlin wrote: "Like Homer's Odysseus, [Mandela] progressed from challenge to challenge, overcoming each one not because he was stronger than his foes, but because he was cleverer and more beguiling. He had forged these qualities following his arrest and imprisonment in 1962, when he came to realize that the route of brute force he had attempted, as the founding commander of the ANC's military wing, could not work. In jail, he judged that the way to kill apartheid was to persuade white people to kill it themselves, to join his team, submit to his leadership." Early on during his long imprisonment, Mandela made it his business to understand the mind-set of the white Afrikaners who ruled South Africa. He studied their history and poetry and learned their language. He treated his thuggish, suspicious warders with respect, in the hope that it would be returned. He would tell his fellow prisoners that the guards were vulnerable human beings who had been turned into brutes by the system in which they worked. It took many years, and many challenges to this approach, but eventually South Africa's white leadership came to see Mandela as the best way out of the corner of apartheid. Mandela is one of those rare creatures the sales academics call naturals, those who possess empathy but are not pushovers, have ego drive but are not bullies.

Two incidents in particular capture Mandela's gifts as a salesman. In 1985, Kobie Coetsee, the then minister of justice, was dispatched by the apartheid government to meet Mandela in prison. Mandela was in the hospital at the time, weakened by an operation, and wearing his prison hospital garb—robe, pajamas, and slippers. Coetsee knew about Mandela only from government files, and feared meeting a man the government believed was determined to take control of South Africa by any means possible. Mandela in turn knew that this was the moment he had been preparing for for years, a chance to open discussions with the government about the future of his country. Mandela greeted Coetsee warmly and the two spoke about people they both knew in the prison service. Coetsee inquired after Mandela's health and mentioned he had recently bumped into Mandela's wife, Winnie. He was impressed by Mandela's knowledge of Afrikaans and Afrikaner history. The content of the meeting was thin, but its polite, affable tone meant everything. It meant that a more serious dialogue could now begin.

Soon afterward, Mandela decided to deploy his charm for a more particular purpose on the officer in charge of the prison where he was being held. Major van Sittert was a large, gruff man with little time for the political prisoners. He also spoke little English, which meant he struggled to communicate with them. So when he next visited, Mandela spoke to him in Afrikaans and then immediately started talking about rugby, a sport adored by white South Africans but loathed by blacks. Mandela had made the effort to study the sport and all the players. He talked about players who were in and out of form and made observations about recent matches. Van Sittert was surprised and then charmed. So much so that when Mandela asked if he might have a hot plate in his cell so he could warm up his dinner each night, van Sittert immediately barked to the nearest guard: "Go and get Mandela a hot plate!"

As these stories show, selling itself is an ethically neutral act. What matters is motivation. Mandela is a masterful manipulator, but his cause is right. The Dalai Lama slips into different modes of communication depending on his audience, but unless you are the

Chinese government you don't call him a cynical chameleon, but a noble man doing his best with a difficult but worthy mission.

Ted Leonsis told me that if there was one thing I should try to do with this book, it was to restore some of the luster to selling. He is right to say that anyone in business who belittles selling should not be in business. Howard Anderson likes to tell the story of John Chambers, the CEO of Cisco and a formidable salesman in his own right. He had not been in his job very long when he arrived half an hour late for a board meeting. Don Valentine, a venture capitalist on the board, began to give him some grief. Chambers explained, "I had an unhappy customer on the phone." Valentine backed off. "You're damned right son. An unhappy customer always trumps a board of venture capitalists." That's true in any organization.

Like all the most interesting things in life, selling is both light and dark. Augie Turak told me "the best salespeople are very insecure. They passionately want success because they think it'll make them a different person. Then they achieve success and it dawns on them they haven't changed at all. What drives salespeople is a need for celebrity. They think that once they're successful, everyone's opinion of them will change, and if they can change everyone's opinion of them, they'll change themselves. Then they succeed, and realize they haven't changed at all." For both the successes and failures, there is the endless rejection, the long line of people saying in so many words "I don't want you, I don't want what you have, I don't want you in my life." If nothing else, selling is an endless confrontation with truth, the truth about yourself and about others. It is raw and uncomfortable and personally exposing in a way other business functions rarely are. This hard truth may help explain why business schools, which prefer to paint a less brutal vision of business life, are so loath to teach it.

But clearly, it need not be so grim. By treating sales with such disdain, business schools prove themselves both foolish and elitist. Without selling, there is no business. It is also the greatest leveler in business. It is open to anyone and it possesses that most democratizing quality, of being wholly measurable. Done well, selling frees people from the oppression of corporate culture and allows them to define their own personalities and destinies. It is a way for people with little formal education, but plenty of perseverance, to do well. Mix a fine education with the desire and talent for selling and the fruits of such hybrid vigor can change the world. Not only should business schools and companies teach more sales, but it should be the starting point of a business education. It is from sales that everything follows: how you make money, how you treat people, how you wish to grow. Every ethical question a businessperson could face comes down to a question you confront in your very first sale: What are you willing to do for a buck?

In *The Godfather*, when the Godfather is shot, his eldest son, Sonny, vows war with the other families unless they turn over Sollozzo, the man who organized the hit. Tom Hagen, the levelheaded Irish consigliere, played by Robert Duvall, tries to calm him down, advising him to separate his personal feelings from the family's business. "They shoot my father and it's business, my ass!" screams Sonny. "Even shooting your father was business not personal, Sonny!" says Hagen. "Well then," says Sonny, "business is going to have to suffer." I'm with Sonny on this. It is all too easy to say it's business not personal when your view of business does not extend beyond the sterility of a spreadsheet or a trading screen. When you sell to another person, business becomes personal very quickly.

I first met Christopher Coleridge at high school in England, and we have remained friends ever since. He is the godfather to my younger son, with all the trust, affection, and respect that implies. He is also a terrific and committed salesman. But if I were to accept what McMurry, the author of "The Mystique of Super-Salesmanship," says about salesmen—that they're greedy, selfish, untrustworthy, that they need constant monitoring and control—then I must have made a terrible mistake in picking him to guide my son's spiritual education. The other possibility is that McMurry's vision is incomplete.

At university Christopher and I both worked on a magazine, I as business manager, he as editor. In truth, he scarcely needed me because he was adept at running the business affairs himself. But he was happy to satisfy my ambitions of moguldom, fantastical as they were. While I viewed drumming up advertisers as a necessary chore, there was little he seemed to enjoy more than cajoling money out of local restaurants and shop owners, and then confronting late payers. We were once owed money by Ford, which had taken out an advertisement for its cars. Two months after publication, they still hadn't paid. Several of my dithering calls had gone unanswered, so one morning Christopher took the matter in hand. After fifteen minutes of badgering, he was speaking to the head of Ford marketing for the whole of Europe, who was baffled as to why he was being disturbed over a bill for a measly £1,500. But the check arrived within days. In social settings, Christopher suffered from an occasional stammer. But when it came to selling, the stammer disappeared to be replaced by an entrepreneurial swagger.

As our university days came to a close, while most of our friends were considering jobs as lawyers and bankers, Christopher dreamt of running his own food company. Whenever we went into a sandwich shop, he would strike up a conversation with whoever was behind the counter. What would they recommend? Which was their best-seller? Where did the cheese come from? How about that taramo-salata? Shouldn't it be beige not bright pink? And he wasn't just being polite. He was interested.

After university, he went into advertising. One of his main accounts was Sugar Puffs, a British cereal brand represented by a large mascot called the Honey Monster. For a couple of years Chris-topher had to accompany this mascot, and the various actors who filled the wooly outfit, to events and shoots, making sure all its body parts reached their destination, a task he performed with remarkably little complaining. He then attended business school at INSEAD in France. At the end of his MBA course, he was passed over by the tra-ditional MBA employers and was itching to start his own business. He and a friend from INSEAD hit on the idea of creating V Water, a vitamin-enhanced water similar to ones selling briskly in the United States. They invented their product, its flavors, and packaging. Then ten INSEAD alumni invested £10,000 each to get the business up and running. The next four years were spent building up a customer base for V Water from the ground up.

Christopher spent his days calling on shop owners across London. One of the firm's first purchases was an old white van, which he would load up with V Water and drive across town. He badly needed distribution, and the shop owners knew it, beating down his profit margin on every sale. Every day, he endured rejec-tion, and even when he succeeded in getting V Water into stores, it tended to be on wretched terms. In the evenings, he would meet friends with jobs in banks, law firms, and politics, who asked him why he did what he did. The answer was that what he did was real. However frustrating, there was something concrete in the arguments over pennies' worth of margin. "They were patronizing, as if sales-people were the dispensable foot soldiers of business. But really it's the highly paid managers who are the dispensable ones. The sales-people, as long as they're managing the customer relationship, are invaluable."

He also found that there was an instant gratification in sales, an immediate yes or no. Every yes, he found, gave him a "child-ish sense of achievement." "There's this amazing thing which hap-pens when you ring somebody up who doesn't really want to hear from you and slowly, you convert them," he said. "You're like David against Goliath and when you win, it's incredibly satisfying." Over five years, V Water steadily grew until one day, just as Christopher was facing having to go out and raise more money from investors, his telephone rang. Pepsi wanted to buy his firm. It was an extraor-dinary reward for his effort, and he and his partner and their inves-tors wasted little time in accepting the offer. V Water became a unit of Pepsi, run by Christopher, and now he no longer had to worry about meeting a monthly payroll or all the other hassles of running his own business.

One warm spring morning we met at an Indian coffee shop opposite Liverpool Street station in London. Every month Christo-pher would try to spend at least a couple of days going door-to-door with one of his salesmen. Even as a managing director at one of the world's largest corporations, he still reveled in the hand-to-hand combat of sales. The salesman we were shadowing was an eighteen-year-old called Sam, who had taken the job to make some money between school and university. He was wearing all black, including a black shirt with the V Water logo. The black outfits were chosen by the sales team because they felt the color made them look like barmen. Christopher had written out a short list of objectives. The salesman would use his list of contacts to check on the existing customers and also go "pioneering," visiting shops in the area code he covered that didn't yet sell V Water.

"Let's have fun and let's get going," said Christopher, clapping his hands. Sam started with the Salad Factory, a small sandwich bar run by two young Polish women. Sam's challenge was to ask them if they'd let him install a set of plastic trays, known as "retention trays," to hold V Water bottles in their refrigerated display. The trays had the V Water logo and were set at a slope, so the bottles would slide forward after one was taken from the front. It created a more aggressive display. "Retention trays have been proved to increase sales," Christopher told Sam. "So create some fear that they'll be missing out if they don't have them." Sam went in and introduced himself. He was not bothered by the awkwardness of the situation, pulling out his trays while customers lined up behind him. He got the owners' approval, installed his trays, and came out. A success. The fact is, Christopher told us, that most shop owners love talking about their products. It is their business, their livelihood. What may seem dull to an outsider is what concerns them every minute of their working day: which products generate the most profit. "Lots of salespeople go in and act all sniveling and they tend to get bullied," he said. The ones who go in and address their customers as peers are the ones who succeed.

When interviewing salespeople, Christopher has a standard routine in which he pretends to be a shopkeeper for five minutes, firing objections and questions at the beleaguered sales rep. "I don't have the space. It's too expensive. It looks like water." He is looking to see if they can think on their feet, not clam up, and above all if they keep smiling. Not that this is anything close to a scientific process. "Reliability is always a big issue," he told me. "There was one guy who was an amazing salesman. He was thirty-two and had had lots of different bar jobs," a warning sign that he rarely stuck with any job for long. "He began by selling V Water into bars he knew, but he quickly became very unreliable." One day, when he was due in for work, he called in and said he had been kidnapped and would be in the next morning. Later in the day, he called Christopher to ask if the job would still be around the next morning. "He finally admitted the kidnapping story was made up and I had to fire him."

Next, we visited a Japanese sushi and sandwich bar. The staff didn't speak great English, but Sam did manage to get the manager out of a back room. Then the conversation went nowhere. She had a senior manager who was at another store. Sam tried to get her on the phone, but she said that they had tried V Water and it hadn't sold well. Sam tried to convince her to try again, but she said no. As we left, Christopher congratulated him. "You want to push it as far as you can without becoming their worst enemy," he said. Sam had spent time to build a relationship, listened to the manager, and tried to get hold of the decision maker. "You were good," said Christopher. "But you can always be even more enthusiastic. You're selling them a dream. To do that you minimize any problems then talk about the future. You should say there's a massive push coming behind V Water. It's all organized, huge promotions, buy one get one free; there's going to be a lot of support."

As we walked along, looking for our next shop, I asked Sam what his friends thought of his summer job. "They think it's hard. There's no buzz about selling, because it's not an easy job. People are afraid to do it. But for me, it's nice not being in an office where there's no real buzz. I like walking around, feeling the buzz, being out on the streets." Initially, he found the experience of going into shops unannounced and talking to owners and managers daunting. "But now, as long as I don't barge in and I'm patient, they don't mind. The only thing is you mustn't be ill-informed. They expect you to have an offer and nine out of ten are willing to listen. You're doing it for their store as well, after all, and then it becomes exciting. If they've got a legitimate reason not to want to hear me, I've realized it doesn't matter. It's not about me."

At the next few shops, Sam had long conversations with the owners and managers, and though he didn't change any minds, he was building relationships. "You have good, long chats, Sam," said Christopher. At a new pasta takeout restaurant, Christopher coached him before he went in. "Go in and tell the manager he'll be the first in his chain to carry V Water. He'll be part of history. Talk about how we're really big and getting bigger." Sam nodded, eyes down, like a boxer readying for a fight, then headed back inside.

Sam came out again empty-handed after what looked like a brave effort. "Doesn't matter," said Christopher. "You've got a new lead and you've made friends." The morning was wearing on and by lunchtime, when the crowds started coming out of the city's offices, the restaurants would be too busy for Sam to sell. Our final stop was a large self-service restaurant. We could see the manager talking to people in the serving area. "This is the kind of place V Water was made for," said Christopher, watching Sam walk up to the counter. "City crowd, busy people. Shops like this are gold." After a few minutes, Sam returned. The manager had told him he liked V Water but there wasn't space for it right now, maybe in the future.

"All right, Sam, you must be very blunt," said Christopher, speaking with a sudden sense of purpose. "When he says he likes it and pauses, you must say 'I'm delighted you like it. What I suggest is I now call your distributor. We can give you twelve bottles free today, which you can sell for profit through your own tills. How many cases shall I put you down for? One case of each flavor?' Get to numbers. Tell him you're going to call his distributor right there and place the order. Use your phone, pass it to the manager. If you just leave it to them, a lot can go wrong. They can't be bothered, other things come up. Sam, if you can get in here, it would be a real achievement. Get him to order one case at least. Tell him 'I don't want to waste your time. I'm here to do business.' Remember that if this all goes well for you over this summer, you'll have it on your CV and you'll have some good contacts. Go on."

While we waited outside, Christopher observed that for all the changes in technology and the size of the company he now works for, it still comes down to this. Finding new stores and following up. Going door-to-door and talking to people in person, not on the phone or via e-mail. Sam is soon back outside, shaking his head.

"All right," said Christopher, fully immersed in the challenge. "Now use some emotion. Tell him you've put your job on the line to get him this special promotion." Christopher pulled out his phone and called the restaurant's distributor to authorize a one-off promotion for the restaurant. He turned back to Sam. "Tell the manager about all the great things we're doing, keep him excited. The distributor has the free samples ready to go. Get him to order. Close, and when you do, send me a text."

Twenty minutes later, Christopher and I had just sat down for lunch. His phone vibrated. He read the text message. It was Sam. He had sold three cases. Christopher beamed with pleasure before turning to the menu. As we talked about this book and my own thrashing around in the moral complexities and emotional challenges of sales, Christopher said: "Your problem is that you think there's some deep truth behind all this and that somehow if you can get to it, everyone will go 'Aha.' The fact is, most of us prefer to believe things are better than perhaps they are. We don't want to be told the whole thing's a lie. We want to compliment each other and say everything's great and get to the end that way. It's just a better way to live than going around saying it's all fake and you're all deluded."

Such optimism might be dangerous if you are an investor, but for a salesperson, it makes a good deal of sense to regard the world as full of customers eager to have their lives improved, rather than sales as some giant scam waiting to be exposed. It came back to Coach's gentle sarcasm about his own homilies to the team on high school game days. They may be cheesy and a little careworn, but wouldn't we all much rather believe them than not? The art of the sale is not contained in *Death of a Salesman*, but in the everyday accumulation of good habits and pleasant behaviors we see in the vast majority of salespeople. It is in their sunny view of life, which they share with the rest of us.

I hope this book has shown that great salespeople come in many different forms. There is no archetype. The common traits are resilience and optimism. But aside from that, there are salespeople who are motivated by money and others who found sales to be the best way to level the walls of worlds that were otherwise closed to them. There is Majid, who revels in the tricks of his trade, but also in the quality of what he sells and his position as king of the Tangier Kasbah. There is Memo and his restless bias for action, for whom selling is a way of keeping score as he propels himself relentlessly through each day, frightened that if he stops, the world he has built for himself will begin to collapse. Coach endured the long days and lonely evenings on the roads of West Virginia for those rare moments when he could call in to the head office and say "Get a pencil!" And he continues to believe there is value in his old sales stump speeches when he delivers them before big games to the high school students of his Connecticut town. There is Carolyn Klemm, for whom selling real estate is an extension of a voracious social appetite and professional ambition. Jeffrey Gitomer's selling tips aren't really actionable. Rather, his purpose is creating a jolly mood for a group of people who always need help keeping their chins up. Every salesperson I met was fascinating to speak with and very likable. Not a bore among them. Some were physically compelling, some not, some persuasive, others quite see-through, each possessed of varying measures of empathy and ego.

But they had all discovered an urgent desire that triggered their ability to sell. The desire is unique to each of them. But there is a similar one, I believe, within all of us. My sons sold lemonade not to sell lemonade but to earn money to buy a go-kart. To sell well, free of unnecessary inhibitions, is to confront the truth of what moves us—and then to turn it loose.

Acknowledgments

My thanks go to the many who agreed to appear in this book, and to the many more who helped me with their time, thoughts, contacts, friendship, and paychecks: Josh and Elena Prentice, who arranged my visit to Tangier. Ed Lyle in Marrakech. Daisuke Iwase for his hospitality in Tokyo, and Eriko Sekiya for her translations and forbearance. Hal Deguchi and Ayumi Kawagoe of Lifenet and the Harvard Business School alumni contingent in Tokyo: Take Takekawa, Ken Kimimori, Go Yamashita, and Yusuke Watanabe. Bill Burke, Larry Goodman, and Joe Uva. Srikumar Rao. Tom and Paul Hardart. Cynthia Shea. Trish O'Reilly and her remarkable father, Gerry, and his wife, Seton. Hugh Lawson, who sketched out the art of selling on a napkin. Joel Podolny, that rare academic bold enough to test himself in the private sector. The remarkable band at the Kauffman Foundation, Carl Schramm, Bob Litan, Dane Stangler, Lesa Mitchell, and Bo Fishback, now of Zaarly, for their friendship and inspiration. James Lyle for many happy midtown lunches. John Churchill and Andrew Stuttaford for their views from the Wall Street trenches. Christopher Coleridge, a great friend and unfailing enthusiast about the art of selling. My trusty newspaper editors: Sarah Sands, Alec Russell, Ravi Mattu, and Erich Eichmann. Jemima McDonnell, Tom Rhodes, Jackie and Dan Higgins, Charlotte and Guy Paisner, and Victoria and Luke Bridgeman for their generosity whenever I'm in London. All at Penguin Press: Eamon Dolan, who acquired and edited this book with thought and care; Emily Graff and Scott Moyers, who gathered it up at first and goal. Svetlana Katz and the brilliant Tina Bennett, that canniest of optimists, who like Leo Castelli makes culture happen. My watchful aunts, Victoria and Ann; my grandfather, Michael, who always thought writing a noble calling, and Cornelia and Cindy, the best of in-laws. My parents, Marcia and Simon, for their unflagging love and example. Augie and Hugo, salesmen in the making, for being such fun, and Margret–well, everything about you just kicks.

Selected Bibliography

BOOKS

Ash, Mary Kay. *The Mary Kay Way: Timeless Principles from America's Greatest Woman Entrepreneur.* Hoboken, NJ: John Wiley & Sons, 2008.

Barnum, P. T. *The Life of P. T. Barnum.* Champaign: University of Illinois Press, 2000.

Barton, Bruce. *The Man Nobody Knows.* Indianapolis: Bobbs-Merrill, 1925.

Benioff, Marc. *Behind the Cloud: The Untold Story of How Salesforce.com Went from Idea to Billion-Dollar Company—and Revolutionized an Industry.* Hoboken, NJ: Jossey-Bass, 2009.

Behrman, S. N. *Duveen: The Story of the Most Spectacular Art Dealer of All Time.* New York: Little Bookroom, 2003.

Bettger, Frank. *How I Raised Myself from Failure to Success in Selling.* New York: Simon & Schuster, 1992.

Biggart, Nicole Woolsey. *Charismatic Capitalism: Direct Selling Organizations in America.* Chicago: University of Chicago Press, 1990.

Carlin, John. *Playing the Enemy: Nelson Mandela and the Game That Made a Nation.* New York: Penguin Press, 2008.

Carnegie, Dale. *How to Win Friends and Influence People.* New York: Simon & Schuster, 2009.

Cialdini, Robert B. *Influence: The Psychology of Persuasion.* New York: Harper Paperbacks, 2006.

Cohen, Annie. *Solal Leo & His Circle: The Life of Leo Castelli.* New York: Knopf, 2010.

Friedman, Walter. *Birth of a Salesman: The Transformation of Selling in America.* Cambridge, MA: Harvard University Press, 2005.

Gitomer, Jeffrey. *The Little Red Book of Selling: 12.5 Principles of Sales Greatness.* Austin, TX: Bard Press, 2004.

Harris, John F. *The Survivor: Bill Clinton in the White House.* New York: Random House, 2006.

Hopkins, Tom. *How to Master the Art of Selling.* New York: Business Plus, 2005.

Iyer, Pico. *The Open Road: The Global Journey of the Fourteenth Dalai Lama.* New York: Vintage, 2009.

Kemp, Giles, and Edward Claflin. *Dale Carnegie: The Man Who Influenced Millions.* New York: St. Martin's Press, 1989.

Mamet, David. *Glengarry Glen Ross: A Play.* New York: Grove Press, 1994.

Mandino, Og. *The Greatest Salesman in the World.* New York: Bantam Books, 1974.

Melville, Herman. *The Confidence-Man: His Masquerade.* New York: W. W. Norton, 2005.

Micklethwait, John, and Adrian Wooldridge. *God Is Back: How the Global Revival of Faith Is Changing the World.* New York: Penguin Press, 2009.

Miller, Arthur. *Death of a Salesman.* New York: Penguin, 1996.

———. *Timebends: A Life.* New York: Penguin, 1995.

Nowak, Martin, and Roger Highfield. *SuperCooperators: Altruism, Evolution, and Why We Need Each Other to Succeed.* New York: Free Press, 2011.

Oakes, Guy. *The Soul of the Salesman: The Moral Ethos of Personal Sales.* Atlantic Highlands, NJ: Humanities Press International, 1990.

Ogilvy, David. *Ogilvy on Advertising.* New York: Vintage, 1985.

Popeil, Ron. *The Salesman of the Century.* New York: Dell, 1996.

Rackham, Neil. *SPIN Selling.* New York: McGraw-Hill, 1988.

Seligman, Martin E. P. *Flourish: A Visionary New Understanding of Happiness and Well-Being.* New York: Free Press, 2011.

Turner, Ted, and Bill Burke. *Call Me Ted.* New York: Business Plus, 2009.

Updike, John. *Rabbit Angstrom: A Tetralogy; Rabbit, Run; Rabbit Redux; Rabbit Is Rich; Rabbit at Rest.* New York: Everyman's Library, 1995.

Vass, Jerry. *Soft Selling in a Hard World: Plain Talk on the Art of Persuasion.* Philadelphia: Running Press, 1998.

Wasserstein, Bruce. *Big Deal: Mergers and Acquisitions in the Digital Age.* New York: Business Plus, 2001.

ARTICLES

Anderson, Erin, and Richard L. Oliver. "Perspectives on Behavior-Based versus Outcome-Based Control Systems." *Journal of Marketing* 51, no. 4 (October 1987): 76–88.

Anderson, Erin, and Vincent Onyemah. "How Right Should the Customer Be?" *Harvard Business Review* 84, no. 7/8 (2006): 59–67.

Behrman, Douglas N., and William D. Perreault Jr. "Measuring the Performance of Industrial Salespersons." *Journal of Business Research* 10, no. 3 (September 1982): 355–370.

Bonanno, George. "Resilience in the Face of Potential Trauma." *Journal of the American Psychological Society* 14, no. 3 (2005): 135–138.

Bonoma, Thomas V. "Major Sales: Who Really Does the Buying." *Harvard Business Review* 60, no. 3 (1982): 111–119.

Chowdhury, Jhinuk. "The Motivational Impact of Sales Quotas on Effort." *Journal of Marketing Research* 30, no. 1 (February 1993): 28–41.

Churchill, Gilbert A., Jr., Neil M. Ford, Steven W. Hartley, and Orville C. Walker Jr. "The Determinants of Salesperson Performance: A Meta-Analysis." *Journal of Marketing* 22, no. 2 (May 1985): 103–118.

Clark, David M. "A Cognitive Perspective on Social Phobia." In *International Handbook of Social Anxiety: Concepts, Research and Interventions Relating to the Self and Shyness.* Edited by W. Ray Crozier and Lynn E. Alden. Hoboken, NJ: John Wiley & Sons, 2001.

Dixon, Andrea L., Rosann L. Spiro, and Maqbul Jamil. "Successful and Unsuccessful Sales Calls: Measuring Salesperson Attributions and Behavioral Intentions." *Journal of Marketing* 65, no. 3 (July 2001): 64–78.

Dubinsky, Alan J., Roy D. Howell, Thomas N. Ingram, and Danny N. Bellenger. "Salesforce Socialization." *Journal of Marketing* 50, no. 4 (October 1986): 192–207.

Dwyer, F. Robert, Paul H. Schurr, and Sejo Oh. "Developing Buyer-Seller Relationships." *Journal of Marketing* 51, no. 2 (April 1987): 11–27.

Hammond, Allen L., and C. K. Prahalad. "Selling to the Poor." *Foreign Policy* 142 (May–June 2004): 30–37.

Kidwell, Blair, David M. Hardesty, Brian R. Murtha, and Shibin Sheng. "Emotional Intelligence in Marketing Exchanges." *Journal of Marketing* 75 (January 2011): 78–95.

Kohli, Ajay K., Tasadduq A. Shervani, and Goutam N. Challagalla. "Learning and Performance Orientation of Salespeople: The Role of Supervisors." *Journal of Marketing Research* 35, no. 2 (May 1998): 263–274.

Kotler, Philip, Neil Rackham, and Suj Krishnaswamy. "Ending the War between Sales and Marketing." *Harvard Business Review* 84, no. 7/8 (2006): 59–67.

Luthans, Fred, and Allan H. Church. "Positive Organizational Behavior: Developing and Managing Psychological Strengths." *The Academy of Management Executive (1993–2005)* 16, no. 1 (February 2002): 57–75.

MacFarland, Richard G. "Crisis of Conscience: The Use of Coercive Sales Tactics and Resultant Felt Stress in the Salesperson." *Journal of Personal Selling and Sales Management* 23, no. 4 (Fall 2003): 311–325.

Mayer, David, and Herbert M. Greenberg. "What Makes a Good Salesman." *Harvard Business Review* 42, no. 4 (1964): 119–125.

McMurray, Robert N. "The Mystique of Super-Salesmanship." *Harvard Business Review* 39, no. 2 (1961): 113–122.

Moynihan, Ray, Iona Heath, and David Henry. "Selling Sickness: The Pharmaceutical Industry and Disease Mongering." *British Medical Journal* 324, no. 13 (April 2002): 886–891.

Peterson, Christopher, Amy Semmel, Carl von Baeyer, Lyn Y. Abramson, Gerald I. Metalsky, and Martin E. P. Seligman. "The Attributional Style Questionnaire." *Cognitive Therapy and Research* 6, no. 3 (1982): 287–300.

Rizzo, John R., Robert J. House, and Sidney I. Lirtzman. "Role Conflict and Ambiguity in Complex Organizations." *Administrative Science Quarterly* 15 (1970): 150–163.

Saxe, Robert, and Barton A. Weitz. "The SOCO Scale: A Measure of the Customer Orientation of Salespeople." *Journal of Marketing Research* 19 (August 1982): 343–351.

Schulman, Peter. "Applying Learned Optimism to Increase Sales Productivity." *Journal of Personal Selling and Sales Management* 19, no. 1 (Winter 1999): 31–37.

Seligman, Martin E., and Peter Schulman. "Explanatory Style as a Predictor of Productivity and Quitting among Life Insurance Sales Agents." *Journal of Personality and Social Psychology* 50, no. 4 (1986): 832–838.

Shapiro, Benson P., and Ronald S. Posner. "Making the Major Sale." *Harvard Business Review* 54, no. 2 (1976): 68–78.

Sujan, Harish. "Smarter versus Harder: An Exploratory Attributional Analysis of Salespeople's Motivation." *Journal of Marketing Research* 23, no. 1 (February 1986): 41–49.

———, Barton A. Weitz, and Nirmalya Kumar. "Learning Orientation, Working Smart, and Effective Selling." *Journal of Marketing* 58, no. 3 (July 1994): 39–52.

Szymanski, David M. "Determinants of Selling Effectiveness: The Importance of Declarative Knowledge to the Personal Selling Concept." *Journal of Marketing* 52, no. 1 (January 1988): 64–77.

Verbeke, Willem, and Richard P. Bagozzi. "Sales Call Anxiety: Exploring What It Means When Fear Rules a Sales Encounter." *Journal of Marketing* 64, no. 3 (July 2000): 88–101.

Walker, Orville C., Jr., Gilbert A. Churchill Jr., and Neil M. Ford. "Motivation and Performance in Industrial Selling: Present Knowledge and Needed Research." *Journal of Marketing Research* 14, no. 2 (May 1977): 156–168.

Weitz, Barton A. "Effectiveness in Sales Interactions: A Contingency Framework." *Journal of Marketing* 45, no. 1 (Winter 1981): 85–103.

———, Harish Sujan, and Mita Sujan. "Knowledge, Motivation, and Adaptive Behavior: A Framework for Improving Selling Effectiveness." *Journal of Marketing* 50, no. 4 (October 1986): 174–191.

Index

PHILIP DELVES BROUGHTON

WHAT THEY TEACH YOU AT HARVARD BUSINESS SCHOOL

What *do* they teach you at Harvard Business School?

Graduates of Harvard Business School run many of the world's biggest and most influential banks, companies and countries. But what kind of person does it take to succeed at HBS? And would you want to be one of them?

For anyone who has ever wondered what goes on behind Harvard Business School's hallowed walls, Philip Delves Broughton's hilarious and enlightening account of his experiences on its prestigious MBA programme provides an extraordinary glimpse into a world of case-study conundrums, guest lectures, *Apprentice*-style tasks, booze luging, burn-outs and high flyers.

And with HBS alumni heading the very global governments, financial institutions and FTSE 500 companies whose reckless love of deregulation and debt got us into so much trouble, Delves Broughton discovers where HBS really adds value – and where it falls disturbingly short.

'Delves Broughton captures an essence of HBS that is part cult, part psychological morass, part hothouse . . . His book is invaluable. Quite brilliant'
Simon Heffer, *Literary Review*

'A funny and revealing insider's view . . . his fascination is infectious' *Sunday Times*

'A particularly absorbing and entertaining read' *Financial Times*

'Horrifying and very funny . . . An excellent book' *Wall Street Journal*